Deleuze and Religion

Gilles Deleuze's philosophy is commonly characterised as materialist and atheistic. It exhibits a recurrent commitment to unleashing philosophy from its historical affiliations with theology so as to release it into a zone of dynamism and becoming. Thus some may consider it a perverse or retrograde act to bring Deleuze's writing into proximity with the discourse of religion. However, Deleuze's philosophical thinking can be seen to engage with notions of Godhead, belief, spirituality, cosmology and biblical research, as well as demonstrating the influence of theist writers and philosophers.

Despite the considerable and ever-expanding body of Deleuzian scholarship, no single volume has yet explored the religious dimensions and implications of Deleuze's writing. Now, Mary Bryden has assembled a team of international scholars to do just that. Their essays illustrate the ways in which Deleuzian thought is antithetical to religious debate, as well as the ways in which it contributes to those debates. In this study, Deleuze's writing is set in the context of a wide spectrum of textual material, including patristics, mysticism, dogmatic theology, hermeneutics, literature and modern critical theory.

This volume will be invaluable for researchers, teachers and students of theology, philosophy, critical theory, cultural studies and literary criticism, as well as to students of French who read Deleuze's work in its original language. The collection offers a stimulating selection of cross-disciplinary approaches towards the varied links between Deleuzian thought and religion.

Mary Bryden is a senior lecturer in the Department of French at the University of Reading. Her book *Women in Samuel Beckett's Prose and Drama: Her Own Other* (Macmillan, 1993) applies Deleuzian analysis to the writings of Samuel Beckett; her other books include *Samuel Beckett and the Idea of God* (Macmillan, 1998) and *Samuel Beckett and Music* (Oxford University Press, 1998).

Deleuze and Religion

Edited by Mary Bryden

London and New York

First published 2001
by Routledge
11 New Fetter Lane, London EC4P 4EE

Simultaneously published in the USA and Canada
by Routledge
29 West 35th Street, New York, NY 10001

Routledge is an imprint of the Taylor & Francis Group

© 2001 selection and editorial matter, Mary Bryden; individual
chapters, the contributors

Typeset in Times by Taylor & Francis Books Ltd
Printed and bound in Great Britain by Clays Ltd, St Ives PLC

British Library Cataloguing in Publication Data
A catalogue record for this book is available from the British Library

Library of Congress Cataloging in Publication Data
A catalogue record for this book has been requested

ISBN 0–415–24028–X (hbk)
ISBN 0–415–24029–8 (pbk)

Contents

Notes on contributors

Eliot Albert currently makes films as well as teaching Philosophy at Goldsmiths College, University of London. His translation of Eric Alliez's *La Signature du monde, ou qu'est-ce que la philosophie de Deleuze et Guattari?* will be published by Athlone Press. He has published essays on Deleuze, Bruno, Nietzsche, and on the heretical nature of materialism. He is currently developing a biopolitical approach to Auschwitz.

Keith Ansell Pearson is Professor of Philosophy at Warwick University and author and editor of books on Nietzsche and Deleuze, including *Nietzsche contra Rousseau* (Cambridge University Press, 1991/6), *The Perfect Nihilist* (Cambridge University Press, 1994), *Viroid Life* (Routledge, 1997) and *Germinal Life: The Difference and Repetition of Deleuze* (Routledge, 1999). He is currently composing a series of essays on Bergson in relation to questions of time, evolution, matter and spirit.

Ronald Bogue is Professor of Comparative Literature at the University of Georgia. He is the author of *Deleuze and Guattari* (Routledge, 1989), as well as of essays on Deleuze that have appeared in *SubStance*, *Criticism*, *South Atlantic Quarterly*, *Man and World*, and several collective volumes. He is also co-editor, with Mihai Spariosu, of *The Play of the Self* (SUNY, 1994) and co-editor, with Marcel Cornis-Pope, of *Violence and Mediation in Contemporary Culture* (SUNY, 1996).

Mary Bryden is a Senior Lecturer in the Department of French Studies, University of Reading. Her books include *Women in the Prose and Drama of Samuel Beckett: Her Own Other* (Macmillan, 1993) and *Samuel Beckett and the Idea of God* (Macmillan, 1998). She has also edited *Samuel Beckett and Music* (Oxford University Press, 1998) and written numerous articles on twentieth-century French literature. She is currently preparing two monographs: one on Deleuze and Literature, and the other on T. E. Lawrence.

Thomas Cousineau is Professor of English at Washington College in Chestertown, Maryland. A graduate of Boston College, he received his doctorate from the University of California at Davis and began his teaching career in French universities, to which he has regularly returned. Along with publishing numerous articles on Beckett in such journals as *Modern Fiction Studies*, *The Journal of Beckett Studies*, and *Samuel Beckett Today/Aujourd'hui*, he is the author of *Waiting for Godot: Form in Movement* and *After the Final No: Samuel Beckett's Trilogy*, and the editor of a special issue of *The Journal of Beckett Studies* devoted to 'Beckett in France'.

Catherine Dale has recently completed her doctorate, 'The Metaphysics of Antonin Artaud', with the University of Western Sydney, Australia. Most of her work is about Artaud, but she has also written about the politics of heroin use, addiction, the liberal subject, and 'viral democracies', as well as articles on literature and art. She is currently preparing a monograph on metaphysics and contemporary art.

Oliver Davies is Reader in Theology at the University of Wales, Lampeter, and Fellow of the Centre for the Study of Christianity and Culture at Regent's Park College, Oxford. He originally studied modern languages, specialising in modern German literature, before moving into the field of theology. He is author of *Meister Eckhart: Mystical Theologian* (1991), and is currently preparing a postmodern Catholic theology.

Maximilian de Gaynesford is Fellow and Tutor in Philosophy at Lincoln College, Oxford. His current research is centred on the first person. He has published on various subjects in the philosophy of mind and language, metaphysics, and epistemology. His interest in Deleuze and Guattari was first stimulated by research in theology at the University of Kent at Canterbury, 1990–3.

N. Robert Glass is Director of Comparative Religion and Culture in the Friends World Program at Long Island University. His articles on Buddhism and postmodern thought have appeared in *The International Philosophical Quarterly* and in *The Journal of the American Academy of Religion*. He is the author of *Working Emptiness: Toward a Third Reading of Buddhism and Postmodern Thought* (Scholars Press, 1995).

Michael Goddard is a PhD candidate in the Department of Art History and Theory, University of Sydney. He trained both in film production and theory, as well as philosophy, at the University of Technology, Sydney, completing several short films as well as a BA (Hons) in Communications. Following this, he completed an MA on the relations between Deleuze's thought, mysticism and cinema, at the University of Otago, Dunedin. At present, his research is focused around the Polish writer Witold Gombrowicz, in relation to East European Modernism, contemporary thought and aesthetic practices.

Philip Goodchild teaches Theology at the University of Nottingham. He is the author of *Gilles Deleuze and the Question of Philosophy* (Fairleigh

Dickinson, 1996) and *Deleuze and Guattari: An Introduction to the Politics of Desire* (Sage, 1996). He is currently preparing a volume entitled *The Price of Piety: Philosophy of Religion and Critical Theory.*

Judith Poxon is a PhD candidate in the Department of Religion at Syracuse University, where she is completing a dissertation that explores the implications for feminist theology of the ways in which difference is articulated in the thought of Gilles Deleuze and Luce Irigaray. She teaches part-time in the Department of Humanities and Religious Studies at California State University, Sacramento, and is co-editing two volumes of French feminist religious thought.

John Protevi teaches contemporary French theory in the Department of French and Italian at Louisiana State University, Baton Rouge. He is the author of *Time and Exteriority* (Bucknell University Press, 1994), and editor of the Post-Structuralism section of the *Edinburgh Encyclopedia of Continental Philosophy* (Edinburgh University Press, 1999). His current book project, *Force and Form: At the Limit of Deconstruction*, deals with the question of hylomorphism in the history of Western philosophy.

Walter Redfern is a Professor of French at Reading University. His monograph on Michel Tournier, *Michel Tournier: Le Coq de Bruyère*, appeared in 1996. He has translated into French his own study, *Puns*, and the novel written in English by Georges Darien: *Gottlieb Krumm*. He is the author of *Clichés and Coinages*, and his other books include studies of Giono, Nizan, Queneau, Darien, Vallès, Sartre, Guilloux, and Brisset. He has also written BBC scripts on figures of speech, and has published a novel, *A Calm Estate*.

Daniel W. Smith received his PhD in philosophy from the University of Chicago in 1997, and has held teaching positions at Grinnell College, Loyola University, and Macquarie University in Sydney, Australia. He is currently a postdoctoral fellow in philosophy at the University of New South Wales, where he is completing a book on the philosophy of Gilles Deleuze. He is the author of numerous articles on continental philosophy, and has translated several books from the French, including Deleuze's *Essays Critical and Clinical* (with Michael A. Greco), and Pierre Klossowski's *Nietzsche and the Vicious Circle*.

Michel Tournier is still one of France's major novelists. His fiction includes: *Vendredi, ou les limbes du Pacifique* (1967: winner of the *Académie française* novel prize), *Le Roi des Aulnes* (1970: winner of the Prix Goncourt), *Les Météores* (1975), *Le Coq de bruyère* (1978), *Gaspard, Melchior et Balthazar* (1980), *Gilles et Jeanne* (1983), *La Goutte d'or* (1985), *Le Médianoche amoureux* (1989). He has also published numerous volumes of essays and autobiography, including *Le Vent Paraclet* (1977), *Le Vol du vampire* (Mercure de France, 1981), *Le Vagabond immobile* (1984), and *Le*

Tabor et le Sinaï (Belfond, 1988). The publisher is Gallimard except where otherwise stated.

Acknowledgements

I am indebted to Paul Patton and Philip Goodchild, who made invaluable suggestions at the beginning of this project. Keith Ansell Pearson has been a tower of strength and encouragement, and Ronald Bogue has oiled the editorial wheels with his professionalism and promptitude. My thanks are due to Tony Simons, who cheerfully ironed out some computer glitches. I am most grateful to Michel Tournier. When I wrote to him in October 1998, asking whether he might contribute an article to this collection, he replied immediately, enclosing a typewritten manuscript of his article on Deleuze, and giving his *imprimatur* for its translation into English for the volume. It is thus appearing here for the first time in English. (The French original was later published in Michel Tournier, *Célébrations* [Paris: Mercure de France, 1999]). The English translation, as well as an introduction to the piece, were undertaken by my colleague, Walter Redfern, who has provided, throughout this project, a ready ear, a perceptive eye, and inexhaustible kindness.

M.B.

Introduction

Mary Bryden

> On peut instaurer une zone de voisinage avec n'importe quoi, à condition
> d'en créer les moyens littéraires [We can establish neighbouring zones with
> absolutely anything, if we provide the literary means to do so].[1]

The topic of Gilles Deleuze and Religion might appear to be a perverse one.
After all, Deleuze's writing recurrently demonstrates a commitment to the
unhinging of philosophy from its complex historical affiliations with
theology, so as to release it into a zone of dynamism, affirmation and
becoming (see Philip Goodchild's essay in this volume). Is it a retrograde act,
even an act of violence, to bring his *oeuvre* into proximity with the discourse
of religion?

Two responses might be made. The first is that, as the epigraph to this
Introduction suggests, writing and thinking, for Deleuze, are expansive and
not contractive. Given the literary means, contact zones may be created
between an infinite diversity of discourses and praxes. Here, Deleuze uses the
term *littéraire* neither in its restricted, elitist sense (that which characterises
fictional, canonical texts) nor in its pejorative sense, as in *Tout ça n'est que
littérature* [That's just waffle]. Rather, he applies it to any form of writing in
which the imagination is deployed. Writing, then, is a medium in which there
are no predetermined correspondences, and in which a process of osmosis
may allow for travel through unfamiliar, exilic spaces towards what is not yet
known. As Deleuze asserts in *Critique et Clinique*:

> Ecrire est une affaire de devenir, toujours inachevé, toujours en train de
> se faire, et qui déborde toute matière vivable ou vécue [Writing is a
> matter of becoming, which is always unfinished, always forging itself,
> and going beyond that which may be, or has been, lived].
>
> (*CC*, p. 11)

Since he himself implemented radical and exhilarating encounters between
apparent contrarieties or incongruities, it is not inappropriate to do likewise.

The second response, however, is a corollary of the first. It concerns the
inevitable particularity within multiplicity at any given moment. If, within
writing, there is no privileged hierarchy of association, then why should

'Deleuze and Religion' be chosen, rather than 'Deleuze and Topiary', or 'Deleuze and Orthodontics'? I am not suggesting that the vibrant inventiveness of Deleuzian scholarship could not produce creditable treatises on the latter two subjects. But 'Deleuze and Religion' has in this instance been chosen because pulses within Deleuze's own writing have themselves suggested it.

As Michael Goddard states in his essay within this volume, 'Deleuze draws heavily on thinkers such as Bergson, Nietzsche, Leibniz and Spinoza, all of whom share a mystical affirmation of nature, joy or life, whatever their conceptual differences'. He goes on to point out that Deleuze and Guattari do themselves advert to 'spiritual' practices such as sorcery and Taoism in, for example, *Mille plateaux*. At other times, as Thomas Cousineau explores in Chapter 9 of this volume, Deleuze seems to overlook or ignore the biblical or spiritual resonance of the text he is discussing.

My own approach to Deleuze is from the standpoint of a literary critic, albeit one with a longstanding interest in theology. Initially interested primarily in Deleuze's response to literary texts, I then discovered that my attention had been colonised by a range of questions and allusions within Deleuze's writing which appeared to be travelling from, or addressed to, spheres which, if not overtly theological, had potential extensions into theological discourses.

I use 'theology' here in its very broadest sense, not intending it to betoken the systematic study of the divine, in relation to specific traditions or schools of thought. (This is not to assert that contributors to this volume do not cite such traditions: of course, they may, and do. See, for example, Oliver Davies's application of apophaticism, and Maximilian de Gaynesford's Christological analysis. But such linkages are optional and not consequential.) Neither is 'theology' to be seen here as necessarily linked with Christian revelation. (Robert Glass's essay in this volume, for example, situates itself within the Buddhist tradition, and that of Ronald Bogue refers to Jewish prophetism.) It is, thus, preferable in this context to think plurally, of 'theologies'. But essentially, I want to interpret theology in terms of its Greek derivation: the practice of 'god-talk'. 'Religion' – the term eventually co-opted for this volume – is perhaps a wider vector for these diversities.

Further, since any proposition implies the possibility of its converse, it will also be necessary to consider Deleuze's 'anti-theologies' (see, for example, Judith Poxon's essay in this volume), his affiliation with Nietzsche in asserting the regime of the Antichrist over and against that of the divine order, and his Nietzschean exposition of the 'molar' instincts of the priestly caste (see my own essay in this volume). In so doing, he demonstrates no great hostility to the person of Christ – whom he brackets with Buddha in terms of his pacific demeanour – but, rather, to the system which installs Christ within a due-exacting regime of judgement (see Catherine Dale's essay in this volume).

It is clearly possible to establish a correspondence (though not an equivalence) between Deleuze's challenge to the influence of Parent-as-God (his anti-Oedipal project) and of God-as-Parent. Indeed, Deleuze himself links the two in *Critique et Clinique*. Here, however, when discussing Melville and D. H. Lawrence, he issues a caveat to the easy assumption that engagement with the horizontal community (that of fraternity) *results from* disengagement from the vertical community (that of [p/m]aternity):

> La fraternité selon Melville ou Lawrence, c'est une affaire d'âmes origi-nales: peut-être ne commence-t-elle qu'avec la mort du père ou de Dieu, mais elle n'en dérive pas [Fraternity, in Melville or Lawrence's terms, concerns original spirits: it might only begin with the death of the father or of God, but it does not derive from it].
>
> (*CC*, p. 112)

Put more loosely, comradeship or humanism is not a *product* of atheism or assimilated orphanhood, but might arise from it.

Whatever its origin or impetus, resistance to the triangulation of desire – (whether it be the *papa-maman-moi* of Oedipal constructs, or the Father, Son and Holy Spirit of Christian Trinitarianism) – remains consistent with the non-hierarchical, horizontal flows which characterise the Deleuzian endeavour. Insofar as the latter subverts the presiding Father at the apex of these triads, Deleuze's challenge to patriarchy has clear affiliations with feminism (problematic as the concept of *devenir-femme* has proved). However, as Claire Colebrook remarks with reference to feminist philosophy: 'How can one speak in such a way as to address the current corpus of concepts while at the same time seeking to think differently?'.[2]

Deleuze, like Nietzsche, approaches theology and ecclesiology with insider knowledge. Thus, for example, when evaluating the poetry of Péguy, he is able to recognise the resonance of litany and liturgy in the stuttering (*bégaiement*) of the complex rhythm of attributes – '(*Mater* purissima, castissima, inviolata, *Virgo* potens, clemens, fidelis)' (*CC*, p. 140) – while not subscribing to its Mariological doctrine. The same powerful image of the Virgin Mother is recruited in his analysis of Sacher-Masoch as a producer of *formations délirantes*:

> Imaginer même que c'est la Vierge, mère sévère, qui met le Christ en croix pour faire naître le nouvel homme, et la femme chrétienne qui conduit les hommes au supplice [Imagine, even, that it is the Virgin, the severe mother, who puts Christ on the cross so that the new man may be born, and the Christian woman who leads men to the torture].
>
> (*CC*, p. 72)

Further, the notion of Godhead recurs in Deleuze's writing within for-mulations which play upon both the cataphatic and the apophatic traditions.

Insofar as deconstruction and postmodernism resist principles of universality, logic, and unity, in order to rehabilitate the marginal, the ephemeral, or the fragmentary, they provide affinities with apophatic theology (broadly speaking, the tradition which holds that understanding of God may be furthered in terms of what he is not, rather than by reference to a taxonomy of positive attributes). For Deleuze, God is *not* the great Bender of Time, the eternal principle in the context of which all human notions of movement and temporality must be set:

> Le temps cesse d'être courbé par un Dieu qui le fait dépendre du mouvement. Il cesse d'être cardinal et devient ordinal [Time has stopped being curved by a God who makes it reliant upon movement. It has stopped being cardinal and become ordinal].
>
> (*CC*, p. 41)

Deleuze-Guattari also engage playfully, however, with positive and visually striking assertions, such as 'Dieu est un Homard ou une double-pince, un *double-bind*' [God is a Lobster or a double-pincer, a double-bind][3] (see the discussion in John Protevi's essay in this volume). Deleuze also quotes in the essay on Louis Wolfson the statement that 'Dieu est la Bombe' (*CC*, p. 31), God being the totality of the nuclear arsenal necessary to sterilise the world.

What God becomes in Deleuze's hands is not a displaced Father, or a tatty remnant such as that which is carried around by the sons of Abel in Tournier's short story 'La Famille Adam',[4] or a mere emptiness. At least, these reference points are not consistent ones. Any God-candidate in Deleuzian terms could not, in any case, be consistent or stationary, but would be apparent only in potentialities and intensities, like that 'clapotement cosmique et spirituel' [spiritual, cosmic lapping] which Deleuze discerns as a goal of the Beckettian character (*CC*, p. 39). Such a God would be borne within the dialectic of immutability and becoming; s/he might be conceived using the insights of process theology or within the evolutionary perspective of Teilhard de Chardin. Daniel Smith's essay in this volume ends with precisely this emphasis: 'What the drama of univocity exemplifies is the *dynamic* nature of Deleuze's thought, which must be defined and comprehended in terms of its *movement*'.

The old God is dead for Deleuze. The spiritual, however, remains (one might compare here the agnostic spirituality which remained as an option for Georges Bataille, who is mentioned in Eliot Albert's essay in this volume). It sometimes hangs or floats in the air – the transparent, colourless air which, in his essay on T. E. Lawrence, Deleuze relates to 'le Dieu des Arabes' (*CC*, p. 144), or the 'lumière blanche livide' [pale white light] (*CC*, pp. 106–7) which Deleuze, following Melville, attaches to the creation narrative of the Book of Genesis. The machinery of the divine order is definitively dismantled, but, as Deleuze asserts in *Critique et Clinique*, visions and perceptions are generated not from rituals and structures, but from the dynamism of the void:

> Ces visions [...] ne sont pas des interruptions du processus, mais des haltes qui en font partie, comme une éternité qui ne peut être révélée que dans le devenir, un paysage qui n'apparaît que dans le mouvement [These visions (...) are not interruptions of the process, but pauses which are part of it, like an eternity which can only be revealed in becoming, a landscape which only appears within movement]
>
> (*CC*, p. 16)

Within a perspective of movement, and of *devenirs*, godness cannot be debarred as easily as godliness. As Keith Ansell Pearson writes in his analysis of Bergson (Chapter 11 of this volume): 'To think the future in terms of a creative evolution is to think in terms of the unforeseeable and the incalculable'.

I have suggested above that any consideration of Deleuze and Religion must necessarily include discussion both of the ways in which Deleuzian thought is antithetical to religious debate, and of the ways in which it contributes to those debates. Given the wide spectrum, then, which these essays cover, I have divided *Deleuze and Religion* into four Parts: 'Judgement and betrayal' (Bogue, Protevi, Poxon); 'Spirituality and mysticism' (Goddard, Glass, Davies, de Gaynesford); 'Literature and religion' (Bryden, Cousineau, Dale); and 'Beyond theology' (Ansell Pearson, Goodchild, Smith, Albert). Michel Tournier's text, and Walter Redfern's introduction to it, appear as an Appendix. In some ways, Deleuze and Tournier, as writers, could hardly contrast more. As Walter Redfern observes: 'Deleuze rears up against synthesis, for which Tournier hankers'; yet 'Deleuze is highly responsive to his friend's slippery ambivalences'. Tournier's essay provides an intriguing glimpse of a philosopher-in-the-making. Notably, the curious early poems by Deleuze which are translated here[5] both contain a mention of God. While one concludes with an appeal to God, the other merely observes the distance between the narratorial voice and the divine: 'I am not God'. The distinction being made here seems to be primarily that between permanence and transience, since the poet refers to a distaste for closure and mortality: 'vile finitude'.

   The Deleuzian corpus is unlikely to be afflicted by 'vile finitude'. Neither, it seems, is Deleuzian scholarship and commentary likely to remain static. I have not attempted in this Introduction lengthily to paraphrase what others have themselves taken pains to explicate, preferring to allow the contributors to this volume to speak for themselves. This they have done multifariously, raising questions which will, I hope, stimulate further investigation into the subject of Deleuze and religion.

Notes

1   Gilles Deleuze, *Critique et Clinique* (Paris: Editions de Minuit, 1993) p. 11. Hereafter referred to as *CC*. All translations from the French are my own.
2   Claire Colebrook, Introduction to *Deleuze and Feminist Theory*, ed. Ian Buchanan and Claire Colebrook (Edinburgh: Edinburgh University Press, 2000) pp. 1–17 (p. 9).
3   Gilles Deleuze and Félix Guattari, *Mille plateaux* (Paris: Editions de Minuit, 1980) p. 54.
4   Michel Tournier, 'La Famille Adam', in *Le Coq de Bruyère* (Paris: Gallimard, 1978) pp. 11–18.
5   The French texts – 'Le Dire du Narcisse médiocre' and 'Les Dires du mime' – appear in *Critique*, 591–592 (August/September 1996) pp. 699–700.

Part I

Judgement and betrayal

1 The betrayal of God

Ronald Bogue

In *A Thousand Plateaus*, Deleuze and Guattari delineate four 'regimes of signs', or regular patterns of power relations that organise sign production: the primitive, presignifying regime; the despotic, signifying regime; the nomadic, countersignifying regime; and the passional, postsignifying regime. The postsignifying regime they identify as 'the regime of betrayal, universal betrayal, in which the true man never ceases to betray God just as God betrays man, with the wrath of God defining the new positivity'. In this regime, God and prophet turn away from one another, averting their faces, and in so doing draw 'a positive line of flight'. God invents 'the reprieve, existence in reprieve, *indefinite postponement*', but also 'the positivity of alliance, or the covenant, as the new relation with the deity, since the subject remains alive'.[1] What I wish to explore is the logic of this mutual betrayal of God and prophet, this aversion of faces that draws a line of flight, this existence in reprieve that signals a new relation. To accomplish this task, two rather lengthy divagations are necessary, one through Jérôme Lindon's *Jonas*, in order to clarify Deleuze and Guattari's account of Jewish prophetism, the other through Jean Beaufret's 'Hölderlin et Sophocle', in order to explain the connection Deleuze and Guattari draw between the Jewish prophets and Oedipus. The mutual betrayal of the passional, postsignifying regime entails a positive alliance of the human and the divine, but betrayal itself, I shall argue, finally provides one a means of subverting what Deleuze refers to as the 'doctrine of judgement', and thereby of breaking free from the God of judgement.[2]

Jonah

Deleuze and Guattari cite Jérôme Lindon as 'the first to analyse the relation between Jewish prophetism and betrayal, in the exemplary case of Jonah' (*TP*, p. 529), and in fact they rely heavily on Lindon's 1955 commentary/translation of the *Book of Jonah*[3] for their exposition of the postsignifying regime of betrayal. At first glance one might understand how Jonah's flight from Nineveh could represent a betrayal of God, and perhaps how God's refusal to destroy Nineveh could stand as a betrayal of Jonah, but the 'exemplary' nature of this complex and enigmatic tale only becomes apparent after one traces the contours of Lindon's ingenious and rather idiosyncratic reading of the biblical text.

Most frequently, the *Book of Jonah* is taken to be the story of a reluctant prophet who preaches doom to the heathens but finally learns of God's universal mercy, which extends even to Israel's enemies. Many have objected to this unflattering reading of a petulant and vindictive Jonah manipulated by a condescending God, but in offering alternative interpretations, they, like all commentators, have had to grapple with several puzzling features of the story. Why, after all, does Jonah flee Nineveh when he knows full well there is no escaping the Lord on the face of the earth? Why does Jonah sleep during the storm at sea? What is the significance of his hymn of praise from the belly of the whale? Why does he seem crestfallen at the salvation of Nineveh? And what lesson is taught through the mysterious *qîq~yôn* plant, which flourishes and dies in a day?

Lindon's answers to these questions spring from his interpretation of *Jonah* in terms of the scapegoat motif, suggested first by the association of *Jonah* with Yom Kippur, the Day of Atonement. Traditional readings on this tenth day of the seventh month open with *Leviticus*, 16, in which Aaron is instructed in the proper sacrifice of the goat of the Lord and in the ritual expulsion of the goat of Azazel. After recitations of *Isaiah*, 57:14–58:14 concerning humility and contrition and *Leviticus*, 18, on sexual purity, Yom Kippur closes with a reading of the four chapters of *Jonah*. According to Lindon, the scapegoat's function is to 'cover and isolate', to take divine punishment upon itself and thereby shield the community from God's wrath. He points out that the unvocalised consonants of *kapper*, 'he covered', are the same as the *kippur* of the Day of Atonement,[4] and that a series of related verbal associations plays through texts connected with *Jonah*. In *Leviticus*, 16, for example, Aaron is instructed to sacrifice the goat of the Lord and sprinkle its blood

> on the *kapporeth* [the cover that is over the Ark of the Covenant; *King James Bible*: 'mercy seat'] and in front of the *kapporeth*; he will thus make a *kapparah* [purgation, cleansing] of the uncleanness of the children of Israel and their sins and their transgressions.
>
> (Lindon, p. 35)

And in the narrative of the Flood, God instructs Noah, 'Make an ark of gopher wood. You will make the ark in cells and you will cover it with *kapper*, an isolating cover, on the inside and on the outside'.[5] Among those covered and protected from the storm is the dove, *yônâ* (the name Jonah means literally 'dove'), the one designated by Noah 'to recognize the dry land amidst the sea, the terrain of men amidst the space of God, to be at the same time the sign that separates and the messenger that connects' (Lindon, pp. 25–6).

Thus, in Lindon's reading, when Jonah hears God's summons to Nineveh and proceeds instead to Tarsis, he deliberately assumes the role of the scapegoat, that which 'covers and isolates'. He knows he cannot flee God's presence; by his flight he takes on the guilt of Nineveh, thereby anticipating God's action and awaiting his punishment. Jonah's sleep during the raging storm is indeed the sleep of the just, for his response to God's call is a voluntary acceptance of God's will, not a rejection of it.[6] The sailors want Jonah to join them and pray to his god, but he thinks to himself, 'safety [*salut*] is theirs, on the contrary, if I cut the ties between us, if I take their affair on myself alone. I will separate them as the *kapper* covers and isolates the ark of men from the waves of God' (Lindon, p. 30). The helmsman asks Jonah where he comes from and who his people are, to which he replies, 'I am a Hebrew' (*Jonah*, 1:9). In this response is the essence of Jewish identity, says Lindon, for there is no physiological, ethnic, cultural or linguistic characteristic that unequivocally differentiates Jews from Gentiles, other than the willingness to say, 'I am a Jew'. When the Nazis gather Jews to be registered, and eventually interred and exterminated, each individual is summoned to say, 'I am a Jew', to accept an imposed separation from others and an unmerited suffering. It is not surprising, then, that Jonah's declaration of his identity is followed by his sacrifice. Indeed, he suggests to the sailors that they throw him overboard (*Jonah*, 1:12), and they fear lest his blood will be on their hands (1:14). Only after appealing to YHWH do they cast Jonah into the sea. When the waves subside, a powerful fear of YHWH overcomes them and they offer sacrifices and vows to the Lord (1:16).

Yet Jonah does not die. Like the goat of Azazel, the scapegoat of *Leviticus*, he is allowed to live. The great fish saves Jonah, and he praises God's mercy, for he knew from the beginning that God was merciful, that through his assumption of guilt Nineveh would be spared, just as the sailors were kept from drowning. But if God wants him to remain alive, he concludes, he will go to Nineveh and proclaim God's warning, 'Forty days and Nineveh will be turned upside down' (*Jonah*, 3:4).[7] Jonah proceeds to the city, and his prophecy leads to Nineveh's penance and God's decision to spare the city. Then 'un mal vient sur Jonas, un grand mal, et cela le brûle' [a trouble comes over Jonah, a great trouble, and it burns him] (4:1). As Lindon notes, the word *r~'â*, which he translates as *mal*, can mean 'sin', 'catastrophe', 'punishment', 'bitterness' or 'error' (Lindon, p. 14). (Sasson adds to the list 'iniquity', 'distress', 'misery of body or mind' [Sasson, p. 272]). But Lindon insists that the line does not mean that 'this greatly displeased Jonah and he was angered', as many translators render the phrase.[8] Rather, Jonah believes that the evil has been placed on him, that he is the covering and isolating scapegoat upon whom the sins of Nineveh have fallen, and the burden of this evil affects him deeply. He prays to God, saying that he knew God was compassionate and good when he fled to Tarsis, and that God would relent from bringing disaster.[9] 'I knew that You would save Niniveh and that You needed someone to assume their evil. It was their evil that I purchased at

Jaffa' (Lindon, p. 44). He therefore accepts his role and asks God, 'take my spirit from me, for my death is worth more than my life' (*Jonah*, 4:3). His death, in other words, is 'le mal de Ninive anéanti, c'est Ninive définitivement sauvée' [the evil of Nineveh wiped out, it is Nineveh definitively saved] (Lindon, p. 45).

Yet once again God spares Jonah. Unsure of the significance of God's action, Jonah reasons that in any case he must not remain among the Ninevites, since he has taken the evil upon himself and become 'an object of opprobrium and terror' (Lindon, p. 46). He therefore isolates himself and leaves the city. At this juncture, God offers Jonah an allegorical lesson (*Jonah*, 4:6–11). God causes a *qîq~yôn* plant to grow over Jonah and give him shade from the sun. The next day, however, the *qîq~yôn* plant dries up and Jonah is so distraught over the plant's demise that he cries out once again for death (4:8). God's point is that Jonah has covered Nineveh and shielded it from God's punishment just as the *qîq~yôn* plant covered Jonah and shielded him from the sun; yet Nineveh can no more endure Jonah's death than Jonah can support the death of the plant. God requires that Jonah survive and that he bear the mark of his expiatory role. The *qîq~yôn* plant, says Lindon, is the 'tree of Cain', and Jonah the Cain of Nineveh.[10] Cain, like Jonah, thought his punishment was greater than he could bear (*Genesis*, 4:13), but 'the Lord set a mark upon Cain, lest any finding him should kill him' (4:15). Likewise, Jonah must continue to live. He must be marked and separated, set aside to wander in the wilderness like the goat of Azazel.[11]

Lindon concludes his translation and study of Jonah with a brief narrative. The Flood marked the failure of Cain. To save His creation, God made a covenant with Noah and subsequently 'invented the Jews' (Lindon, p. 54), a people distinguished only by God's choice of them as the people before whom he would appear. For centuries, the goat of the Lord was sacrificed, and a second goat, as if a living replacement for the first, was sent forth to Azazel. In this way, the 'rupture in the equilibrium of Creation' caused by Cain's bloodshed was overcome, and 'the knife of Aaron, making the goat untouchable, forced God Himself to assume the impurity of Israel' (Lindon, p. 56). One day, however, Israel rejected God's commandments; sacrifices ceased and the Temple was destroyed. Thereafter a new mode of salvation was necessary. The people themselves assumed the evil that befell them, yet in their misery they cried to the Lord, 'Why hast thou forsaken me?' (*Psalms*, 22:1; *Matthew*, 27:46; *Mark*, 15:34). And God remembered His covenant and protected His people, though thenceforth they would be eternal scapegoats condemned like Cain to live with the burden of their woe. In this sense Jonah, 'irremediably isolated in his turpitude, justly condemned to death and each day resuscitated', proved the exemplar of his people, 'the one called Israel, "wrestling with God" and with men' (Lindon, p. 58). The Covenant of Noah was sustained, though it 'no longer rested on anything but its betrayal' (p. 59).

Lindon speaks of the son of Amittai as 'the absurd and criminal Jonah, traitor to that for which he dies and living his continual death' (Lindon, p. 61), but in what regard is he a traitor? Only, it would seem, in his decision to go to Tarsis, to flee the Lord and his command. Yet for Lindon, this betrayal is actually an act of faith, not its breach. True betrayal would only arise if Jonah were to say, 'I am not a Hebrew, I am like you', if he were to refuse to say, 'let misfortune befall me'. Lindon's primary concern is with the scapegoat, and betrayal is but another name for the assumption of that role. Time and again throughout the Pentateuch, of course, God's 'stiff-necked people' break His covenant, and in this sense they betray God and incur guilt, but Jonah's betrayal has little to do with renegade crime and just punishment. Rather, it concerns the willingness to 'cover and protect', to be the scapegoat, already condemned yet marked for survival.

What Deleuze and Guattari see in this story, however, is something else. They treat the scapegoat as the link between two regimes of signs. In the despotic, signifying regime, signs are centred on the frontal face of the omnipotent despot, from whom all signification emanates; he is surrounded by ever-widening circles of priests, officials and bureaucrats interpreting his pronouncements; and at the limits of the system, at the walls of the city, the path of escape is blocked, the faceless, accursed scapegoat being the only creature allowed to wander outside the sphere of despotic control. The scapegoat

> incarnates that line of flight the signifying regime cannot tolerate, in other words, an absolute deterritorialization [...]. Anything that threatens to put the system to flight will be killed or put to flight itself. Anything that exceeds the excess of the signifier or passes beneath it will be marked with a negative value.
>
> *(TP*, p. 116)

In the passional, postsignifying regime, however, the scapegoat is transformed. What was purely negative becomes a positive source of semiotic organisation. Rather than tracing a line of absolute deterritorialisation, the scapegoat marks discrete stages whereby an unoriented wandering is momentarily coded, then set adrift, only to be fixed and coded again. At each stage, an obsessive point of subjectification (such as God) defines a subject of enunciation (in this case, the prophet) and a subject of the statement (the people), the signs of a given stage functioning in terms of this limited, temporary, tripartite structure.[12]

For Deleuze and Guattari, then, it is this positive encoding of the wandering scapegoat that defines the regime of signs of Jewish prophetism:

> Let misfortune befall us: this formula punctuates Jewish history. It is we who must follow the most deterritorialized line, the line of the scapegoat, but we will change its sign, we will turn it into the positive line of

our subjectivity, our Passion, our proceeding or grievance. We will be our own scapegoat.

(*TP*, p. 122)

In their elaboration of this history, Deleuze and Guattari recapitulate the phases of Lindon's account while stressing the theme of betrayal. Cain, 'the true man', 'turns away from the God who turns away from him'; he 'already follows the line of deterritorialization, protected by a sign allowing him to escape death' (*TP*, p. 123). The dove of Noah's ark occupies 'the limit of separation or line of flight' between land and water. Moses, before his death, 'receives the great song of betrayal' (this phase Lindon does not mention). And Jonah betrays God in all the ways detailed in Lindon's reading (*TP*, p. 123). The final figure in Deleuze and Guattari's narrative – Jesus – 'universalizes the system of betrayal: he betrays the God of the Jews, he betrays the Jews, he is betrayed by God ("Why hast thou forsaken me?"), he is betrayed by Judas, the true man' (*TP*, p. 124).

If for Lindon, then, betrayal is a way of being faithful to God and assuming the scapegoat's role, for Deleuze and Guattari betrayal is the moment of flight, the break in the order of things. The scapegoat is first and foremost the wanderer in the desert, and the history of Jewish prophetism is that of a continual departure from any prescribed course and a continual remapping and recoding of that errant path. Crucial to Jonah's betrayal is his anticipation of God's actions, his orientation towards the future. 'But Jonah, in fleeing from the face of God, did exactly what God had wanted: he took the evil of Nineveh upon himself; he did it even more effectively than God had wanted, he anticipated God' (*TP*, pp. 123–4). Though he travels towards Tarsis, his flight is uncharted, his destination unknown – or, at any rate, insignificant, since his orientation is his point of departure, not his point of arrival. Like other prophets, 'his relation to God is passional and authoritative rather than despotic and signifying; he anticipates and detects the powers [*puissances*] of the future rather than applying past and present powers [*pouvoirs*]' (*TP*, p. 124). Jonah's flight is an underdetermined movement whose sense God will determine through his response. God's reaction, however, is not a betrayal, at least not in the same sense as Jonah's. God stops Jonah's wandering and returns him to Nineveh, thereby reinstating him within a regulated order. If God betrays the prophet, it is in the general sense that he seems to forsake him, to abandon him in his position of scapegoat. But the relation between prophet and God is one of only partial and limited betrayal, for God preserves the prophet in a state of 'reprieve, existence in reprieve, *indefinite postponement*' (*TP*, p. 123). Each betrayal is a brief rupture in the order of God's reason, which then serves as the beginning of a new order, a new disclosure of the divine will and plan. Betrayal is subsumed within a *regime* of signs, a systematic organisation of practices that produces regulated speech acts. But in itself, betrayal stands outside the semiotic realm, a gap in the fabric of signs.

Oedipus

In Lindon's reading of *Jonah*, the prophet betrays God, but only in a partial sense, and God's betrayal – if such there is – is even more limited than the prophet's. Deleuze and Guattari by contrast stress the mutuality of human and divine betrayal in the history of Jewish prophetism, a motif they see culminating in the narrative of the life of Jesus. But Deleuze and Guattari cite another narrative that provides the best model of the mutual betrayal of humankind and God, one outside the Judaic tradition – that of Oedipus. Deleuze and Guattari note that the first part of Oedipus' story is 'imperial, despotic, paranoid, interpretive, divinatory' and hence best understood in terms of the despotic, signifying regime of signs; but that the second part, detailed in *Oedipus at Colonus*, concerns 'Oedipus's wandering, his line of flight, the double turning away of his own face and that of God' (*TP*, p. 124). Oedipus' name

> is *atheos*: he invents something worse than death or exile, he wanders and survives on a strangely positive line of separation or deterritorialization. Hölderlin and Heidegger see this as the birth of the *double turning away*, the change of face, and also the birth of modern tragedy, for which they bizarrely credit the Greeks: the outcome is no longer murder or sudden death but survival under reprieve, unlimited postponement.
>
> (*TP*, pp. 124–5)

The full sense of this observation depends on a familiarity with Jean Beaufret's essay 'Hölderlin et Sophocle', a brilliant Heideggerian explication of Hölderlin's abstruse 'Remarks on Oedipus' and 'Remarks on Antigone'.[13] A brief summary of Beaufret's exegesis should help clarify the nature of Oedipus' relationship to the divine and the extent to which it may be seen as one of mutual betrayal.

Beaufret begins with an analysis of Hölderlin's conception of art, which is framed in terms of an Aristotelian opposition of *technē* (art) and *physis* (nature). Aristotle speaks of art imitating nature, but also of art surpassing nature and thereby completing it. Hölderlin distinguishes clearly between nature – the native, the natural, the innate – and culture, regarding culture's proper task as that of separating itself as much as possible from nature and thereby bringing to completion what nature could not achieve on its own. Yet when culture reaches its highest goal, it reunites with the essence of nature through what Hölderlin refers to as a *vaterländische Umkehre*, a return to one's native land, 'the turn-about [*volte*] which comes back to the very essence of the native' (Beaufret, p. 8).[14] Hence, art may be said both to oppose nature and to imitate it, to distance itself from nature but eventually to reveal nature's essence through a *vaterländische Umkehre*.

Hölderlin regards the ancient Greeks as 'sons of fire', by nature passionate, ecstatic, 'aorgic'.[15] Thus the proper task of Greek artists is to go beyond their 'oriental' nature and attain lucidity, sobriety and clarity of exposition, yet eventually to return to their 'aorgic' nature (though very few are successful in reaching this highest aim). Conversely, Hölderlin sees Germans (and modern Europeans in general) as naturally lucid and therefore faced with the cultural task of creating passionate, ecstatic art, with the modern artist's eventual (and hitherto unachieved) goal that of returning from the ecstatic to become again *knowingly* what one is *naturally*, i.e. clear and composed (Beaufret, p. 11). It is in this context that Hölderlin approaches Sophocles' *Oedipus the King*,[16] viewing the play as a model of the lucid tragedy modernity should seek to create as its highest *vaterländische Umkehre*.

Hölderlin finds the essence of Sophocles' tragedy in 'the retreat or the distancing of the divine' (Beaufret, p. 12). One may say that Greek tragedy as a whole is concerned with the limit or the border between humans and the gods. Yet in Aeschylus, for example, if humans transgress the limit of the divine (one thinks especially of Agamemnon and Prometheus), the limit itself remains clearly demarcated, the mortal's crime being that of a patent exceeding of limits. In Sophocles, by contrast, the limit *qua* limit is in question, and the hero falls into a dangerous gap in which the divine and human are undifferentiated. Thus in his 'Remarks on Oedipus' Hölderlin speaks of the tragic moment in which 'God and man couple [*sich paart*], and without limits [*grenzenlos*] natural force [*Naturmacht*] and man's innermost [*des Menschen Innerstes*] become one in wrath'. 'The presentation of the tragic rests primarily on this', he says, 'that the unlimited becoming-one [*das grenzenlose Eineswerden*] purifies itself through unlimited separation [*durch grenzenloses Scheiden*]' (*SWB*, II, pp. 395–6).

What Hölderlin means by the 'unlimited becoming-one' of humankind and God is suggested in the second section of his 'Remarks on Oedipus'. The intelligibility of *Oedipus the King*, says Hölderlin, rests on a proper understanding of Oedipus' response to the oracle reported by Creon. The oracle charges the Thebans to purify the city and drive the corruption from the land, but Oedipus 'interprets too infinitely' [*zu unendlich deutet*] (*SWB*, II, p. 391). Though the oracle might simply call for a rigorous trial and the maintenance of 'good civil order' [*gute bürgerliche Ordnung*], Oedipus goes beyond his civic, human role and speaks in a 'priestly' [*priesterlich*] fashion of the need for rites of purification. He also asks for particular details (of whom is the oracle speaking?) and leads Creon's thoughts to the murder of Laius. In this manner, Oedipus links the oracle and Laius' death, 'which are not necessarily connected to one another'. At this point, Oedipus enters a realm in which the human order of the state and the divine order of the oracle interpenetrate, and the subsequent scenes of the drama are so many demonstrations of the suffering, mad furore of man-and-god's 'endless becoming one': the 'wonderful angry curiosity' [*wunderbare zornige Neugier*] (*SWB*, II, p. 392) of Oedipus before Tiresias, as his knowledge, 'after it has broken its barriers', seeks that which it cannot bear or contain; the 'joyous destruction' of his words to Creon as his 'unbound' thought rages under the weight of 'tragic secrets'; the 'imbecility' [*Blöde*] and 'pathetic naive error of the powerful man' as he tells Jocasta of his efforts to avoid killing Polybus and marrying Merope; the 'desperate struggle' to 'come to himself' in the second half of the play, the 'foolishly wild search for a consciousness' [*das närrischwilde Nachsuchen nach einem Bewußtsein*] (*SWB*, II, p. 393); and the 'insane questioning for a consciousness' [*das geisteskranke Fragen nach einem Bewußtsein*] (*SWB*, II, p. 394) evident in his final interrogation of the messenger.

The tragedy of *Oedipus* thus dramatises the unlimited becoming-one of humankind and God, but that becoming-one also 'purifies itself through unlimited separation' [*durch grenzenloses Scheiden*] (*SWB*, II, p. 396). By purification Hölderlin clearly refers to tragic catharsis, but what he means by 'unlimited separation' is less evident. Beaufret finds a clue in Hölderlin's reference later in the Remarks to the 'categorical turn/reversal' [*kategorischen Umkehr*] whereby humankind responds to the moment when the god 'categorically turns' [*sich kategorisch wendet*] (*SWB*, II, p. 396). He argues that Hölderlin's 'categorical turn' echoes the categorical imperative of Kant, whom Hölderlin in a letter calls 'the Moses of our nation, who has led us out of Egyptian torpidity into the free desert of his speculation, and who has brought back from the sacred mountain the vigorous law'.[17] Kant's categorical law, in Hölderlin's view, is a sobering force that returns moderns to their native lucidity and disabuses them of their pretensions to understand the divine language of intuitive reason. Kantian morality is devoid of theophany, and hence 'it is no longer a vision of God, but already the retreat of the divine. The law is the most proper document of such a *retreat*. If God is presence, it is to the exclusion of any "intuitive representation" ' (Beaufret, pp. 14–15).

The categorical turn, then, is the moment of divine abandonment, 'when the Father turned his face from men' [*als den Vater gewandt sein Angesicht von den Menschen*] ('Brot und Wein', stanza 8, l. 127, *SWB*, I, p. 313), but also the moment when humans must assume the burden of the law and 'endure this *lack of God* that is the most essential figure of his presence' (Beaufret, p. 15). Although Oedipus is seized by an 'unlimited becoming-one' with God, he is also *atheos* (Sophocles, *Oedipus the King*, l. 661), 'not *atheist*, but deserted as much as possible by the god who separates himself and turns away from him' (Beaufret, p. 16). Even when Oedipus' crime is revealed, the heavens remain silent. Oedipus exacts his own punishment, but then embarks on an extended terrestrial wandering that only concludes in *Oedipus at Colonus*. This second life of Oedipus is that of the 'categorical turn of the divine', in which Oedipus must 'learn to lead a life of death in postponement' [or 'in reprieve', *une vie de mort en sursis*] (Beaufret, p. 17). As the drama of maximum separation of the human and the divine, *Oedipus* represents the furthest cultural distancing of Greek art from its native aorgic roots. As a 'tragedy of slow death' (Beaufret, p. 17), it serves as a model for modern tragedy, which should go beyond its culturally created enthusiasm and ecstasy and aim at a higher lucidity through a *vaterländische Umkehr*, or return to the native land of modern clarity.

Oedipus is the exemplary drama of the categorical turn, and this turn Hölderlin associates with infidelity and betrayal. In the 'frighteningly festive forms' of the drama, which is 'like a heresy trial' [*wie eines Ketzergerichtes*], God and humankind 'express themselves in the all-forgetting form of infidelity' [*in der allvergessenden Form der Untreue sich mitteilt*]. They do so in order that 'the memory of the Heavenly ones [*der Himmlischen*] not fade', for 'divine infidelity is the best to retain' [*göttliche Untreue ist am besten zu behalten*]. In the moment of such a turn, 'man forgets himself and forgets God, and turns around, indeed in a holy manner, like a traitor' [*wie ein Verräter*] (*SWB*, II, p. 396). This mutual betrayal entails a mutual forgetting, which Hölderlin describes in a passage that Beaufret declares as dense as any written *depuis que le monde est monde*:

> Inside it [the moment of the utmost limits of suffering], man forgets himself, because he is entirely in the moment [*weil er ganz im Moment ist*]; God [forgets himself], because he is nothing but time [*weil er nichts als Zeit ist*]; and each is unfaithful [*untreu*], time, because at such a moment it turns categorically, and beginning and end no longer rhyme at all; man, because within this moment he must follow the categorical turn, and thus cannot at all equal the beginning in what follows.
>
> (*SWB*, II, p. 396)

Man forgets himself in the sense that at the height of his tragic suffering he ceases to focus on past and future, to orient himself in terms of memories and projected plans, and instead exists solely within the present moment. But he also forgets in that he 'decisively liberates himself from *dead customs and opinions, devoid of spirit or sense*' (Beaufret, p. 19), as Hölderlin puts it in a letter of 1799 (*SWB*, II, p. 798). The tragic moment is a caesura in the rhythm of man's life, a break that makes past and future incommensurable from that instant on. Continuity is ruptured; beginning and end no longer rhyme; the beginning cannot equal what follows.[18]

God forgets himself in that he 'is nothing but time', a phrase that is clarified somewhat by Hölderlin's comment in the preceding paragraph that in the moment of the utmost limit of suffering, nothing remains but 'the conditions of time or space' [*die Bedingungen der Zeit oder des Raums*] (*SWB*, II, p. 396). The reference to Kant is evident, as Beaufret points out. 'The *conditions* of time or space signify in Kantian language that by which time and space are essentially themselves, an abstraction made of "affections" that alone give them a content' (Beaufret, p. 21). Kant also speaks of the condition of time or space as the pure and empty form of time or space. Hence, argues Beaufret,

> the god *who is nothing but time*, time being itself reduced to that in it which is a pure 'condition', that is, its pure and empty form, isn't this

indeed the retreat or the turning-away of God, such that he leaves man faced with the empty immensity of the endless sky?

(Beaufret, p. 21)

God's infidelity, then, is in the manner of his revelation. No longer a father, a friend, or even an enemy, He manifests himself solely as the pure and empty form of time, a blank and featureless sky. Man's infidelity is in his separation from God, his voluntary assumption of the task of living in this pure and empty form of time. Man turns from God as a traitor, but he does so in a holy manner. His effort is to be adequate to God's manifestation and thereby preserve 'the memory of the Heavenly ones'. That memory is one of divine infidelity, which is 'the best to retain', a memory of God's forgetting of man in that moment in which man forgets himself by entering into an unoriented time devoid of past and future coordinates. Man's turn from God is a 'categorical turn', and hence one that leaves him without divine intuition in the determination of his ethical judgements. His turn entails fidelity to a separation of the divine and the human, a discrete differentiation of what Kant calls the noumenal and the phenomenal.

The God of Judgement

Lindon's Jonah betrays God in fleeing towards Tarsis, but God betrays Jonah only to the extent to which he abandons the prophet to the role of scapegoat. In Hölderlin's account of Oedipus, by contrast, the betrayal of humankind and God is much more decidedly mutual: if Oedipus is a saintly traitor who turns from God, it is simply because 'the Father has turned his face from men' and set them adrift in the pure and empty form of time. In both Lindon's Jonah and Hölderlin's Oedipus, Deleuze and Guattari find the themes of the scapegoat and betrayal, but in Hölderlin alone does the turn from God take on an explicitly temporal dimension. For Deleuze and Guattari, I have argued, Jonah's betrayal *per se* rests in his flight towards an unknown future, and hence in his entrance into an uncharted and uncoded space and time. The precise nature of that time of betrayal now requires our attention.

Deleuze expands on this theme of the pure and empty form of time in his essay 'On four poetic formulas that might summarize the Kantian philosophy' (*ECC*, pp. 27–35), citing specifically Hölderlin's Oedipus (and Beaufret's commentary). Before Kant, says Deleuze, time is traditionally subordinated to movement. The world is seen as a great revolving door, spinning in an eternal circle, and time is conceived of as the measure of the passage between discrete and fixed points. With Kant, however, 'time is no longer related to the movement it measures, but rather movement to the time that conditions it' (*ECC*, p. 28). Time is the condition of possibility of movement, that within which movement can appear. Thus time itself proves to be a form whose content is unspecified. No longer can time be thought of in terms of succession, for 'things succeed each other in diverse times, but they are also simultaneous in the same time, and they subsist in an indeterminate time' [*un temps quelconque*] (*ECC*, p.28). That indeterminate time is neither eternal (time-less) nor changing (a qualitatively different time now than at some other moment). 'It is the form of everything that changes and moves, but it is an immutable form that does not change – not an eternal form, but precisely the form of what is *not* eternal, the immutable form of change and movement' (*ECC*, p. 29). And this new time has a theological dimension, for in it 'time ceases to be curved by a God who makes it depend on movement' (*ECC*, p. 28).

Time, then, is a pure and empty form, 'the immutable form of change and movement', which is not subordinate to an organizing god. Nor is it subsumable within some unifying self, which, as Deleuze often comments, is but a substitute for God.[19] In Deleuze's analysis, Kant revolutionises the Cartesian formula *cogito, ergo sum* by showing that the self is forever doubled – *fêlé*, split, or fractured – and precisely through the pure and empty form of time. The self (the *ego sum*) exists in time as something changing; it passively receives impressions and experiences itself through those changing impressions. The *cogito*, or thinking 'I', is an act, a determining activity, itself undetermined, that determines its existence only as something existing in time. Thus the active I (*cogito*) and the passive self (*ego sum*) are

> separated by the line of time, which relates them to each other only under the condition of a fundamental difference. My existence can never be determined as that of an active and spontaneous being, but as a passive 'self' that represents to itself the 'I' – that is, the spontaneity of the determination as an Other that affects it.
>
> (*ECC*, pp. 29–30)

Though time is the form of interiority, time is not within us but we who are within it. 'Interiority constantly hollows us out, splits us in two, doubles us, even though our unity subsists' (*ECC*, p. 31). The I and the Self are a two-in-one, a *Je fêlé*, or constitutively split I/self, and it is this split that Hölderlin identifies when he speaks of the caesura that separates the no-longer-rhyming beginning and end. Hölderlin, Deleuze says in *Difference and Repetition*, 'discovers the emptiness [*le vide*] of pure time, and in this emptiness, simultaneously the continued diversion [*détournement*, 'turning away'] of the divine, the prolonged fracture of the I [*Je*] and the constitutive passion of the self [*Moi*]' (*DR*, p. 87).

One might think that this discovery of the split self in the pure and empty form of time would be an emancipating event, yet Hölderlin treats it as 'the essence of tragedy' [*l'essence du tragique*], a kind of 'death instinct' (*DR*, p. 118) whereby Oedipus is condemned to the 'slow death' of a 'life of death in postponement' [*une vie de mort en sursis*] (Beaufret, p. 17). Oedipus and

God's mutual betrayal takes place in a 'categorical turn', which both Beaufret and Deleuze identify with the categorical imperative of Kant's *Critique of Practical Reason*. As Beaufret argues, the turn of God and man is categorical for Hölderlin since it reflects the Kantian absence of theophany in ethical judgements, the end of any 'intuitive representative' of the divine. Deleuze adds that the categorical imperative implies a new relationship between Law and the Good, a reversal whereby Law no longer derives from the Good, but the Good issues from the Law as 'a pure form that has no object, whether sensible or intelligible. It does not tell us what we must do, but what subjective rule we must obey no matter what our action' (*ECC*, p. 32). Kant's ascetic insistence that ethical action be devoid of interest and based solely on the principle of the categorical imperative leads to the curious resemblance of Kant's Law to Kafka's – blank, featureless, implacable. It is a law that never acquits us, 'neither of our virtues nor of our vices or our faults: at every moment there is only an apparent acquittal, and the moral conscience, far from appeasing itself, is intensified by all our renunciations and pricks us even more strongly' (*ECC*, p. 32). As Titorelli informs K. in *The Trial*, there is no possibility of acquittal before the Law, only 'ostensible acquittal' or 'indefinite postponement'.[20] The application of the Law is unending, but its process is never concluded. Rather than announcing immortality, 'it distills a "slow death", and continuously *defers the judgement of the law*' (*ECC*, p. 33).

Hölderlin's categorical turn, then, far from emancipating human beings, condemns them to an endless judgement without release or execution. In this regard, Deleuze and Guattari see a basic continuity between Jewish prophetism as traced by Lindon and Hölderlin's lineage of Oedipal abandonment that eventuates in the modern Kantian Law as 'pure form that has no object' (*ECC*, p. 32). In both, betrayal leads to the perpetual judgement of God, albeit in different guises. The passional, postsignifying regime of signs, we will recall, is a regime of the mutual betrayal of humankind and God, but one that involves as well a positive relation between the two. It would seem that this relation is based on a perpetual yet endlessly deferred judgement. How, then, is judgement related to betrayal?

In 'To have done with judgement' (*Essays Critical and Clinical*), Deleuze offers a brief genealogy of judgement based largely on Nietzsche's remarks on debt in *The Genealogy of Morals* and his analysis of the 'doctrine of judgement' in *The Antichrist*. All exchange has its origin in debt, and debt itself first comes into existence when individuals make promises but do not fulfil them. The debt owed the creditors is paid through the extraction of pain from the debtors, that pain giving the creditors pleasure. Tribal rites in which initiates are marked or scarred are merely extensions of the creditor/debtor relation, the elders extracting a measure of pleasure from the unit of communal debt inscribed in the bodies of the debtor-initiates. The creditor/debtor relationship is a cruel system of justice, but one devoid of judgement, and it is exclusively human, the gods at most serving as passive witnesses or advocates for one of the parties involved. Gradually, however, debt is transferred to the gods, as humans and gods begin to judge. Judgement presupposes 'that the gods give *lots* to men, and that men, depending on their lots, are fit for some particular *form*, for some particular organic *end*' (*ECC*, p. 128). Humans stake claims to certain lots, and the legitimacy of their claims is judged by mortals and gods. Human actions are measured according to the higher standard of divine forms, judgement assessing the extent to which an ideal form is realised. Thus judgement initially appears 'in the form of the *false judgement* leading to delirium and madness, when man is mistaken about his lot, and in the form the *judgement of God*, when the form imposes another lot' (*ECC*, p. 129). In Christianity, says Deleuze, 'a final bifurcation takes place: there are no longer any lots, for it is our judgements that make up our only lot; and there is no longer any form, for it is the judgement of God that constitutes the infinite form' (*ECC*, p. 129).[21] The Christian's only role is that of perpetual self-judge, and the sole form against which that role is measured is the infinite form of the deity, that form being one with an all-pervasive judgement. Ultimately, this form of judgement culminates in Kafka's blank law of perpetual postponement and in the tragic destiny of Hölderlin's Oedipus living a death in continual reprieve. 'At the limit, dividing oneself into lots and punishing oneself become the characteristics of the new judgement or modern tragedy' (*ECC*, p. 129).

The 'doctrine of judgement', as Nietzsche outlines it, requires a debt to the deity that is infinite and thus unpayable. But an infinite and endless debt requires an infinite and endlessly indebted debtor – hence the necessity of the doctrine of the soul's immortality. 'The debtor must survive if his debt is to be infinite' (*ECC*, pp. 126–7). The debtor's debt can never be discharged, and in this sense judgement, as final judgement (or Last Judgement), is perpetually deferred. Judging, then, as an endless and forever uncompleted process, is directly related to deferral: 'it is the act of postponing [*l'acte de différer*], of carrying to infinity, that makes judgement possible' (*ECC*, p. 127). Judgement's condition of possibility is a relation 'between existence and the infinite following an order of time: the existing being as having a debt to God' (*ECC*, p. 127). Thus an infinite debt to God entails not only the immortality of the soul, but also a specific conception of time and the relationship between existence and the infinite. Deferral is the act whereby existence is put in relation to the infinite, 'carried to infinity', and this act takes place within an order of time, an infinite straight line of moments extending towards a perpetually receding end point. Judgement, then, does not create but instead presupposes this relation between existence and infinity and this order of time: 'the power to judge and to be judged is given to whomever stands in this relation' (*ECC*, p. 127).

If we return to Hölderlin's Oedipus, we can perhaps see more clearly how betrayal is related to judgement and its condition of possibility. When man and God turn from one another, man forgets himself in time and God reveals himself as time. This temporal turn Deleuze identifies with Kant's reversal of the relation between movement and time, an unbending of the divine circle of time. Time ceases to be organised around the hinge [*cardo*] of a revolving door and becomes a straight line. 'It ceases to be cardinal and becomes ordinal, the order of an empty time' (*ECC*, p. 28). The order of an empty time is a simple but terrifying labyrinth, an infinite, inexorable, incessantly extending line, and it is this line that Deleuze finds in Hölderlin's Oedipus: 'Hölderlin portrayed Oedipus as having already entered into this strict march of the slow death, following an order of time that had ceased to "rhyme" ' (*ECC*, p. 28). Hölderlin calls the mutual betrayal of God and man a 'categorical turn', and hence ties it to the judgement of Kant's categorical imperative. Deleuze sees Kant's law as an opaque, self-enclosed principle, which imposes a perpetual and endless judging without final judgement. But that process of continual judging itself has as its condition the act of deferring, which puts existence in relation to the infinite in an order of time. In the turn of mutual betrayal, then, when time becomes a straight line, 'we have to renounce the ancient cycle of faults and expiations in order to follow the infinite route of the slow death, the deferred judgement, or the infinite debt' (*ECC*, p. 33).

It would seem, then, that the betrayal of God, in which man and God turn away from one another, has the peculiar effect of confirming a moral and theological relationship – that presupposed by the doctrine of judgement. In the turn of mutual betrayal, time may no longer be 'curved by a God', but the disclosure of a time that is 'unilinear and rectilinear' (*ECC*, p. 28) leads finally to an endless connection between the human and the divine, one based on the act of deferral and infinite debt. Yet once again we must question whether betrayal *per se* brings the human and the divine into a relation of perpetual deferral, since the mutual aversion of man and God does not *necessarily* issue in a regime of endless judgement. Kant's 'rectification of time' (*ECC*, p. 28) unbends the divine temporal circle, but it also discloses the condition of time as a pure and empty form. Further, time as the 'form of interiority', as the 'Affect of self by itself' (*ECC*, p. 31), is that which creates the *Je fêlé*, which 'constantly hollows us out, splits us in two, doubles us, even though our unity subsists' (*ECC*, p. 31). The pure and empty form of time need not issue in the straight line of an 'order of time'. The determining action of the I need not be joined with the passive determinable self in a regulated constitution of knowledge. This, says Deleuze, is the surprising discovery Kant makes late in life in the *Critique of Judgment*. What Kant discloses is a 'pathos beyond all logic', an aesthetic

which will grasp time as it bursts forth [*dans son jaillissement*], at the very origin of its thread and its vertigo. This is no longer the Affect of the *Critique of Pure Reason*, which linked the Self to the I in a relation-ship that was still regulated by the order of time; it is a Pathos that lets them evolve freely in order to form strange combinations as sources of time, 'arbitrary forms of possible intuitions'.

(*ECC*, p. 34)

The possibility exists, therefore, that the categorical turn of mutual betrayal need not inaugurate the 'form of judgement', that act of deferral that puts existence in relation to the infinite through an order of time and an unpayable debt. Nor need the 'universal betrayal' of the passional, postsignifying regime of signs necessarily inaugurate a process of subject formation, whereby a point of subjectification determines a *sujet d'énonciation* and a *sujet d'énoncé*. With a deregulation of the senses and a disordering of time, the *Je fêlé* may escape reconstitution and enter into asubjective relations, apersonal and anindividual, 'strange combinations as sources of time, "arbitrary forms of possible intuitions" '.

The passional, postsignifying regime of signs is a regime of universal betrayal, in which God averts his face as man turns away from God. It is a regime that territorialises the wandering of the scapegoat, submits the wanderer to a process of subjectification, and surrenders the subjected subject to the slow death of an indefinite postponement and perpetual reprieve. Lindon's reading of *Jonah* provides Deleuze and Guattari with an account of Jewish prophetism that makes it readily assimilable to the passional, postsignifying regime. Not only does Lindon transform what is often regarded as a tale of human disobedience and universal divine mercy into a story of faithful betrayal, showing Jonah to be a willing scapegoat who 'covers and protects', but he also relates Jonah to Cain, who is marked for a life in perpetual reprieve, to Noah's dove, which separates earth and heaven while assuring their mutual relation, and to Jesus, who reiterates the Psalmist's cry, 'Why hast thou forsaken me?'. In Hölderlin's Oedipus, Deleuze and Guattari find a continuation of the themes of Jewish prophetism – betrayal, the scapegoat, indefinite postponement. The betrayal of man and God, though, is much more clearly mutual in Hölderlin than in Lindon; the turn of God discloses the divine solely as the pure and empty form of time, and man's turn from God is but a means of preserving the memory of God's forgetfulness. In that categorical turn of man and God, a fundamental connection is established between betrayal and indefinite postponement. The infinite and unpayable debt to God is structured by a form of judgement, an act of deferral that puts existence in relation to the infinite in an order of time. Yet the turn also makes possible a disordering of time, a form of interiority that desubjectifies and shatters the *Je fêlé*.

What, then, is meant by 'the betrayal of God'? The passional, postsignifying regime may involve universal betrayal, but the moment of betrayal itself is a break in the regime, an uncoded and unmapped gap that is then recoded and remapped in terms of a specific configuration of power relations. The mutual betrayal of Hölderlin's categorical turn is likewise a rupture, an opening in time and a split in the subject, albeit one that can initiate the 'hell here below' (*ECC*, p. 33) of slow death and the indefinite deferral of the law. The God who is betrayed is the God of Judgement, whose principle is that of an ubiquitous evaluation of life by otherworldly standards. Everywhere life is judged guilty, and everywhere people are invited to judge others and themselves, to engage in an endless judgement that has as its aim a world of total social control and conformity to a dominant, homogeneous order. In the passional, postsignifying regime, the betrayal of God is fed back into the semiotic machine, made a part of a regular order of signs. In the modern form of tragedy outlined in Hölderlin's categorical turn, betrayal leads to an inexorable order of time and an implacable, blank law that makes life a slow death in continual reprieve. Yet the moment of betrayal itself, that mutual aversion of the human and the divine, makes possible a break with the form of judgement. Ultimately, then, betrayal is a way of having done with the judgement of God, and thereby doing away with the God of Judgement.

Notes

1 Gilles Deleuze and Félix Guattari, *A Thousand Plateaus*, trans. Brian Massumi (Minneapolis: University of Minnesota Press, 1987) p. 123. Hereafter referred to as *TP*.

2 I should note that Deleuze and Guattari also associate betrayal with the warrior, a central figure in the nomadic, countersignifying regime. The warrior 'is in the position of betraying everything, including the function of the military' (*TP*, p. 354); there is 'a fundamental indiscipline of the warrior, a questioning of hierarchy, perpetual blackmail by abandonment or betrayal, and a very volatile sense of honor' (*TP*, p. 358). Further, the nomadic is linked to the invention of 'a people to come' (*TP*, p. 377), a motif that Deleuze also ties to betrayal in an essay on T. E. Lawrence, who 'betrays England as much as Arabia, in a nightmare-dream where everything is betrayed at once' [*dans un rêve-cauchemar de tout trahir à la fois*]: Gilles Deleuze, *Essays Critical and Clinical*, trans. Daniel W. Smith and Michael A. Greco (Minneapolis: University of Minnesota Press, 1997), p. 117. Hereafter referred to as *ECC*. Unfortunately, the issues raised by these passages – those of the relation between the postsignifying and countersignifying regimes, the passional and the nomadic, the mutual betrayal of God and prophet, the warrior's betrayal of everything, and the universal betrayal inherent in the invention of a people to come – are beyond the scope of this essay. My reading of 'betrayal' as a break or gap in power relations, however, should suggest the lines I would follow in exploring these questions.

3 Jérôme Lindon, *Jonas* (Paris: Editions de Minuit, 1955). English translations from Lindon's translation (from Hebrew into French) are my own.

4 Bernard Bamberger comments that 'In Scripture, this holy day is called the Day of the *Kippurim* (*Lev.* 23:27f., 25:9). The word probably comes from a root meaning "to cover up". It refers to the process by which guilt or impurity is canceled out, made nonexistent' (Bernard J. Bamberger, *The Torah: A Modern Commentary. III: Leviticus* [New York: Union of American Hebrew Congregations, 1979] p. 162).

5 *Genesis*, 6:14. Lindon's French translation of the passage reads: 'Fais-toi une arche d'arbres de gopher. Tu feras l'arche en cellules et tu la couvriras de *kapper*, d'une couverture isolante, au-dedans et au-dehors' (Lindon, p. 23). The King James version of the verse is 'Make thee an ark of gopher wood; rooms shalt

thou make in the ark, and shalt pitch it within and without with pitch'. In a note on the word *kapper* at the conclusion of his translation, Lindon remarks

> Let us remember that *kapper*, which gives its name to the ark of the Covenant and to the day of *Kippur*, was, first, the *pitch* that covered-and-isolated the dove in the ark of Noah, and that it is represented here [in *Jonah*, 4] by the *sap* that covers-and-isolates Jonah under the *qîq~yôn* plant.
>
> (Lindon, p. 61, my translation)

6 In his exhaustive Anchor Bible commentary on *Jonah*, Sasson reviews various interpretations of the significance of Jonah's puzzling sleep. In wisdom literature, 'we do have a citation or two in which *r~dam* and *tardemâ* refer to the sleep of the irresponsible. [...] In stories about prophets, however, 'deep sleep' is said to overtake a prophet only *after* signs and wonders of God's presence become manifest'. Sasson's own reading is that

> prophets come to be *nird~mîm* when, upon recognizing signs of God's presence, they make themselves ready to receive the divine message. In this way, they readily accept divine control over their future behavior. Jonah's situation is not, however, similar to the abandoned prophets upon whom an angry God pours deep sleep (cf. *Isa* 29:10); rather, his condition is that of a prophet who realizes that there is no escaping God. It is at this juncture in our narrative, therefore, that Jonah capitulates and runs away no more.
>
> (Jack M. Sasson, *Jonah: A New Translation, with Introduction,*
> *Commentary, and Interpretation* [The Anchor Bible]
> [New York: Doubleday, 1990, pp. 101–2]).

7 Lindon's translation is 'Encore quarante jours et Ninive sera bouleversée' (Lindon, p. 40). Lindon adds in a footnote: 'As in French, the word [*nehp~ket*, rendered as *bouleversée*] has a literal and a figurative sense (*I Samuel*, 10:6: "You will be changed into another man")'. The King James version reads 'Yet forty days, and Nineveh shall be overthrown'. Sasson's wording is 'Forty more days, and Nineveh overturns' (Sasson, p. 224). The sense of *nehp~ket*, 'overturns', says Sasson, 'is crucial to the development of the plot' (Sasson, p. 234) for it renders Jonah's proclamation fundamentally ambiguous. Jonah could mean that in forty days Nineveh will be destroyed, but he could mean as well that Nineveh will be transformed. Often Jonah is viewed as a disgruntled prophet who predicts the demise of Nineveh and then is angered that God's mercy makes him a liar (or worse yet, that God's mercy spares those whom Jonah wants dead). Sasson argues that Jonah thinks he is foretelling destruction but that God is announcing repentance through words whose true meaning Jonah (and the reader) will only understand later. What Lindon implies is that Jonah is aware of the double meaning of his prophecy and that he is therefore not disappointed at its fulfilment in God's mercy.

8 Sasson also rejects the attribution of anger to Jonah, arguing that 4:1 should be translated, 'This outcome was so terribly upsetting to Jonah that he was dejected' (Sasson, p. 270). In his comment on the verse, Sasson notes that the line refers literally to the heating sensation that accompanies emotion. He observes that, though the Vulgate unequivocally identifies Jonah's emotion as anger (*iratus est* is Jerome's phrase), the Septuagint says that 'Jonah was terribly saddened, and was confused/shaken up'; the Arabic translation renders the line, 'he was very much grieved by all this'; the Targum reads, 'Jonah felt extremely bad and it affected him severely'; and the Syriac translation says that 'it distressed him exceedingly' (Sasson, p. 275). Sasson observes as well that the attribution of anger to Jonah, besides helping to shape a decidedly unappealing portrait of the

prophet's character, has all too frequently been marshaled in anti-semitic discourse: 'Jonah's alleged incapacity to share God's love with anyone who is not a Hebrew has unfortunately become a metaphor by which to censure Judaism and Jewish attributes'. Sasson's hope, he adds, is that 'most heavy-handed manifestations of this repugnant disposition are behind us' (Sasson, p. 274).

9 Sasson translates Jonah's prayer (4:1–3) as follows:

> Please, Lord, this certainly was my opinion, while yet in my own homeland; accordingly, I planned to flee toward Tarshish because I realized then that you are a gracious and compassionate God, very patient and abundantly benevolent, who would also relent from bringing disaster. Now then, Lord, take away life from me, because for me death is better than life.
>
> (Sasson, p. 270)

As Sasson notes, commentators have struggled considerably with the logic of this passage. He himself concludes that Jonah is angrily saying, in effect, that he knew God would be merciful to Nineveh, so he ran away, but God made him come to Nineveh anyway and prophesy its destruction; and now that God has done as Jonah expected, Jonah is so humiliated he wants to die. Sasson also remarks, 'It is not easy to offer a good reason for Jonah's feeling that only his own murder would adequately compensate for Nineveh's survival' (Sasson, p. 296). Clearly, Lindon is arguing that the reasoning in question is that of the scapegoating mechanism, a line of thinking that must at times seem void of 'good reason'.

10 The word *qîq~yôn* occurs only in *Jonah*, and there is considerable debate concerning its meaning. Most frequently it is said to be either a type of gourd or the *ricinus*, or castor-oil plant. In his lengthy review of the debate, Robinson concludes that 'if the choice is between the *ricinus* and the gourd (and there is not much to be said for the other traditional candidates), the gourd has perhaps the stronger case' (Bernard P. Robinson, 'Jonah's Qiqayon plant', *Zeitschrift für alttestamentliche Wissenschaft*, 97 [1985], pp. 390–403 [p. 402]). However, neither is a particularly suitable match for the plant described in *Jonah*. He suggests that perhaps the author had heard of a mythical Assyrian plant, the *kukk~nṣtu(m)*, and had included it to lend Assyrian authenticity to the story, or that it 'may be a nonce-word, newly coined to give an exotic flavour to the story', in which case the coinage may be 'derived from the root meaning "to spew" ' (Robinson, p. 402), since the whale had 'spewed' Jonah from its mouth. Robinson does not mention the possibility that *qîq~yôn* might be a nonce word echoing the name of Cain.

11 Lindon notes that the same word denotes Abel, the 'vanity of vanities' of *Ecclesiastes*, and the 'mists' of the second chapter of *Jonah*. Conversely, Cain comes from *'kaniti*, "I have acquired" ' (Lindon, p. 48). Hence Lindon's conclusion that in God's eyes 'Abel was nothing, it was Cain who was man' [*Abel n'était rien, c'était Kaïn, l'homme*] (Lindon, p. 48).

12 The specific workings of the point of subjectification, the subject of enunciation [*sujet d'énonciation*] and subject of the statement [*sujet d'énoncé*] need not concern us here. I discuss these concepts in my *Deleuze and Guattari* (London: Routledge, 1989), pp. 139–45.

13 Jean Beaufret, 'Hölderlin et Sophocle', in Friedrich Hölderlin, *Remarques sur Oedipe/Remarques sur Antigone*, trans. François Fédier (Paris: Christian Bourgois [10–18], 1965).

14 The phrase *vaterländische Umkehre* occurs in 'Anmerkungen zur Antigone' [Remarks on Antigone], §3, in Friedrich Hölderlin, *Sämtliche Werke und Briefe*, II, ed. Günter Mieth (München: Carl Hanser, 1970) p. 454. Hereafter referred to as *SWB*. In Thomas Pfau's translation (*Essays and Letters on Theory* [Albany

NY: SUNY Press, 1988]), the phrase is rendered as 'patriotic reversal' (Pfau, p. 114), a literal rendering that is potentially misleading, I believe. Fédier's French translation, 'retournement natal' (Fédier, p. 83), though somewhat freer, conveys more clearly Hölderlin's point. Citations from Hölderlin's 'Anmerkungen zum Ödipus' and 'Anmerkungen zur Antigone' will be from the Mieth edition, but translations are my own.

15 Pfau says of his translation of *aorgisch* that

> Hölderlin's distinction [between *organisch* and *aorgisch*] must be understood in the context of Swabian Pietism and the energetically inspired concept of nature of German Romanticism. Unlike Schelling's distinction between *organisch* and *anorganisch*, Hölderlin's 'organic' implies not a natural organism or the like, but designates the organized, reflected principle of the spirit and of art. Similarly, the term *aorgisch*, subsequently translated as 'aorgic', does not refer to the merely lifeless but designates, in the course of this translation, the unreflexive, unrepresented, disorganizing manifestation of nature.
>
> (Pfau, p. 168)

The *aorgisch* is close to what Nietzsche calls the Dionysian, though as Beaufret notes, Hölderlin associates it with Apollo, 'not as the absolute contrary of Dionysus, but rather its highest accomplishment as the extreme of virile force' (Beaufret, p. 9).

16 See Sophocles, *Oedipus the King, Oedipus at Colonus, Antigone*, trans. F. Storr (Loeb Classical Library) (New York: G. P. Putnam, 1912).

17 Letter to Karl Gock, 1 January 1799, *SWB*, II, p. 797; cited in Beaufret, p. 14.

18 Hölderlin speaks at length of the rhythm of the action of *Oedipus* and *Antigone*, seeing each as a single metrical structure divided by a caesura. In both dramas, the appearance of Tiresias marks the caesura of the action. The beginning and ending are of unequal length in the two works, he notes, the beginning shorter than the ending in *Oedipus*, and vice-versa in *Antigone*. It would seem that by the inequality and disharmony of beginning and ending Hölderlin refers to a radical discontinuity in the action signalled by the caesura of the prophet's appearance. Deleuze makes extensive use of Hölderlin's remarks on the caesura and the lack of rhyme between beginning and end in *Difference and Repetition*. See Gilles Deleuze, *Difference and Repetition*, trans. Paul Patton (New York: Columbia University Press, 1994) pp. 87–9. Hereafter referred to as *DR*.

19

> More generally, the supposed identity of the I has no other guarantee than the unity of God himself. For this reason, the substitution of the point of view of the 'I' for the point of view of 'God' has much less importance than is commonly supposed, so long as the former retains an identity that it owes precisely to the latter. God survives as long as the I enjoys a subsistence, a simplicity and an identity which express the entirety of its resemblance to the divine. Conversely, the death of God does not leave the identity of the I intact, but installs and interiorises within it an essential dissimilarity, a 'demarcation' in place of the mark or the seal of God.
>
> (*DR*, pp. 86–7)

20 Franz Kafka, *The Trial*, trans. Willa and Edwin Muir, rev. by E. M. Butler (New York: Modern Library, 1956) p. 201.

21 Deleuze expands on the Christian 'system of judgement' in his study of D. H. Lawrence's *Apocalypse*, 'Nietzsche and Saint Paul, Lawrence and John of Patmos' (*Essays Critical and Clinical*, pp. 36–52). The Christian rage to judge is at once a will to destruction and a will to penetrate every nook and cranny of the

world and the soul with a conforming power. A collective Self seeks both the destruction of an unspecified enemy, defined as 'anyone who does not conform to God's order' (*ECC*, p. 45), and the creation of a New Jerusalem of total social control. The 'postponed destiny' so central to Jewish prophetism is transformed from an open-ended expectation of an unforeseen future into a pre-programmed, destructive destiny, ' "postferred", placed *after* death, after the death of Christ and the death of each and every person' (*ECC*, p. 41).

2 The organism as the judgement of God

Aristotle, Kant and Deleuze on nature (that is, on biology, theology and politics)

John Protevi

God has been called many things, but perhaps nothing so strange as the name of 'Lobster' which he receives in *A Thousand Plateaus*.[1] Is this simple profanation a pendant to the gleeful anti-clericalism of Deleuze,[2] for whom there is no insult so wretched as that of 'priest'?[3] Certainly, on one level. But it is also a clue to Deleuze's ability to use a traditional concern of theology, the name of God, to intervene in the most basic questions of Western philosophy, in this case, the interchange of theology, biology and politics inherent in the question of nature and the organism.

The unity and finality of nature as a whole and the organism as a microcosm have always been patterned on God. Deleuze acknowledges this tradition in his concept 'the organism as the judgement of God' (*ATP*, p. 159), and then breaks with it with the concept of 'God is a lobster'. This essay will explain how the first of these concepts, 'the organism as the judgement of God', demonstrates a fundamental structure in one stream of Western philosophy,[4] as exemplified in Aristotle and Kant, while the second, 'God is a lobster', shows Deleuze's radical break with this traditional nexus of theology, biology and politics.

Why Aristotle and Kant? Why not Plato and Hegel? Or any other pair of great canonical figures whose linkage of theology, biology and politics was equally thoughtful and influential? Precisely because the very arbitrariness of the pairing will demonstrate the solidity of the theo-bio-political structure expressed by the concept 'the organism as judgement of God' and thus the utility of Deleuze's insightful formulation of it. I cannot demonstrate it here, but I am confident that a reading of the *Timaeus* and the *Encyclopedia* could demonstrate that, for Plato and Hegel as well, the organism is the judgement of God. So showing that two philosophers as disparate in time, method, and cultural presuppositions as Aristotle and Kant share a profound similarity in the way God provides the model of the organism, demonstrates that structure in a way that a simple point of reference, say Aristotle alone, would not.

The concept of 'the organism as the judgement of God' could only have come from the wild syncretism of Deleuze and Guattari, who gleefully bring the rantings of Artaud to bear on the deepest questions of Western philosophy. The key for understanding how the organism is the judgement of God for Aristotle, Kant and Deleuze is to unearth the connections in their thought of biology, theology and politics. In a word, to think nature. But nature is conceived differently in the three thinkers, and thus so will God be, for the question of God is inextricably linked to the question of nature. For Aristotle, nature is unidirectional: it is oriented to the best, to self-direction, *autarkeia*. Deviation from this natural striving for self-direction is unnatural: it is monstrosity, femininity, slavishness. Thus for Aristotle, the god, the most perfectly realised instance of self-direction, is the prime mover of cosmic locomotion and its lesser analogue, species reproduction, and is also the model for organismic unity. For Kant, nature is the field in which mechanism and purposiveness must be reconciled via the thought of an architect God. For Kant, God is the architect whom we must presuppose to understand the self-organising unity of part and whole in nature and in the organism. For Deleuze, nature is the abstract machine of stratification and destratification, or, in another formulation, coding/overcoding/decoding. There is a double direction to Deleuzean nature, towards unity and towards dispersion, towards capture and towards escape. For Deleuze, however, God is a lobster, the double-pincered abstract machine of natural stratification, and thus part, but only part, of nature. It is precisely this restriction of God to a part of nature that constitutes Deleuze's break with the tradition represented in this essay by Aristotle and Kant, and that enables his critical stance (in the technical sense of critique as separation of the discourse of production from the discourse of products) towards the theo-bio-politics of the organism as judgement of God.

The most important questions are at stake in the question of nature as the interchange of biology, theology and politics. Are natural theology and theologically modelled nature hidden forms of politics? Does Aristotle project the ideal of the adult citizen male onto a nature – onto a biology and theology – that he then will claim justifies his political decision to favour the interests of adult citizen males? Is mechanistic nature for Kant the projection of alienating modern industrial production, and political and moral freedom as self-determinating organic unity a reactive bourgeois fantasy? A good case can be made for each of these points, but the defenders of the interests of the state and of capital are such that this 'dialogue' would be fruitlessly unending. But, on another level, investigating just how this interchange of biology, theology and politics in nature works brings us to the very cutting edge of contemporary philosophy, the question of complex systems, in ways that vitiate the sterile oppositions of what passes for contemporary political discourse.

With the question of discourse, we come to the question of the *logos* underlying this theology and biology. For Aristotle and for Kant, the key to the conceptual interchange in the term 'nature' is analogy. For Aristotle, nature is the universal pull to realising the good as the internal *telos* of things, and the unidirectional orientations to self-direction in biology, theology and the political are analogous to one another. For Kant, owing to the acknowledged limits of his conceptual system, natural organicism is an 'analogue of life', posing questions that can, in lieu of an unthinkable thought of living matter, only be answered by the supplement of an architect God.

For Deleuze, on the other hand, there is no analogy in nature, but a single dual-action abstract machine operating in, between, and beyond different strata. There is thus no room for metaphor in Deleuze; there is no privilege given to the order of discovery and the cultural sedimentation of significa-tion over the order of being. Crossing these orders is the condition of metaphor. That is, one discovers an analogy between concepts in the sensible order that were indicated by an older sedimentation of signs (the proper signification) and concepts in the intelligible order (the figurative meaning), and then effects a transfer between sensible propriety and intelligible figuration. Rather than metaphor, for Deleuze there is only the simultaneity of the abstract machine and the multiplicity of machinic assemblages that work on, in, and between strata.

Aristotle

David Balme and Pierre Pellegrin, those who have done the most to rehabilitate Aristotle's biology in the last forty years, rescuing it from those who would denigrate it as a confused grab-bag of empirical observation and fantastic gullibility, insist on the unity of Aristotle's thought, that is, that one see the interchange between the natural science writings and the logi-cal/metaphysical writings.[5] They neglect, however, the ethical/political thought and *its* relation both to biology and to the highest point of 'first philosophy', theology. We must correct this omission and think through the reasons why Aristotle will say that *autarkeia* is the condition of both the adult citizen male and of 'the god', *ho theos*, the prime mover. *The unity of theo-bio-political thought.*

As the theology of *Metaphysics*, Lambda 7–9 teaches us, the highest being is pure activity, pure being-at-work, *energeia*. This work or function, *ergon*, has nothing of externally directed labour about it; it is purely self-directed and purely self-oriented, insight into insight, *hê noêsis noêseôs noêsis* (*Metaphysics*, 12.9.1074b34).[6] In fact, the very activity of insight is itself life, *hê gar nou energeia zôê* (12.7.1072b27), and furthermore, this purely interior activity of insight into insight is a life of pure constant pleasure (1072b24–26). The god who enjoys such a life is the highest substance, *ousia*; it is not merely unified, but simple (1072a32). *Divine biology.*

We learn from the same passage that the god serves as the erotic spur of cosmic locomotion and biological reproduction, *kinei hôs erômenon* (1072b3). Stars desire the simplicity of life of the god, but can only move in circles, the perfect motion. As such, they must settle for mere unity rather than simplicity, as they contain a matter susceptible of locomotion. Divine life is the first mover, erotically provoking the circles of stellar locomotion and species-generation, which mimetically supplement, in their motion and generation, the unreachable constancy of divine life (*De Anima*, 2.4.415a25–b7; *Metaphysics*, 9.8.1050b28). *Erotic mimetology*.

Generation is change within the protective borders of the circle of the species, oriented to the ideal case in which the superior male principle, working in the spermatic motions of the father that victoriously overcome the motions inherent in the maternal material on which it works, provokes the appearance of the same form in a father-resembling male child (*On the Generation of Animals*, 4.3.767b15–17). *Patriarchal semenology*.

We have a prephilosophical intuition that men and higher animals are substances, *ousiai*. The search for *ousia* in the great central books of the *Metaphysics* 7–9 is the search for a schema that will reveal the substantiality of those things our prephilosophical intuition has named as *ousiai*. *Dialectical ousiology*.

'Substance' is a misnomer for *ousia*. An *ousia* is a thing, but also the thinghood of the thing, *to ti estin kai tode ti* (*Metaphysics*, 7.1.1028a12). First subject, then matter, and most difficultly, form, are disposed of as candidates for *ousia*. Matter is the unlimited, the indeterminate, *hylê*. Form, *morphê* or *eidos*, is limit, *peras*. Formation is selection from a pool of potentials, cutting off some functions while selecting others. *Eidetic selection entails hylomorphic limitation*.

The stumbling block in the identification of *ousia* is always the question of particular unity. Matter is indeterminate; form is general. The hylomorphic composite enjoys a good run, but questions remain as to the ground of the vertical unity of the hylomorph and horizontal unity of generation. Hylomorphism, the imposition of form on matter, must be supplemented by the functionalising of potential, *dynamis*, in a unity wholly devoted to an activity, *energeia*. After the travails of the ousiology, the successful candidate for this thinghood, this substantiality, is activity: *hôste phaneron hoti hê ousia kai to eidos energeia estin* (9.8.1050b1). Activity is not motion; it is self-directed, *praxis*, not *poiesis*, practice not production. *Ousia* is not static; it is active and powerful, the ability to rule over parts, to form a unity of heterogenous materials. Substance is not stasis, nor is it motion; it is self-directed activity. *Energetic dynamism entails energetic unification*.

The soul is the principle of energetic unity in living creatures. Bodily fatigue prevents it from being pure activity. Rather, it is *hexis*, the capability of a body to perform its characteristic functions (*De Anima*, 2.1.412a27). Under the rule of the soul, the body becomes unified, a single organ, *panta yar ta physika sômata tês psychês organa* (2.4.415b18). Any formation of a unity is always that of ruler/ruled, and the unification of the animal body under the rule of the soul is masterly rather than political (*Politics*, 1.5.1254a30). *Psychic organisation entails somatic enslavement*.

The *ergon* of humans, our peculiar activity, is living the life in which the soul works with *excellent reason* (*Nicomachean Ethics*, 1.7.1098a13–16). If the human body is to be an organ for the soul working with *logos*, it must be prepared so that this potential is selected and cultivated. Such preparation of the body is the ethical training of the appetites to display a body that is self-directed. Only the adult male citizens are self-directed: slaves lack decision-making ability, while in women it is not strong enough to rule the appetites, and in [male] children it is incomplete (*Politics*, 1.13.1260a10). Education is the selection and consolidation of self-directing traits in citizen male children. *Pedagogic masculinisation.*

Politics is the science of arranging the city so the citizens can live well. The character of the citizens is the most important task of the legislator (*Politics*, 8.1.1337a10). He must form the bodies of the male children of citizens so they can reproduce the model of their fathers. The most self-directed of all citizens is the theoretician (*Nicomachean Ethics*, 10.7.1177a28). Politics is the necessary supplement to safeguard the production of leisure necessary for theory. Although the most self-directed of all humans, the theoretician needs a leisured body (not a lazy one, as our slavish notion would have it, but a fit and healthy body, an organic body achieved via a balance of exercise, food, rest) (10.8.1178b35). The leisured body of the theoretician is organised so that it can become effaced before the object of *nous*, its enslaved appetites complacent and quiet. The model of a self-directed living being whose life is theory is the god. *The organism as judgement of God.*

Kant

Kant brings into transcendental subjectivity the categories of Aristotelian *logos*, categories that were both, and thus neither, subjective and objective. In the *Critique of Judgment* he subjectivises the concept of natural purpose or organism, the *ousia* which Aristotle located in those natural things that had their principle of motion within them, that is, those with an internal final cause and thus those pulled along to be themselves, to make their matter match their form, which their paternal efficient cause passed on by organising maternal material. Now, since, *grosso modo*, the science of Kant's time outlawed final cause and had only a billiard-ball notion of efficient causality, a mechanism or blind pushing is all Kant could think in nature, given the tools of his time. Nonetheless, he wants to save natural purposes, but without paying the price of naive realism. His solution: natural purposes can only be thought in the mode of postulates. *Think* as if *nature were purposive.*

The *Critique of Judgment* is Kant's masterpiece, even if he cannot follow through on all the promise of its radicality. In it, he attempts to mediate theory and practice, nature and freedom. The subject of the *Critique of Judgment* is no longer the merely theoretical knower of the *Critique of Pure*

Reason nor the rational moral agent of the *Critique of Practical Reason*, but a natural and embodied subject throughout whom surges a 'feeling of life', *Lebensgefühl*, the raising and lowering of the intensity of which is felt as pleasure and pain.[7] *The felt intensity of life.*

Such pleasures and pains are brought forth by reflective judgement, which, in contrast to determinate judgement, does not subsume a sensory manifold under a pre-given concept, but instead arrives at its judgement, its way of making sense, in the very process of exploring the manifold given it (*CJ*, p. 190). In other words, reflective judgement is the escape from stereotyped cultural categories; it is the fresh encounter with the novel, an encounter that is felt before it is thought, or, even more radically, felt in excess of any recuperative thought. *Kant, the father of Romanticism.*

The *Critique of Judgment* has two main sections, a discussion of aesthetic judgement, that is, the judgements of beauty and of the sublime, and a discussion of teleological judgement, that is, the judgement of the purposiveness (the way in which the whole is greater than the sum of its parts and in fact determines the meaning and function of the parts) of organisms and of nature as a whole. *Think art and nature together.*

In the aesthetic judgement of beauty, an external object is judged as capable of provoking a harmonious interplay of imagination and understanding; the sublime, on the other hand, is the judgement that an external object is capable of provoking a disharmony of imagination and reason. In beauty, nature appeals to us as a pleasant stimulus, as provoking a disinterested non-sensuous pleasure; the sublime is the feeling that nature overpowers us, that we are radically insufficient to match its physical power. But for Kant, this very same physical insufficiency both provokes a violent torsion of our faculties and reminds us of our radical moral superiority to violent nature. Thus sublimity becomes the feeling of pleasure through or even in painful violence (*CJ*, pp. 244–6). *Beautiful harmony; sublime violence.*

The 'antinomy of teleological judgment' (*CJ*, pp. 386–8) states that we must think nature as mechanistic and yet as contingent in its particulars – there are no mechanistic laws of biology, no 'Newton of a blade of grass' (*CJ*, p. 400) – and in relation to us. The solution is to determine the supersensible basis of nature's lawfulness (that which was precisely left indeterminate but thinkable by the *Critique of Pure Reason*) as the negative idea of a non-discursive intellect (*CJ*, p. 410). But this is inscrutable, so we must have recourse to the idea of a moral architect God as the practical determination of the supersensible. Thus nature and freedom are finally related in the thought of a moral architect God who guarantees that nature must at least cooperate with our moral action (*CJ*, p. 444). *Architect God.*

In teleological judgement, organisms are not primarily seen as art, but as an 'analogon of life', that is, a being in which each part is an end and means of itself, as in the thought of a certain body politic, a *Staatskörpers* (*CJ*, p. 375n). Yet, Kant insists, such self-organising is inscrutable to us, because it would rely on the thought of a 'living matter', *hylozoism* (*CJ*, p. 374).

Therefore, to understand organisms, even though we have there a 'remote analogy' with human purposes (*CJ*, p. 375), we must ultimately, just as with nature as a whole, invoke the necessary presupposition of an external moral and divine producer. *The organism as judgement of God.*

Deleuze

For Deleuze, nature is singular yet bi-directional, the abstract machine of stratification and destratification. Nature operates both in, on and between the strata, and also beyond them, on the place of consistency. *Bi-polar nature.*

Professor Challenger[8] tells us that stratification is a lobster-god, the double articulation of content and expression, each of which has both substance and form. A substance is a 'formed matter', and refers to territorialities or spatial bindings; a form, on the other hand, implies a 'code', or temporal ordering. Content is production of 'formed matter', matter selected (territorialised) and formed (coded), while expression is production of a 'functional structure' that utilises this content to produce a new entity by an 'overcoding', resulting in 'phenomena of centering, unification, totalization, integration, hierarchization, and finalization' (*ATP*, p. 41). *Double articulation is the working of the Lobster-God.*

More detail is necessary, for the Lobster-God is complex. The abstract machine of stratification has four processes in two articulations. The first process is sedimentation, which determines: (a) substance of content, that is, the selection of homogeneous materials from a subordinate flow; and (b) a form of content, that is, the deposition of these materials into layers. The second process is 'folding,' in which there is: (c) a form of expression, that is, the creation of new linkages; and (d) a substance of expression, the creation of new entities with emergent properties (*ATP*, p. 43). *Sediment and fold.*

A body is any economic system considered as a mechanism of capture and appropriation, a region of matter-energy flow that has a relative consistency even as it is plugged into a network of other flows, slowing them down, cooling them off. But bodies are not all-powerful in their captures. A body is also defined by what overpowers it, by what escapes it. Deleuze uses the Nietzschean language of 'dominant and dominated forces', to explain that 'every relationship of forces constitutes a body – whether it is chemical, biological, social, or political'.[9] A social body: the student body, the Corps of Engineers. A political body: the body politic. A body is a differential ratio of rate of capture over rate of escape. *Differential corporeal systems.*

An organ is that which regulates the rates of capture and escape for a body. Organs are machines, that is, flow/break couplings in which a matter-energy flow is interrupted and part siphoned off to flow in the slower economy of the body. Organs are a body's way of negotiating with the outside, appropriating and slowing down a bit of matter-energy flow. Organs are points of intensity of matter-energy, a place of activity less intense than the surrounding outside but more intense than the body's other organs (with regard to its particular flow, that is). *Organs as liminal intensities.*

An organism is a particular organisation of organs, one that is centralised and hierarchical, appropriating the matter-energy of the organs and funnelling a surplus portion of them to the benefit of the organism as a transcendence relative to its organs, a superior body that has appropriated the organs as labour. Through its organisation of the organs, each one biting into and regulating a flow, an organism is a thickening or coagulation of flows of biomass and genetic material.[10] The organism is thus a stratum with regard to those flows, 'a phenomenon of accumulation, coagulation, and sedimentation that, in order to extract useful labor from the BwO ['Body without Organs'], imposes upon it forms, functions, bonds, dominant and hierarchized organizations, organized transcendences' (*ATP*, p. 159). *The organism profits from the labour of the organs.*

Organisms occur in at least two registers: one strictly biological, the other political. But it is the same abstract machine of stratification, the same Lobster-God operant in any register from geological to social as the way to appropriate matter-energy flows from the Earth and build a layer that slows down the flow and funnels a surplus to a transcendently organised body. The abstract machine of stratification is biological and political at once. *The geology of morals set forth by the Lobster-God is bio-political organisation.*

The political sense of organism means the oedipalised body of *Anti-Oedipus*, that is, one whose desire has been captured and patterned by a social machine. The organism as oedipalised body is a selection of a subset of the possible connections of the body, orienting it to docile reproductive labour. What is reproduced? Either products at work (hylomorphic labour reproducing form given by the master's organ of voice) or species reproduction via heterosexual penile-vaginal intercourse. The political organism can be on the scale of the 'individual' or on the scale of the body politic. The body politics organised as an organism: the totalitarian body. *Oedipal desire entails the organisation of an organism.*

Culture, or the social machine, is a recompensatory reterritorialisation or stratification to make up for a previous deterritorialisation on the organic stratum. Culture, that is, machinic assemblages operating on the alloplastic stratum, selects from a vastly larger pool of potential connections, opened up due to the deterritorialisation of some of our organs (*ATP*, p. 61). Thus culture is a huge reterritorialisation to compensate for our deterritorialisation on the organic stratum. Oedipalisation is the form of that reterritorialisation. It is stratification, that is, selection and consolidation. The social machine selects from the set of potential organ connections and consolidates them, via a series of exclusive disjunctions, into fixed and seemingly irrevocable patterns of allowable organ connections. *Compensatory cultural reterritorialisation.*

A body without organs, or BwO, is a misnomer. No body can do away with its organs. Rather, a BwO is a non-organismically organised body. Or rather 'it' is not at all, but is only the limit of a given process of destratification, the point at which a particular organisation of organs called an organism no longer holds and matter-energy flows are arranged immanently without reference to a transcendence profiting from the siphoning action of the organismically organised organs. A BwO cannot be wished into existence; it is an object of construction, a practice; it is 'what remains after you take everything away' (*ATP*, p. 151). It is not approached by regression, since it is there all along, besides the organism as its 'road not taken'. Thus the BwO is approached not through regression but by a systematic practice of disturbing the organism to unlock its forgotten potentials: 'The BwO is not at all the opposite of the organs. The organs are not its enemies. The enemy is the organism' (*ATP*, p. 158). *The immanence of the BwO to the organism.*

One might think a BwO is the matter-energy flow itself subtending a body, but this is only a representation of what might have been a BwO had it been left alone, but instead became a substratum viewed from a stratum.[11] Strictly speaking, a BwO is the limit of the process of destratification of a stratum or organism, and hence the 'phase space' of the body that suffered being made into an organism, its virtual field, the pool of potentials for any organisation of that body – organismic organisation, and other types of organisations as well.[12] What we really have is organism as limit of a process, just as a BwO is limit of a process. The organism and the body without organs are limits of the opposed processes of stratification and destratification. There is no such thing as an organism or a BwO. Both are representations of limits of processes. 'An organism' is only a representation of pure molar fixity, just as 'a BwO' is only a representation of pure molecular flow. The organism *versus* the BwO is only a *de jure* distinction, but Deleuze insists that such ideal purity never obtains in the world. All we have are *de facto* mixes, bodies consisting of varying ratios of stratifying and destratifying. After all, a stratum is itself only a ratio of capture *versus* escape. *The non-existence of the organism and of the body without organs.*

Why are there only representations of bodies that have reached the limit of the process of stratification (an organism) and destratification (the body without organs)? Because of the relation of actual and virtual: we expand the actual by incorporating more of the virtual, but the two can never fully overlap; the virtual must remain as adjacent, as the road not taken, as the nagging reminder of what might have been. Thus working towards your BwO is not regression, but tapping into previously deselected potentials, a refreshing dip into the pool of the virtual in order to re-organise in a non-organismic fashion, to gain a new non-organism body. That not all BwOs are ethically worth selecting is not the point here.[13] The organism is pure actuality, pure selection that has dispensed with disturbance from the virtual deselected option, while a BwO is pure virtuality, the never-never land of never having to make choices. Neither exists. *The non-equivalence of the actual and the virtual.*

To note the non-existence of organism and BwO is not to say that bodies cannot move towards either limit. Approaching the BwO is expanding the virtual realm and incorporating it into the actual organisation of the body with inclusive disjunctions that do not shut off a potential, even when another is temporarily selected. A body must be organised to some extent: it must have a coordination of organs that negotiate with the external flows. But with inclusive disjunctions those organs can have roles that shift about, experimentally, over time. Approaching the organism, on the other hand, is organising a body with exclusive disjunctions, so that, once the organismic pattern of organs is set up, its virtual options are forbidden. The difference between inclusive and exclusive disjunctions in organisation is easy to see in the political sense of organism as oedipalised desire – (in this context, inclusive disjunction is nothing more than the ability to make connections that are not reproductive) – but a little harder to see in the biological. But exactly that biological fluidity is the whole point of creative involution.[14] *Incorporation of the virtual via inclusive disjunction is the criterion of ethical selection for the organisation of bodies.*

Deleuze appears as a philosophical joker or *provocateur* when he says God is a Lobster (*ATP*, p. 40). But as refreshing as Deleuze's introjection of humour into philosophy is,[15] he is also serious about the Lobster-God. In keeping with his Lucretian, Nietzschean, Spinozist heritage, he is committed to the immanence of natural processes. Now for Spinoza, God and Nature were equivalent, *Deus sive Natura*. Deleuze's commitment to Spinoza is not to his notion of God, however, but to his insistence on the immanence of natural processes. Given his historical context, which defined God as transcendent, Spinoza's insistence on immanence was seen as atheism. So if for us, God is defined as transcendent, then Deleuze and Spinoza are indeed atheists. Now Deleuze does not say that the abstract machine is God, rather that God is a Lobster. The lobster as organism is doubly articulated, the result of the process of stratification symbolised by the Lobster-God. But the abstract machine of nature is not just stratification producing organisms, but also destratification producing the plane of consistency. So the Lobster-God is neither transcendent, nor is he all of nature, but only one aspect of nature as abstract machine of stratification *and* destratification. *The partiality of the Lobster-God.*

When God is not being a Lobster for Deleuze, he is the name of a transcendental illusion sometimes occurring in alloplastic strata. The overcoding of earth/tribe codes pushes the social recording surface onto the body of despot filiated with a sky god (*AO*, p. 194). All credit for production goes to this transcendent God. But this is a transcendental illusion produced by an immanent process. Critique is the refusal to use concepts derived from products to discuss their own production process. Thus the ground cannot resemble that which it grounds: the virtual cannot resemble the actual.[16] The stratification process as part of the abstract machine of nature does not resemble strata; God as part of the abstract machine, as the Lobster-God of stratification, is responsible for, but does not resemble, that which it produces, God as transcendent entity on which the organism is modelled. *'God is a Lobster' is a critical statement that exposes the illusion of the organism as the judgement of God.*

Notes

1 Gilles Deleuze and Félix Guattari, *A Thousand Plateaus*, trans. Brian Massumi (Minneapolis: University of Minnesota Press, 1987) p. 40. Hereafter referred to as *ATP*.

2 For purposes of orthographic simplicity I shall use 'Deleuze' in this essay to indicate both his singular thought and that of Deleuze and Guattari. The emergent effects of their collaboration should not be underestimated, but cannot be dealt with in this format.

3 For example, the inspired and beautiful rant at *Anti-Oedipus*, pp. 268–9. Gilles Deleuze and Félix Guattari, *Anti-Oedipus*, trans. Robert Hurley, Mark Seem and Helen R. Lane (Minneapolis: University of Minnesota Press, 1983). Hereafter referred to as *AO*.

4 Deleuze's explicit lack of interest in the thesis of the end of philosophy or the closure of metaphysics – 'I've never been worried about going beyond metaphysics or any death of philosophy', Deleuze says in 'On philosophy,' in *Negotiations, 1972–90*, trans. Martin Joughin (New York: Columbia University Press, 1995), p. 136 – does not mean that he would not acknowledge fundamental structures in what he calls state philosophy. He merely wants to highlight the arbitrary nature of the Heideggerian and Derridean canons that allow that thesis to be constructed. Deleuze will affirm the existence of a current of philosophers – the Stoics, Lucretius, Spinoza, Hume, Nietzsche (his –Deleuze's – Nietzsche, to be sure!), Bergson, Foucault – who do not fit the Heideggerian and Derridean canon and whose 'thought of the outside' provides resources for novel creation of concepts, the ongoing life of philosophy.

5 See the bibliography of David Balme's writings in *Aristotle on Nature and Living Things: Philosophical and Historical Studies Presented to David M. Balme on his Seventieth Birthday*, ed. Allan Gotthelf (Bristol: Bristol Classical Press, 1985); Pierre Pellegrin, *Aristotle's Classification of Animals*, trans. A. Preus (Berkeley: University of California Press, 1986).

6 Citations from Aristotle are from the Oxford Classical Text editions. The standard English translation is *The Complete Works of Aristotle*, ed. Jonathan Barnes (Princeton: Princeton University Press, 1984).

7 Immanuel Kant, *Critique of Judgment*, trans. Werner Pluhar (Indianapolis: Hackett, 1987), p. 204. Pluhar puts the *Akademie Ausgabe* (AA) pagination in the margins. I cite the AA pages. Hereafter referred to as *CJ*.

8 'Professor Challenger' is the *nom de plume* adopted by Deleuze and Guattari in the 'Geology of morals' plateau of *A Thousand Plateaus*.

9 Gilles Deleuze, *Nietzsche and Philosophy*, trans. Hugh Tomlinson (New York: Columbia University Press, 1983), p. 40.

10 On these and other points in my reading of Deleuze, see Manuel A. DeLanda, *A Thousand Years of Nonlinear History* (New York: Zone Books, 1997).

11 One of my few criticisms of DeLanda's *A Thousand Years of Nonlinear History* is the passage at 261–2 naming a variety of BwOs as if they were entities.

12 On the reading of BwO as virtual, see Brian Massumi, *A User's Guide to Capitalism and Schizophrenia* (Cambridge MA: MIT Press, 1992).

13 See my 'A problem of pure matter: Deleuze and Guattari's treatment of fascist nihilism in *A Thousand Plateaus*', in *Nihilism Now!: 'Monsters of Energy'*, ed. Keith Ansell Pearson and Diane Morgan (Macmillan, forthcoming).

14 See Keith Ansell Pearson, *Viroid Life* (London: Routledge, 1997); and *Germinal Life* (London: Routledge, 1999).

15 Friedrich Nietzsche: 'I should actually risk an order of rank among philosophers depending on the rank of their laughter', *Beyond Good and Evil*, trans. W Kaufmann (New York: Random House, 1966) §294.

16 See Alistair Welchman, 'Deleuze,' in *Edinburgh Encyclopedia of Continental Philosophy*, ed. Simon Glendinning (Edinburgh: Edinburgh University Press, 1999).

3 Embodied anti-theology

The body without organs and the judgement of God

Judith Poxon

> We must make up our minds to strip [ourselves] bare in order to scrape off that animalcule that itches [us] mortally, god, and with god [our] organs.[1]

What is the body without organs, and what, if anything, is its theological significance? Gilles Deleuze observes that 'The *judgment of God*, the system of the judgment of God, the theological system, is precisely the operation of He who makes an organism, an organization of organs called the organism',[2] and that, because this is so, 'the way to escape judgment is to make yourself a body without organs, to find your body without organs'.[3] The body without organs, in other words, diverges from the body-as-organism in such a way as to undo the judgement of God and the theological system. While, at first reading, these claims may be incomprehensible, they yield their sense when situated in the context of Deleuze's critique, in *The Logic of Sense*, of 'the order of God'[4] – an order within which the self-identical nature of God authorises the analogous identities or integrities of language, subject and body. Against this divine order, Deleuze affirms an order of the Antichrist (*LS*, p. 292), an order expressive not of identity but of difference as such, and in so doing undoes the order of God and the judgement on which it is based and which it in turn enforces. In this essay, then, I will argue that the body without organs – the BwO – emerges out of the order of the Antichrist as a vital anti-theological trope, challenging the divine order and expressing the creative power of pure affirmation.

Deleuze develops his critique of the order of God within the context of an extended reading of the work of philosopher and novelist Pierre Klossowski (*LS*, pp. 280–301). Here he explores the opposition in Klossowski's thought between reason, seen as essentially theological, and the body, seen as essentially perverse (*LS*, p. 280), in order to show the ways in which the perverse Klossowskian body undermines both the divine system and, more immediately, the identity of the self which that system authorises. Within the divine system, for Deleuze–Klossowski, each of the identities that comprise it – identities of God, world, self, body, and language – both rests on and underwrites the identity of each other element, while the identity of God serves as the ultimate foundation of the system as a whole (*LS*, p. 292).

According to Deleuze, then, 'Klossowski insists that God is the sole guarantor of the identity of the self and of its substantive base, that is, of the integrity of the body' (*LS*, p. 294). Moreover, God is able to guarantee this interlocking order of identities by virtue of being a Kantian master of the disjunctive syllogism – a divine judge who serves as both the totality of all possible realities and the determination of that subset of reality that constitutes the conceptual identity of any given person or thing (*LS*, p. 295). After Kant, in other words, the Christian God is revealed as that principle according to which all embodied reality is *either* this *or* that, but never this *and* that, and, as Klossowski shows, it is precisely on account of reality's being embodied that God is able to impose this limitative identity.

Clearly, however, both Deleuze and Klossowski are working with two different conceptions of 'body' here. On the one hand, there is the *theological* body, whose integrity forms the 'substantive base' of the interlocking identities of the order of God:

> The order of divine creation depends on bodies, is suspended from them. In the order of God, in the order of existence, bodies give to minds (or rather impose on them) two properties: identity and immortality, personality and resurrectibility, incommunicability and integrity. [...] God must depend upon the body.
>
> (*LS*, p. 292)

The integrity of this theological body provides an objective, material guarantee that the essential attributes of an individual self will not be predicable of other individual selves, and that the mind, or soul, will have – by virtue of being tied to a particular body – its own unique identity. And even more, the theological body guarantees the immortality of the mind or soul, for 'it is insofar as it is brought back to its body that the mind acquires immortality' (*LS*, p. 292).

In contrast to this theological body stands the *perverse* body, which is perverse 'precisely [because of] this objective power of hesitation [...]: this paw which is neither left nor right; this determination by fits and starts; this differentiation never suppressing the undifferentiated which is divided in it' (*LS*, p. 281). In other words, the perverse body is perverse to the extent that it keeps open all of its possible determinations, refusing to assert what it is at the expense of suppressing what it is not, refusing *identity*.

In order to indicate the significance of this distinction between theological and perverse bodies, then, Deleuze (re)turns from Klossowski to Kant – in particular, to Kant's linking of God with the disjunctive syllogism. For Kant, says Deleuze,

> God is defined by the sum total of all possibilities, insofar as this sum constitutes an 'originary' material or the whole of reality. The reality of each thing 'is derived' from it; it rests in effect on the limitation of this

> totality, 'inasmuch as part of it (reality) is ascribed to the thing, and the
> rest is excluded – a procedure which is in agreement with the "either-or"
> of the disjunctive major premise and with the determination of the
> object, in the minor premise, through one of the members of the divi-
> sion'. In short, the sum total of the possible is an originary material
> from which the exclusive and complete determination of the concept of
> each thing is derived through disjunction. God has no other sense than
> that of founding this treatment of the disjunctive syllogism.
>
> (*LS*, pp. 295–6; citing Kant, *Critique of Pure Reason*)

That is, the process by which the reality of each thing is derived from and
guaranteed by God, understood as the 'whole of reality,' is a process of
limitation and negation. The 'either-or' of disjunction, according to this
process, resolves the ambiguity of its 'or' in favour of exclusion: each thing is
what it is, and only what it is, and is not what it is not. Within the order of
Kant's God, (P Q) always means (P Q). 'In Kant, therefore', says Deleuze,
'we see that God is revealed as the master of the disjunctive syllogism only
inasmuch as the disjunction is tied to [...] a *negative and limitative use*' (*LS*,
p. 296). It is this 'negative and limitative use' of the disjunctive syllogism that
must, for Deleuze–Klossowski, depend on the body, and in particular on the
identity or integrity of the theological body. In fact, this is the essence of the
theological body: that it underwrite the Kantian understanding of the
disjunctive syllogism, that it provide the material guarantee of the identity
and immortality of the self that is constituted by negation, limitation,
exclusion.[5]

But if 'it is precisely inside God's order, and only there, that disjunctions
have the negative value of exclusion', then 'it is on the other side, inside the
order of the Antichrist, that the disjunction (difference, divergence,
decentering) becomes as such an affirmative and affirmed power' (*LS*, pp.
296–7). And here lies the significance for Deleuze of the Klossowskian
perverse body: in its 'differentiation never suppressing the undifferentiated
which is divided in it' (*LS*, p. 281), it instantiates the *inclusive* force of the
order of the Antichrist. Against the exclusionary force of the 'either-or', of
which the Kantian God is the master, in other words, Klossowski proposes a
Nietzschean 'anti-theology,' in which, because 'several souls [may] enter
together into the same body, and the same soul may possess several bodies
[...] God can no longer guarantee any identity!' (*LS*, p. 293).

Within this 'anti-theology', depending not on the integrity of the theological body but rather on the *dis*-integration, the difference and divergence
of the perverse body, 'it is not God but the Antichrist who is the master of
the disjunctive syllogism [because] the anti-God determines the *passage* of
each thing through all of its possible predicates' (*LS*, p. 296). The result of
such a *passage* – that is, of the refusal to settle on one, or even several,
possible predicates, the insistence on the constant flux of a truly infinite
becoming – is that:

The disjunction is always a disjunction; the 'either-or' is always an 'either-or.' Rather than signifying that a certain number of predicates are excluded from a thing in virtue of the identity of the corresponding concept, the disjunction now signifies that each thing is opened up to the infinity of predicates through which it passes, on the condition that it lose its identity as concept and as self. [Thus] the disjunction is affirmed for itself without ceasing to be a disjunction; divergence or difference become objects of pure affirmation, and 'either-or' becomes the power of affirmation, outside the conceptual conditions of the identity of a God, a world, or a self.

(*LS*, p. 296)

In other words, in order to subvert the exclusionary force of the 'either-or', in order to affirm difference itself, all claims to the possibility of an identity established within the 'order of God' must be surrendered. And if the God of the divine order 'must depend upon the body' (*LS*, p. 292), then the identity or integrity of the body – in other words, the body understood as organism – will be the first to go.

How, then, does the body without organs correspond to, or resonate with, this perverse Klossowskian body that has the power to undo the order of God? Indeed, what is the body without organs?

First of all, according to Deleuze (and Guattari), the BwO is 'not a concept but a practice, a set of practices', and as such it is not something that is ever accomplished or realised: 'You never reach the Body without Organs, you can't reach it, you are forever attaining it, it is a limit'. Rather, it is continually constructed in processes of experimentation, carried out across biological, social and political registers (*ATP*, pp. 149–50). In contrast to the body-as-organism, the theological body, the BwO is 'an affective, intensive, anarchist body that consists solely of poles, zones, thresholds, and gradients. It is traversed by a powerful, nonorganic vitality' and is defined not in its wholeness, its identity, but rather 'in its becoming, in its intensity, as the power to affect or to be affected' (*ECC*, p. 131). As Elizabeth Grosz writes:

[The] notion of the BwO is Deleuze and Guattari's attempt to denaturalize human bodies and to place them in direct relations with the flows or particles of other bodies or things. [...] It is thus not a question of what the BwO *is*, what composes it, but what it does, how it functions, what it affects, what it produces.[6]

That is, what is highlighted in the BwO is process, flux, function, as opposed to the static identity of the theological body, the body-as-organism. Strictly speaking, the BwO cannot be said *to be* at all; rather, it always *becomes*. It is, as Dorothea Olkowski points out, 'a field of becomings'.[7]

If, however, the BwO stands in contrast to the wholeness of the theological body, it is nevertheless, for Deleuze and Guattari, 'not at all a question of a fragmented, splintered body, of organs without the body (OwB). The BwO is exactly the opposite. There are not organs in the sense of fragments in relation to a lost unity, nor is there a return to the undifferentiated in relation to a differentiable totality' (*ATP*, pp. 164–5). That is, the BwO is not the mark of regression to an illusory pre-Oedipal wholeness, a state in which the 'self' exists in an undifferentiated union with the maternal body. Indeed, such a regression would place the BwO squarely within the psychoanalytic perspective that Deleuze, with Guattari, is at such pains to discredit.[8]

Rather than representing an imaginary pre-Oedipal state, the BwO 'is what remains when you take everything away. What you take away is precisely the phantasy, and signifiances and subjectifications as a whole' (*ATP*, p. 151). In other words, it is the opposite of the psychoanalytic body, the mythological body, the religious body. It is, as Grosz points out, 'a body without a psychical interior, without internal cohesion or latent significance'. It is 'the body before and in excess of the coalescence of its intensities and their sedimentation into meaningful, functional, organized, transcendent totalities'.[9] Thus, the BwO is emphatically not made in the image of God, nor in any other image. Or rather, like the Deleuzean simulacrum, it supports a demonic image, an 'image without a likeness […], stripped of resemblance'.[10] If the BwO is 'not a concept but a practice', it is precisely the set of practices that refuse to subject the body to mythological or religious imaginings. On the contrary, 'the body is now nothing more than a set of valves, locks, floodgates, bowls, or communicating vessels' (*ATP*, p. 153) – a desiring-machine, an anti-'human' process.

Thus, despite appearances, the BwO is not opposed to the organs. Indeed, as Deleuze and Guattari note, 'the BwO is not at all the opposite of the organs. The organs are not its enemies. The enemy is the organism. The BwO is opposed not to the organs but to that organization of the organs called the organism' (*ATP*, p. 158). This is so because, unlike the organism that is unified in its organisation, the BwO is multiple, and that multiplicity constitutes the source of its vitality, its force. 'The body without organs is not a dead body but a living body all the more alive and teeming once it has blown apart the organism and its organization. [… It] is a body populated by multiplicities' (*ATP*, p. 30). Olkowski notes that the BwO, existing outside of the divine order, without limits, is 'a crowd; a multiplicity; a pack in smooth, that is unorganized and unstable, space' (Olkowski, pp. 137–8). But this multiplicity, for Deleuze, 'is a problem not of the One and the Multiple but of a fusional multiplicity that effectively goes beyond any opposition between the one and the multiple' (*ATP*, p. 154) – or, to put it another way, 'not the unity of the One, but a much stranger unity that applies only to the multiple' (*ATP*, p. 158). The multiplicity of the BwO, then, is irreducible to a numeric quantity of organs that would be subsumable into the unity of the organism; while not the enemy of the organs, the BwO is nevertheless also *not* the organs. In this context, Deleuze gestures towards Artaud's world of 'crowned Anarchy' – a world 'where no gods go' (*ATP*, p. 158) – in order to contrast it with 'this, our world', linking the former with the BwO and the latter with the body-as-organism, in which flows of vital energy or force are blocked, stratified, thwarted.

Thus the BwO, like Klossowski's perverse body, is clearly a body opposed to the order of God, since it is God who makes the organism, who imposes his divine image and order on the machinic BwO in order to remake it as organism. The body-as-organism, the theological body, is 'a stratum on the BwO [...] that, in order to extract a useful labor from the BwO, imposes upon it forms, functions, bonds, dominant and hierarchized organizations, organized transcendences' (*ATP*, p. 159) – in other words, all of the marks of the order of God. The 'powerful, nonorganic vitality' of the BwO, its irreducible multiplicity, is submitted to the organ-ised integrity or identity of the theological body, so that the theological body in turn is able to provide the material base for the interdependent identities of God, self and language. 'For the judgment of God weighs upon and is exercised against the BwO; it is the BwO that undergoes it. [...] The judgment of God uproots it from its immanence and makes it an organism, a signification, a subject' (*ATP*, p. 159). The BwO, on the contrary, undoes the divine order, and this comes as no surprise, given that

> the judgment of God, the system of the judgment of God, the theologi-cal system, is precisely the operation of He who makes an organism, an organization of organs called the organism, because He cannot bear the BwO, because He pursues it and rips it apart so He can be first, and the organism be first. The organism is already that, the judgment of God.
>
> (*ATP*, pp. 158–9)

But it is precisely because the body that refuses its status as organism asserts instead of divine judgement its own 'powerful, nonorganic vitality' – a vitality that is 'the relation of the body to the imperceptible forces and powers that seize hold of it, or that it seizes hold of' (*ECC*, p. 131) – that it is able to undermine the judgement of God. This is why Deleuze can argue that to make oneself a BwO – a body that celebrates the intensity of its multiple becomings – is 'the way to escape judgment' (*ECC*, p. 131).

But what, exactly, is the relation between the *judgement* of God, to which the BwO is explicitly opposed, and the Deleuzean–Klossowskian *order* of God? According to Deleuze, it is divine judgement that imposes divine order: 'Judgment implies a veritable organization of the bodies through which it acts: organs are both judges and judged, and the judgment of God is nothing other than the power to organize to infinity' (*ECC*, p. 130). Judgement imposes order both on and through the organs: divine judgement produces the order of the organism by judging the organs, while the organs in their turn support God's order by judging the BwO. In other words, judgement is precisely that power that is productive of order, and the judgement of God is productive of the order of God, with the complicity of the theological body, the body-as-organism. 'At bottom, a doctrine of judgment presumes that [God gives] *lots* to men, and that men, depending on their lots, are fit for some particular *form*, for some particular organic *end*' (*ECC*, p. 128). Whereas, as Grosz points out, the BwO 'resists any equation with a notion of identity or property' ('A Thousand tiny sexes', p. 201), God's judgement acts through the body-as-organism to impose a particular form, or *identity*, on each individual person, and it is that identity, linked as it is to a particular function, that underwrites and gives expression to the entire order of God.

This, then, is precisely what is at stake for Deleuze in his claim that Klossowski's formulation of the perverse body aims at the dissolution of personal identity, and it is here that the perverse body, which is also the body without organs, reveals its theological import. If identity and the order of God are mutually constitutive constructs, and both are opposed to the affirmative, creative force of the body without organs, just as to Klossowski's perverse body, then, conversely, the BwO not only undoes the divine order but also opens onto the order of the Antichrist, an order in which personal identity has no foundation because the self-identical nature of God and the divine judgement that expresses and authorises it have been cancelled out. This anti-divine order, then, 'is characterized by the death of God, the destruction of the world, the dissolution of the person, the disintegration of bodies, and the shifting function of language which now expresses only intensities' (*LS*, p. 294). It is an order in which the identity of the self has fractured beyond recognition, and the body-as-organism – object and product of divine judgement, foundation of divine order – gives way to the powerful nonorganic or machinic vitality of the body without organs. Within the order of the Antichrist, personal identity is replaced by 'pre-individual and impersonal singularities' and 'the identity of the self is lost, not to the benefit of the One or the unity of the Whole, but to the advantage of an intense multiplicity and power of metamorphosis, where relations of force play within one another' (*LS*, p. 297). Indeed, 'the system of the Antichrist is the system of simulacra opposed to the world of identities'; that is, this Deleuzean simulacrum, like the BwO, 'dismisses identity' and 'opens up to its difference and to all other differences' (*LS*, p. 298). The order of the Antichrist, in other words, is the order of the 'affective, intensive, anarchist' body without organs.

For both Deleuze and Klossowski, then, the order of the Antichrist is the order of Nietzsche's eternal return, an order in which 'there is no longer any originary reality'. The disjunction of divine judgement is released from its Kantian limitations, allowed to remain a disjunction, and, as noted earlier, 'affirmed for itself without ceasing to be a disjunction [so that] divergence or difference become objects of pure affirmation, and "either-or" becomes the power of affirmation' (*LS*, p. 296). In its irreducibly affirmative force, the Nietzschean repetition of the eternal return stands, for Deleuze, in sharp contrast to the Christian repetition of Kierkegaard, which more nearly resembles the theology of resurrection. This, as Deleuze's reading of Klossowski shows, depends on the integrity of the body-as-organism, 'for what the Christian repetition brings back, it brings back once, and only once: the wealth of Job and the child of Abraham, the resurrected body and the recovered self' (*LS*, pp. 300–1).[11] The eternal return, in guaranteeing that the 'either-or' of disjunction remains an 'either-or,' undermines the coherence of the organism, and banishes the order of God: '*All of that which is founded on God and makes a negative or exclusive use of the disjunction is denied and excluded by the eternal return*' (*LS*, p. 301). Thus Deleuze's anti-theology does not leap with Kierkegaard but rather dances with Nietzsche (*DR*, p. 10); it celebrates the moment in which the God who guarantees identity dies and the self dissolves, in order that the nonorganic vitality of the BwO might emerge.

Of course, Deleuze is not unaware of the dangers entailed in an anti-theology that is (un)grounded in the disintegration of the body-as-organism and the dissolution of the self, and he warns his readers to experiment cautiously as they assemble the set of practices that constitute the BwO. Explicitly, there is always the possibility of making for oneself an 'empty BwO' – the BwO of the drug addict, the schizophrenic, the masochist (*ATP*, p. 150). Indeed, Artaud compares making a BwO with suicide.[12] For Deleuze, however, 'the dissolution of the self ceases [within the order of the Antichrist] to be a pathological determination in order to become the mightiest power, rich in positive and salutary promises' (*LS*, p. 283). This is so because the anti-theology of the BwO, understood as a 'line of flight'[13] leading away from the judgement of God, expresses the power of pure creative affirmation in a way that the theology of the order of God cannot. Divine judgement, the foundation and guarantee of the divine order, 'presupposes preexisting criteria (higher values), criteria that preexist for all time (to the infinity of time), so that it can neither apprehend what is new in an existing being nor even sense the creation of a mode of existence'. In other words, 'judgment prevents the emergence of any new mode of existence' (*ECC*, pp. 134–5).

Within the order of God, creation has its one historical moment, recorded in Genesis; thenceforth, because divine judgement operates according to its own eternal and transcendental values, imposing personal identity and bodily integrity on its creatures, nothing new may emerge to challenge those values and that order. Freed from the judgement of God, on the other hand, the body without organs traverses a different order, within which the circular movement of a Nietzschean eternal return has only difference at its centre (*LS*, p. 300), and the creative force of difference itself refuses identity to play with endlessly divergent series of pre-individual singularities.

According to Deleuze, finally, the secret of the body without organs, and thus of the order of the Antichrist, lies here: 'to bring into existence and not to judge [...], because what has value can be made or distinguished only by defying judgment' (*ECC*, p. 135). The system of God, and the divine judgement on which it is based, has everything to do with a will to dominate, to impose upon, to limit, to organ-ise. In its place, a Deleuzean anti-theology celebrates the nonorganic vitality of the body without organs, understood as the refusal of personal identity and the irreducible affirmation of difference itself. And perhaps in this gesture it reveals itself as a 'true' *liberation* theology.

Notes

1 Antonin Artaud, 'To have done with the judgment of God', in *Selected Writings*, trans. Helen Weaver, ed. Susan Sontag (New York: Farrar, Strauss and Giroux, 1976) p. 571.
2 Gilles Deleuze and Félix Guattari, *A Thousand Plateaus: Capitalism and Schizophrenia*, trans. Brian Massumi (Minneapolis: University of Minnesota Press, 1987) p. 158. Hereafter referred to as *ATP*.
3 Gilles Deleuze, *Essays Critical and Clinical*, trans. Daniel W. Smith and Michael A. Greco (Minneapolis: University of Minnesota Press, 1997) p. 130. Hereafter referred to as *ECC*. It is well known that Deleuze developed the conception of the body without organs in collaboration with Félix Guattari; see, for example, *Anti-Oedipus: Capitalism and Schizophrenia*, trans. Robert Hurley *et al.* (Minneapolis: University of Minnesota Press, 1983). However, Deleuze also uses this figuration in his individual work, as exemplified in the essay cited here.
4 Gilles Deleuze, *The Logic of Sense*, trans. Mark Lester and Charles Stivale (New York: Columbia University Press, 1990) p. 292. Hereafter referred to as *LS*.
5 Against the power of the disjunctive syllogism (understood as limitation and exclusion) to recuperate the integrity of self, world, and God, however, Deleuze notes that Kant's putting into question of rational theology 'introduces a kind of disequilibrium, a fissure or crack in the pure Self' that, at least momentarily, allows to erupt 'that schizophrenia in principle which characterizes the highest power of thought, and opens Being onto difference': Gilles Deleuze, *Difference and Repetition*, trans. Paul Patton (New York: Columbia University Press, 1994) p. 58. Hereafter referred to as *DR*.
6 Elizabeth Grosz, *Volatile Bodies: Toward a Corporeal Feminism* (Bloomington: Indiana University Press, 1994) pp. 168–70, emphasis added.
7 Dorothea Olkowski, 'Nietzsche's dice throw: tragedy, nihilism, and the Body without Organs', in C. Boundas and D. Olkowski (eds) *Gilles Deleuze and the Theater of Philosophy* (New York: Routledge, 1994) pp. 119–40 (p. 138).
8 See especially Gilles Deleuze and Félix Guattari, *Anti-Oedipus: Capitalism and Schizophrenia*, trans. Robert Hurley *et al.* (Minneapolis: University of Minnesota Press, 1983).
9 Elizabeth Grosz, 'A Thousand tiny sexes: feminism and rhizomatics', in C. Boundas and D. Olkowski (eds) *Gilles Deleuze and the Theater of Philosophy* (New York: Routledge, 1994) pp. 187–210 (p. 201).
10 *DR*, p. 127. While a full discussion of the link between the BwO and the Deleuzean simulacrum is beyond the scope of this paper, it will be touched on again later. A particularly rich site of discussion of the simulacrum can be found in *LS*, pp. 253–79.
11 As noted earlier, the integrity of the theological body is the material guarantee of resurrectibility (see *LS*, p. 292).
12 Antonin Artaud, *Artaud Anthology*, ed. Jack Hirschman (San Francisco: City Lights Books, 1965) p. 56.
13 See *ATP* for Deleuze and Guattari's development of the figuration of 'lines of flight'.

Part II
Spirituality and mysticism

4 The scattering of time crystals

Deleuze, mysticism and cinema

Michael Goddard

Introduction: mystical experience, deconstruction and subjectivation

'Mysticism' has proved to be one of the most elusive yet most recalcitrant words used in discussing religious experience and discourse. [...] Widely disseminated throughout history and across cultural boundaries, 'mysticism' [...] can refer to an entire spectrum of particular experiences, ranging from the prayer of quiet to the soul's union with God. [It] can refer, with equal ease, to a diverse body of writings which straddles literature and philosophy or seems to slip between their dividing lines.[1]

As the above quotation illustrates, mysticism is a particularly troubling term, and one that tends to elude any simple definition. At the same time, mysticism has given rise to a plethora of theoretical approaches which seek to understand it from theological, philosophical, psychological, sociohistorical or deconstructive points of view, and there is considerable controversy between and within these various positions.[2] Many contemporary accounts of mysticism insist on the contextuality of mysticism in relation to religious practices and cultural traditions, as opposed to earlier accounts which focused on the unity of all forms of mystical experience regardless of their context. Similarly, the assumption that mystical experience is based on oneness, unity and the presence of God has also been challenged, particularly from a deconstructive perspective.[3] The many contributions to the links between deconstruction or postmodernism and negative theology as a privileged textual expression of mystical experience constitute a scholarly and daunting discourse that threatens to consume mysticism whole without leaving so much as a trace.

What is disconcerting about this deconstructive meta-discourse on the discourse of negative theology is that it seems to foreclose any understanding of mysticism prediscursively and reduces mystical experience to its textual traces in much the same way that psychoanalysis reduces dreams, or films for that matter, to their latent textual content. A different way to approach mysticism is as an existential practice of subjectivation, neither reducing it to its textual forms nor ascribing to it a universal essence. In accordance with Deleuze's approach to cinema, particularly in *Cinema 2: The Time-Image*,[4] mysticism can be understood as a practice which actualises a prediscursive seeing and hearing, a vision and a voice that otherwise would have remained virtual and which constitutes an ecstatic experience of the outside. This proximity between the understanding of mysticism as a process of subjectivation and Deleuze's account of cinema will be used in this essay to generate a relationship between Deleuze's thought and mystical experience around the concept of the crystalline regime of signs. As Deleuze does not directly refer to mysticism in his works on cinema, it will be necessary to proceed by way of other writers, whose works on mysticism are particularly resonant with Deleuze's account of cinema. By means of these mediators, I hope to generate a synthetic Deleuzian approach to mysticism, based on the resonance between mysticism and cinema as two forms of visionary subjectivation or instances of the crystalline regime of signs.

Deleuze, mysticism and pathological forms of subjectivity

The understanding of mystical experience as a process of subjectivation, involving a considerable disordering of conventional subjectivity, places it in proximity with other, frequently marginalised, forms of subjectivity, particularly schizophrenia, masochism, drug use, especially of hallucinogens, and the paranormal. These are all modes of experience that Deleuze and Guattari have associated with becomings or creative breakdowns of conventional structures of subjectivity and of which to some extent they have been understood as advocates.[5]

What must be borne in mind when considering these practices, however, is the need for rigorous care: for Deleuze and Guattari, without 'doses of caution',[6] many of these practices result in botched attempts at creating lines-of-flight from conventional forms of subjectivity and failed becomings whose ultimate consequences are often worse than the conventional forms of subjectification they seek to escape: 'Why such a parade of sucked dry, catatonicised, vitrified, sewn-up bodies, when the BwO [Body without Organs] is also full of gaiety, ecstasy and dance?' (*A Thousand Plateaus*, p. 150). This is particularly apparent in Deleuze and Guattari's valorisation of schizophrenia as a process which is sharply distinguished from the schizophrenic entity who arrives for treatment in a psychiatric facility. Schizophrenia and mystical experience share many common features, to the extent that the latter might provide a framework whereby the desubjectification inherent in the schizophrenic process could be not only endured but also find a fertile form of expression.

This linkage between mystical experience and schizophrenia goes back as far as William James, who saw schizophrenia as a 'diabolical mysticism',[7] and it includes both the ascription of mystical properties to valorise schizophrenia in the work of Laing, and the emphasising of the hallucinatory, psychotic properties of mysticism, in numerous psychological works including those of Freud. The much quoted case of Judge Schreber, whose account of his mental illness is nothing less than the creation of a mystical cosmology, is a celebrated example demonstrating the co-existence of mysticism, perversion and schizophrenia.

In Kenneth Walpnick's highly informative comparative reading of the experiences of Teresa of Avila, the sixteenth-century mystic, and Lara Jefferson, a contemporary schizophrenic, the main difference that seems to emerge between their respective experiences is that whereas the mystic undergoes a strict training that enables both a social reintegration and a conceptual understanding of a heightened or 'deautomatised' experience, the schizophrenic has a terrifying encounter with the unknown, and is thrown into an experience she is completely unprepared for and from which she has no guarantee of ever returning.[8] Essentially, for Walpnick, schizophrenia is a form of unconscious mysticism, and mysticism a conscious or chosen schizophrenia: 'The mystic provides the example of the method whereby the inner and outer may be joined; the schizophrenic, the tragic result when they are separated' ('Mysticism and schizophrenia', p. 337).

One of the troubling aspects of this account of the relations between schizophrenia and mystical experience is that it invokes the conventional idea of schizophrenia as a tragic separation from the world,[9] rather than as a process of perceptual metamorphosis and fuller immersion in the world as it is understood by Deleuze and Guattari. If schizophrenia and mystical experience refer to processes that are not only perceptually similar but identical, is the only difference between the two to be found in the reterritorialisation of mysticism onto conventional religious ideas, as opposed to the violent reterritorialisation of schizophrenia through psychiatry and medication? Are schizophrenics merely misunderstood mystics, so that Lara Jefferson would be revered alongside Teresa of Avila given a different set of cultural circumstances?

It is difficult to respond definitively to these questions, but one crucial difference between the subjective experiences of schizophrenics and mystics is that whereas mystical experiences involve intense focusing or recollection, schizophrenic experience is generally characterised by extreme distraction whereby any form of focus becomes impossible. Similarly, the experiences afforded by the use of hallucinogens seem immune to the powers of recollection and instead drift from one hallucinatory perception to another in a seemingly random fashion. In other words, while hallucinatory or ecstatic experience can be arrived at by different means, producing perceptual states that can be remarkably similar, it is only through mystical practices, and not schizophrenia or drug use, that processes of recollection can maintain and extend their sensory metamorphoses into sustainable processes of subjectivation. In Deleuzian terms, all these processes attempt to fabricate time crystals, but only mysticism succeeds, not because it reterritorialises subjectivation onto religious traditions, but because it provides a mode of expression whereby these experiences of the unknown, of the virtual, can be reintegrated and redeveloped as spiritual experiences, and thereby extended into social life and discourse, without sacrificing their singularity.

This is not to say that mystics return from their ecstatic experiences unscathed and are able to adopt an unproblematic reintegration into their cultural world. The experience of the 'dark night of the soul' where the mystic experiences an irremediable loss of the ecstatic experience and is plunged into a sense of futility and emptiness has many resonances with the pathological experience of narcissistic depression.

This resonance between the experience of mysticism and depression can perhaps best be summed up by the medieval term *acedia* in which the melancholy experience of the absence of God can paradoxically form the basis of an affirmation of faith by means of ascetic practices; as with schizophrenia, while the contemporary depressive may have an affective experience resembling that of the mystic, he or she is unlikely to have access to adequate expressive practices capable of extending these experiences into a mode of life. Hence, for Julia Kristeva, depressives remain prisoners of affect whose only line-of-flight involves their own extinction: 'the delights of reunion that a regressive daydream promises itself through the nuptials of suicide'.[10] Unlike the depressive, the mystic retains a recollection of the ecstatic experience, however distanced, and, even if they are unable to recreate or reexperience the ecstatic sense of the loss of self, it can still be maintained in another form by finding a crystalline mode of expression with which to communicate the ecstasy. Thus mysticism is not only a process of affective metamorphosis, but also the transmission of this experience via the fabrication of a crystalline regime of signs.

This discussion of mysticism as an ecstatic process takes us very close to the way it is understood by Michel de Certeau. What de Certeau can add to this discussion, in proximity to the work of Deleuze, is an understanding of mysticism in terms of the body and temporality. For de Certeau, not only does mysticism have recourse to a social language whereby singular experiences are returned to the social world from which they originate, at times in the form of a minor language,[11] but mystics are themselves the embodiment of a spiritual 'language', a writing of gestures, movements and sensations, of which mystical writings will only ever be a translation:

> The mystic 'somatises', interprets the music of meaning with his or her corporeal repertoire. One not only plays one's body, one is played by it. [...] In this regard, stigmata, visions, and the like reveal and adopt the obscure laws of the body, the extreme notes of a scale never completely enumerated, never entirely domesticated, aroused by the very exigency of which it is sometimes the sign and sometimes the threat.
>
> ('Mysticism', p. 22)

For de Certeau, mystical experience is primarily an experience not of consciousness but of the depths of the body and its unknown potentialities, an attempt to experience what lies before and beneath language in the deeper body that threatens stable structures of language and social convention. Crucial to this conception is a sense of temporality, for if mysticism was limited to certain extreme corporeal experiences then there would be nothing to distinguish it from pathology. For de Certeau, mystical discourse interprets the phenomena it describes as unessential, as the mere trace or sign of a temporal process of metamorphosis. In other words, mysticism is not limited to the remarkable event or events of which it consists, but is a temporal linkage of these events that moves beyond them into a possible history, a 'history yet to be made' ('Mysticism', p. 19).

In Deleuzian terms, this is a process of becoming, in which the virtual forces that a given event activates are in excess of what the event actualises. Like an iceberg, the majority of which remains submerged beneath the surface of the ocean, mystical experience gives rise to a form of temporality that crystallises powerful virtual forces, beyond the power of an individual body or discourse to actualise: the body plunges into the virtual or spiritual depths which exceed it, rather than containing the spiritual within as a personal property. This is what differentiates mystical experience understood as a spiritual process from conventional religious understandings of spirit:

> A process is 'spiritual' when it is not confined to a single moment, no matter how intense or exceptional that moment may be, when it does not dedicate everything to its revival, as if it were a paradise to recover or preserve, when it does not lose its way in imaginary fixations. [...] It relatavises the ecstasy or stigmata as a sign that would become a mirage if one were to stop there.
>
> ('Mysticism' p. 19)

In other words, mysticism is not solely concerned with the singularity of ecstatic corporeal and affective experiences, but the virtual forces that these experiences actualise, and how these experiences might be translated into other modes of expression. The crystallising of virtual forces through a metamorphic corporeal process and their extension into some form of semiotic expression and social existence is, then, the essential component of mysticism understood in terms of this crystallisation. It is in this way that mystical experience leads to the development of a crystalline regime of signs, however much this may be obscured by conventional religious precepts or the mirages of ecstatic phenomena.

In order to develop more fully the relations between mysticism and the crystalline regime, it is worth examining the thought of Henri Bergson, who provides the clearest account of how mysticism, like artistic creation, requires a crystalline method of composition, an account which is of central importance to Deleuze's crystalline account of the cinema of the time-image.

From dynamic religion to the crystalline regime of signs: mysticism according to Bergson

For Bergson, there are two distinct sources of religion and morality which are not merely different expressions of the same impulse, that of differences in degree, but expressions of completely distinct tendencies or differences in kind, which have become confused in practice because they often exist together in a composite form. These two sources are referred to by Bergson as static religion, which corresponds to conventional institutional religious practices, the religions of churches and temples, and dynamic religion, which finds its expression in the various forms of mystical practices whose common feature would be a distance or movement away from static religions.

For Bergson, both sources of religion can be defined in relation to the *élan vital*. This concept, which Bergson elaborates most fully in *Creative Evolution*,[12] can perhaps best be understood as the virtual creative force that propels life forwards, to develop ever new forms in a process of perpetual invention and becoming. This force can be defined neither with reference to any ultimate origin, nor in relation to any pre-given end, but instead follows several directions or lines at once, tending always in the direction of greater complexity and differentiation.[13] What distinguishes human forms of life, in relation to this principle, from other species is not necessarily a greater complexity of organisation, or a capacity to form larger social groupings, as these capacities are also evident in insect life. For Bergson, human life is based on the development of individual intelligence, rather than collective instinct, as the form of expression of the *élan vital*. This results in a capacity for reflective awareness, beyond the dictates of immediate survival needs, and hence the liberation of an unrivalled capacity for invention.

For Bergson, the myth-making function of static religion provides, in the form of fictions of spiritual transcendent figures that threaten, punish and demand obedience, a variety of defence mechanisms against the possibly self- or socially destructive operations of intelligence. In this sense, the myth-making function is closely tied to the operations of political power from which it borrows its forms. The result of these defensive mechanisms is that the intelligence, which responds to problems through acquiring information, is given a believable story which it accepts as true rather than experience a primal anxiety based on a sense of limitation and mortality. For Bergson, these stories are 'tales on a par with those with which we lull children to sleep' (*The Two Sources*, p. 179) and, like neurotic defence mechanisms, they have several unpleasant side-effects. The principal effect of static religion is to induce a somnolence, which led Marx to diagnose religion as the opiate of the masses, and which tends to foster an atmosphere of blind obedience and conformity to social and religious norms.

The solution of the myth-making function to the problems generated by the development of intelligence is not the only one possible; nor is it without its own inherent problems: by attempting to turn back the flow of creative evolution or at least to check its forward momentum, the myth-making solution is in constant conflict with the creative development of intelligence and with the *élan vital* itself. It can never constitute more than a temporary holding pattern, continually shattered by some new invention or discovery, only to be hastily reassembled in readiness for the next attack. Hence the continual conflict between demands for progress in the name of reason or science, and demands for a return to conventional religious values, which are merely the two sides to the myth-making function itself.

In contrast, by following the movement of the *élan vital*, a different way of experiencing an attachment to life, and one based on perceiving and extending the very movement of life, rather than in a defence against it, presents itself in what Bergson refers to as dynamic religion. In dynamic religion, the *élan vital* becomes directly perceptible through the intensification of the otherwise dormant and contemplative faculty of intuition which for Bergson constitutes a veritable leap into the virtual flow of life itself.

This is Bergson's account of mysticism in terms of the *élan vital*: static religion is the maintenance of transcendence as a defence against the becoming of life or the creative evolution of the *élan vital*, while the attempt to directly perceive, incarnate[14] and extend the *élan vital* in a domain of pure immanence is mysticism. This distinction renders clearly the affinity between Deleuze and Guattari's concept of the plane of immanence and the practice of mysticism, in that mysticism is understood entirely in terms of immanence.

For Bergson, mysticism is as yet a rare phenomenon, only realised in a few individuals, who attain what the 'spiritual current, in its passage through matter, probably desired to reach but could not' (*The Two Sources*, p. 182). This, however, does not render mysticism an elitist, obscurantist phenomenon, for inasmuch as mysticism corresponds to an innate potential of human existence to grasp the spiritual current that flows within it, the lives of mystics strike a chord within the masses of humanity by living out in reality what static religion can only represent in the form of mythological fictions. This point is demonstrated by the appropriation of the lives of mystics by static religion, which then retells the stories of its 'saints' in accordance with conventional religious truths. Whatever the distortions that result from these fictionalisations, there is a secret resonance between the mystic's direct perception of the *élan vital* and its immanence in all living beings. In other words, for Bergson, what mysticism does is to actualise the creative powers that inhere in all forms of life in a virtual state, which renders mystical experience potentially comprehensible to anyone. The development of a crystalline regime responds to the question of how mystical experience, which in one language would be that of the divine love of God, while in another would be the direct perception, affect and extension into action and expression of the *élan vital*, can be transmitted to those who only have the vaguest of notions of what such an experience might be.

One solution to this problem of expression is to use the resources of conventional religious and cultural traditions, to translate into a habitual framework the singular experiences of mystical illumination. While such a method has the advantage of reaching large numbers of people, its reliance on convention tends to distort its 'content' beyond recognition. In effect, mystical experience undergoes an operation of the myth-making function that renders it almost identical to the static religion in which it is embedded. This method corresponds to an organic regime of signs, or narrativisation, whereby the ecstatic perceptions of visions and voices are interpreted in terms of the religious tradition in which they take place, and both affective metamorphoses and the virtual forces they actualise have only a rudimentary existence. This organic regime is entirely reliant on sensory-motor schemata, which are habitual images that stand in for any direct experience of the spiritual.

Bergson identifies very clearly, however, another method by which mystical experience can be communicated, a method that requires the development of a different regime of signs:

> There is another method of composition, more ambitious, less certain, which cannot tell when it will succeed, or even if it will succeed at all. It consists in working back from the intellectual and social plane to a point in the soul from which there springs an imperative demand for creation. [...] To obey it completely new words have to be coined, new ideas would have to be created, but this would no longer be communicating something, it would not be writing. Yet the writer will attempt to realise the unrealisable. He will revert to the simple emotion, to the form that yearns to create its matter, and will go with it to meet ideas already made, words that already exist, briefly social segments of reality. All along the way he will feel it manifesting itself in signs borne of itself [...]. He will be driven to strain the words, to do violence to speech.
>
> (*The Two Sources*, pp. 217–18)

This passage is the most precise description of the emergence of the crystalline regime of signs in mystical experience. As with the development of crystals themselves, a profound metamorphosis affects not only the form of the content that is expressed, but also the form of the expression itself. A violence must be done to language, resulting in 'signs borne of itself', which is the only way that mystical experience can be transmitted in its fullness.

Deleuze, 'the spiritual' and mysticism

To claim that there is a mystical component to the thought of Bergson is fairly straightforward: not only *The Two Sources of Morality and Religion*, but many of his other works, frequently refer to and are conceptually dependent on a conception of the spiritual, while taking into account research into the paranormal and frequently affirming mystical experience as a privileged expression of the *élan vital*. In the case of Deleuze, however, such a claim is a good deal more controversial. Deleuze draws heavily on thinkers such as Bergson, Nietzsche, Leibniz and Spinoza, all of whom share a mystical affirmation of nature, joy or life, whatever their conceptual differences, and Deleuze and Guattari discuss spiritual phenomena such as sorcery, vampirism and Taoism in key sections of *A Thousand Plateaus*. However, Deleuze, both in his work with Guattari and in his own work, has tended to be read through a materialist lens, whereby even concepts with a strong spiritual resonance such as the virtual are understood in an almost scientific, positivistic way.

A telling example of this is Philip Goodchild's attempt to distinguish the thought of Bergson from that of Deleuze and Guattari, in order to remove any spiritual resonance from the latter.[15] Rather than seeing Deleuze's relation to Bergson as a creative process of becoming, Goodchild identifies points in Bergson's work that Deleuze is supposed to either accept or reject. Whereas notions such as multiplicity or difference as differentiation are acceptable to Goodchild's Deleuze, the concept of the *élan vital* is not: 'For Deleuze, Bergson's thought generated its own incorrigible illusion. [...] Bergson invented the notion of the *élan vital* as the creative, driving force of all life, in a kind of Monism of desire' (*Deleuze and Guattari*, p. 27). This is a serious misreading of Deleuze's *Bergsonism*[16] which extends Bergson's thought and subjects it to a metamorphosis, but is not a deconstruction of Bergson's key concepts, including the virtual and the *élan vital*:

> There is no contradiction between this monism [of the *élan vital*] and dualism. [...] The coexistence of all the levels is virtual, only virtual. The point of unification is itself virtual. This point is not without similarities to the One-Whole of the Platonists.
>
> (*Bergsonism*, p. 93)

Furthermore, when it comes to the cinema books, not only does Deleuze base a considerable part of them on a 'return to Bergson', but, in the second volume at least, he places a considerable emphasis on film as a technology of the virtual in a Bergsonist, spiritual sense. Hence it is a curious point that Goodchild makes when he underscores Deleuze's rejection of Bergson's monism, as well as his supposed insistence on 'the Whole or One of mysticism' (*Deleuze and Guattari*, p. 27). For Bergson, monism is only arrived at by a rigorous understanding of difference and multiplicity, and by no means resolves these into a higher, transcendent unity. The mystical experience of God or 'oneness' is similarly an intensification of difference and an experience of ecstatic subjectivation or metamorphosis. For Bergson, what the mystic experiences is pure immanence as a creative emotion, which is not a precursor but an equivalent to 'Deleuzian desire' (*Deleuze and Guattari*, p. 27). According to Deleuze: 'At the limit, it is the mystic who plays with the whole of creation, who invents an expression of it whose adequacy increases with its dynamism' (*Bergsonism*, p. 112). What this example demonstrates is how the spiritual is effectively excluded from Deleuze's work in the name of difference and multiplicity because it is conventionally understood in terms of unity and transcendence.

Instead, the 'spiritual' or 'spirits', rather than Spirit[17] can be conceived of as virtually inhering in the material world in the form of temporalities, or conversely the material world can be conceived of as existing in the spiritual or in God in the same way that it exists in time. The spiritual and the material are simply two distinct yet indiscernible sides of the same fold. This way of thinking is in line with the immanent 'spiritual philosophies' of both Bergson and Spinoza, and, unlike the transcendent conception of Spirit, does not betray Deleuze's own thought. This entirely immanent relation to the spiritual is also what mysticism actualises through a complete immersion in life and in love as a process of metamorphic subjectivation and the elaboration of a crystalline regime of signs.

I have already stressed the links between mysticism and the emergence of a crystalline regime of signs; while mysticism is not referred to explicitly by Deleuze in his works on cinema, the centrality of the crystalline regime, and its operation of opening to a direct image of time and of the virtual, is a parallel process to the mystical metamorphosis of subjectivity identified by Bergson. It is as if the cinema, beginning life shrouded in sensory-motor schemata, underwent a spiritual crisis in the realm of action, and cast off its schemata, its habits of perception one by one, thereby unearthing the extraordinary virtual forces of affect and expression that would animate its later development. Of course, this would remain just another mythic story if it did not lead back out of the cinema into a re-spiritualisation of life itself, through the transmission of this experience via the crystalline regime of signs to the spectator, who can then be directly affected by the spiritual experience that this new technology of the virtual facilitates.

This is not to say that going to the movies will provide an experience of enlightenment, for even in the relatively rare cases where the crystalline regime affords the potential transmission of a spiritual experience, there are many factors that can block this from being received, and, even when received, it can only form a minute part of a subject's own process of subjectivation. Nevertheless, as in the case of the mystic, cinema, in its crystalline forms, can become a spiritual tool, capable of facilitating an experience of ecstatic subjectivation in which spectators experience cinema as a pure optical and sound situation, a vision and a voice, a scattering of time crystals that leads them beyond the boundaries of their static selves and into profound contact with the outside. If static religions always operate strategically by means of recollection-images, whereas mysticism attempts to relay spiritual movement through the direct perception of the spiritual, virtual dimensions of life, then the cinema of the time-image is uniquely placed to tactically disperse the relatively contained time crystals of mysticism, across the extended circuits of contemporary, secular mass-media communications.

In conclusion, what a close attention to mysticism as a process of subjectivation and the creation of a crystalline regime of signs reveals is that mysticism provides an opening to the processes of life itself, to a spiritual dimension wholly immanent to life in which processes of creation and differentiation, virtualisation and actualisation are continually taking place. It is through this immanent, crystalline understanding of the spiritual that the resonance between Deleuze's thought, mysticism and the contemporary semiotic regime of the cinema can gain the fullest expression: an understanding that also problematises the deconstructive approach to religion and postmodernity and suggests a creative alternative in which the affirmation of belief would no longer depend on scientific or religious traditions but on inventive practices or a scattering of the crystals of time.

Notes

1 Kevin Hart, *The Trespass of the Sign: Deconstruction, Theology and Philosophy* (Cambridge: Cambridge University Press, 1985) pp. 174–5.
2 For a wide variety of these approaches, see *Understanding Mysticism*, ed. Richard Woods (New York: Image Books, 1980).
3 See especially *Derrida and Negative Theology*, ed. Hart and Harold Coward and Toby Foshay (Albany: State University of New York Press, 1992).
4 Gilles Deleuze, *Cinema 2: The Time-Image*, trans. Hugh Tomlinson and Robert Galeta (Minneapolis: University of Minnesota Press, 1989).
5 See Gilles Deleuze and Félix Guattari, 'How do you make yourself a body without organs?', *A Thousand Plateaus*, trans. Brian Massumi (Minneapolis: University of Minnesota Press, 1987) pp. 149–66.
6 See *A Thousand Plateaus*, p. 150: 'What happened? Were you cautious enough? Not wisdom, caution. In doses. As a rule immanent to experimentation: injections of caution'.
7 William James, *The Varieties of Religious Experience* (New York: The Modern Library of New York, Random House, 1902, 1927) p. 334.
8 Kenneth Walpnick, 'Mysticism and schizophrenia', in *Understanding Mysticism*, ed. Richard Woods (New York: Image Books, 1980) pp. 321–37.
9 This is not to diminish the pain or distress suffered by actual 'clinical' schizophrenics, but to insist that this painful separation is caused by an arresting of the schizophrenic process and not by the process itself.
10 Julia Kristeva, *Black Sun: Depression and Melancholia*, trans. Leon S. Roudiez (New York: Columbia University Press, 1989) p. 14.
11 See Michel de Certeau, 'Mysticism', trans. Marsanne Brammer, *Diacritics*, 22, 2 (summer 1992) pp. 11–25:

> In the case of the shepherdess Catherine Emerich (1774–1824) a complete language emerges. [...] The discourse of the 'visionary' woman brought the 'savage' tongue of a rural world to the surface of a written 'literature'. A subterranean organisation was brought to light, unveiling and multiplying the resources of a peasant tradition within the very mystical experience that sprang from it.
>
> (p. 21)

12 Henri Bergson, *Creative Evolution*, trans. Arthur Mitchell (London: Macmillan, 1922).

13 Henri Bergson, *The Two Sources of Morality and Religion*, trans. R. Ashley Audra and Cloudesley Brereton (London: Macmillan, 1935) pp. 91–5.

14 On incarnation of the flesh as immanence, see Michael Hardt, 'Exposure: Pasolini in the flesh', *Canadian Review of Comparative Literature*, 24, 3 (1997) pp. 581–7.

15 Philip Goodchild, *Deleuze and Guattari: An Introduction to the Politics of Desire* (London: Sage, 1996).

16 Gilles Deleuze, *Bergsonism*, trans. Hugh Tomlinson and Barbara Hammerjam (New York: Zone Books, 1988).

17 On the problematics of the word 'spirit' see Jacques Derrida, *On Spirit: Heidegger and the Question*, trans. Geoffrey Bennington and Rachel Bowlby (Chicago and London: Chicago University Press, 1989).

5   The *Tibetan Book of the Dead*

Deleuze and the positivity of the
second light

N. Robert Glass

> The blue light of the skandha of consciousness in its basic purity, the wis-
> dom of the dharmadhatu, luminous, clear, sharp and brilliant, will come to-
> wards you from the heart of Vairocana and his consort, and pierce you so
> that your eyes cannot bear it. At the same time, together with it, the soft
> white light of the gods will also come towards you and pierce you. At that
> time, under the influence of bad karma, you will be terrified and escape from
> the wisdom of the dharmadhatu with its bright blue light, but you will feel an
> emotion of pleasure towards the soft white light of the gods. [...] Do not
> take pleasure in the soft white light of the gods, do not be attracted to it or
> yearn for it [...] but feel longing for the bright blue light.[1]

In the Buddhist tradition, the text of the *Bardo Thodol* is used to instruct
beings on how to make wise decisions in the interval between death and
rebirth. Though popularly known in the West as the *Tibetan Book of the
Dead*, bardo really means something closer to gap or interval. As Robert
Thurman translates, it is the 'Book of Liberation Through Understanding in
the Between'.[2] The central issue in the text is this: a few days after the death
of the physical body, beings are continually faced with a choice between two
lights, one luminous and brilliant and the other much softer. The text
instructs us not to take pleasure in the soft light – which initially seems
attractive – but rather to choose the bright light, which at first elicits fear.

While the *Bardo Thodol* is a book of death, it is also a book of birth, a
book of space or a book of the between. The choice one faces in the gap
between birth and death is essentially no different from the choice one faces
in the gap between one breath and the next. The Buddhist tradition works
with many such gaps – the gap between thought and word, or word and
deed, or stimulus and response, or one thought and the next. The gap is not
neutral, but marks the intersection of multiple lines of thought and multiple
dimensions of force. Indeed, the gap or between might be seen as the very
location of Buddhist practice.

This essay suggests that Gilles Deleuze might be seen as a theologian of
the between. His work with concepts such as climax and plateau, the
possible and the potential, and the actual and the virtual, can aid us greatly
in exploring the philosophical potential of the *Tibetan Book of the Dead*.

While the central issue in the between is a choice between two lights, it might also be seen as a choice between two forms of desire, between a world with others and a world without others, or between becoming more of what we already are and becoming something new.

However, there is a problem here: initially, the second world exists in and is seen through the gaps of the first world. The challenge is to see and understand it in a way not framed by the first world. That is, the second world is most often understood by negating terms used in the description of the first. In Buddhism, the 'goal' is often described as becoming egoless, selfless, desireless, thoughtless, and purposeless: one seeks a state of no-mind or no-thought. In Deleuze's essay, 'Michel Tournier and the world without others',[3] an imaginative analysis of a reworked Robinson Crusoe story, it is the negation of a term from the first world (others) that defines the second (without others). But if it is a world without others, what is it 'with'? How does one present a second world with a positivity of its own?[4]

If there is to be a theology of the between, then one of the primary tasks is the inversion of its defining term: the whole notion of 'between' panders to what we already are rather than to what we might become. The theological problem in Buddhism is this: how to see and understand the world of the second light in terms not taken from the first. Drawing from both Deleuze and Buddhism, this essay explores the positive potential of a 'theology of the between'. After situating the problem within Buddhism, it attempts to construct a vision of the positivity of the second world – in this case the world of the second light of the *Tibetan Book of the Dead*.

According to the Tibetan Buddhist tradition, there are two aspects of mind, only the first of which dissolves at death. Part of the purpose of Buddhist practice is to work with and cultivate the second aspect of mind during life so that one may make wise choices in the bardo realms between death and rebirth. Though technically there are a number of bardos here, the manifestations of light and energy in the first two betweens after death are so subtle that most beings do not recognise them. The quotation which opens the article is taken from the third between – the Mild Deity Reality Between.[5] The essential issue is whether or not one's choices will be governed by forces or desire with a centre or forces or desire without a centre. This section of the *Tibetan Book of the Dead* assumes beings will be confused by habitual tendencies or past karma (forces with a centre), and attempts to guide them in the right direction.

The Mild Deity between is not significantly different from other betweens. The habits or forces that orient and determine one's thinking and decision-making at this period of death are the same as those that appear in life. There is, however, one important difference: at the moment of death, these governing forces become seven times more intense and the relationship between forms and forces inverts. That is, while, in the 'life between', forms are primary and light or energy is secondary, in the Mild Deity between this situation reverses and light and energy become primary. While in life one made decisions on the basis of distinctions between forms, one is now asked to make decisions on the basis of distinctions between energies or desires. Cultivating a sensitivity to and awareness of this alternate dimension is one of the goals of Buddhist practice.

This new awareness is pursued in two ways: first, one works to pacify the strength of past karmic tendencies (represented in the negative force of the first light); second, one works to cultivate sensitivity to the qualities of centreless forces or energy (represented in the positive force of the second light). These two aspects of practice correspond roughly to *trekcho* and *togal*, two forms of meditation. The former works to cut away delusion while the latter works to cultivate the presence of Clear Light.[6] The two practices might also be seen to be working with the two different aspects of mind, the relative and the absolute. To sum up, one works to pacify the coding or awareness which responds to the first light while cultivating and activating the coding or awareness that will respond to the second. The tension between the two lights represents the tension between these two different qualities of energy, one which fixes a self and one which does not. The practice is difficult because it involves abandoning one's identity or ego without having an alternative: we understand what we are losing, but not what will replace it.

In Buddhist literature, suggestions regarding what is 'gained' through Buddhist practice use language from the first world: nirvana is the 'blowing out of desire' or the 'non-leaking realm'. Through practice, one cultivates the 'the two wisdoms of emptiness' – the wisdom of the empty and the wisdom of the non-empty.[7] In both these cases, the second world is described through the presence or absence of terms drawn from the first world. One wonders again: if the second world is without (without desire, without leaks, without ego, without a centre) what is it with? If the second world has a positivity of its own, what is it?

It is at this point that constructive theological work is necessary and Deleuze's work can be most helpful. Deleuze's essay, 'Michel Tournier and the world without others' is a philosophical analysis of Tournier's novel *Friday*, a retelling of the Robinson Crusoe story.[8] Deleuze explores the perceptual and affective changes that a being might undergo while spending years on a desert island where there are no others. How much of what we see, feel and desire is structured by the presence of another being? Would the continual absence of others eventually allow one to enter into an alternate perceptual and affective world? A second essay, 'How do you make yourself a body without organs?', explores the tension between two forms of desire, desire-as-lack which seeks climax, and another form of desire which seeks to circulate or maintain itself.[9] Here again, our understanding of the second world is framed by the first. Though a distinction is made between desire-as-lack and a more positive state of desire, for most readers 'desire' is still a term understood through our experience of the first world. In both these essays, Deleuze hints at an alternate world of radically different coding, perception, force and desire.

The intent of this essay is not to match terms from Deleuze with terms from Buddhism, but to pursue the links suggested above to create an understanding of the world of the second light in its own terms. Drawing from both Deleuze's work and Buddhism, I suggest that this second world can be characterised positively in five ways. Let me take up each of these in turn.

1   *It is field-sensitive rather than figure-dependent. That is, while in*
    a negative sense it is not oriented around a figure abstracted
    from the field, in a positive sense it sustains and expands the
    field.

> But the Other is neither an object in the field of my perception nor a subject who perceives me: the Other is initially a structure of the perceptual field, without which the entire field could not function as it does. That this structure may be actualized by real characters, by variable subjects – me for you and you for me – does not prevent its preexistence, as the condition of organization in general, to the terms which actualize it in each organized perceptual field – yours and mine.
>
> (*Logic of Sense*, p. 307)

In 'Michel Tournier and the world without others', Deleuze distinguishes between two notions of the 'other'. The first 'other' is the obvious other that exists through the presence of another being in my perceptual field. The second 'other' is less obvious – the structure-other or perceptual field which is organised and maintained as a result of being habitually governed by actual others. The short-term presence or absence of the former (the actual other) has no effect on the regulatory presence of the latter (the perceptual structure within which actual others are or are not present). This essay is an extended speculation on one question: what might be the long-term effects of the absence of actual others?

The concepts of field dependence and field independence, borrowed from the psychology of perception, can help us here. The two terms lie on a spectrum, with field independence measuring how well a being can abstract an object from the perceptual field (e.g. a hunter seeing a deer quite clearly against an ambiguous forest background) and field dependence used mainly in a negative sense to denote a weak ability in field independence (hunters who can never seem to see the deer). Inverting the terms, however, is of great use in constructing the positivity of the second world. In this case, field independence is not an advantage, but a liability – one might call these people *figure-dependent* (or even figure-addicted). Perception is dependent upon and regulated by the other which grounds the structure-other framework. Those able to free themselves of this dependence (as Robinson does eventually does on the island) are able to become *field-sensitive or field-oriented*.

One can distinguish among practices of meditation by seeing how each answers the question: how does one relate to that which arises in the heart-mind? If the goal is to become less figure-dependent and more field-sensitive, then meditation would be the attempt continually to let go of or dissolve the vectors of force which maintain the images or figures which arise. Since these vectors of force, in turn, maintain the structure-other perceptual field, their dissolution helps create a world governed not by others – a field-sensitive world.

2 *It is oriented towards maintaining an affective plateau, rather than seeking a climax. That is, while in a negative sense it does not 'leak', in a positive sense energy is maintained and circulated.*

> When we desire Others, are not our desires brought to bear upon this expressed small possible world which the Other wrongly envelops, instead of allowing it to float and fly above the world, developed onto a glorious double?
>
> (*Logic of Sense*, p. 313)

In 'How do you make yourself a body without organs?', Deleuze introduces the notion of circulating and non-circulating bodies and speculates on the difference between activities that might empty bodies and activities that might fill bodies. Negative desire, or desire-as-lack, is a restricted and limited form of positive desire. Borrowing Deleuze's use of the concepts climax and plateau allows us to extend the notions of figure dependence and field sensitivity into the realm of desire and affect.

In distinguishing between negative and positive desire, one of the issues is whether or not an object is present. The affective distinction between forces with objects and forces without objects then follows from the perceptual distinction between figure-dependent and field-sensitive worlds. The move from a 'conditional bliss dependent on the senses' to a more vital state requires going 'beyond desires dependent on sense objects'.[10] While negative desire seeks an end or climax, positive desire seeks to maintain or even build upon itself in order to create a plateau of intensity. From this perspective, the second world is then not without desire, just without the negative desire of the first world – a desire with a centre or a desire focused on objects. The goal of Buddhist practice is then not the absence of desire, but the absence of negative desire and the presence of positive desire. The energy of desire has been transformed in its shift from one state to another.

This suggests a different understanding of the Buddhist term 'defilement'. The word 'defile' is usually listed with two meanings in the dictionary. The first is the common understanding: to make impure, to desecrate or to stain. The second meaning is not so common: marching in a line or file, a narrow passageway, or a pass through which troops must march in a narrow column. I suggest here that the Buddhist notion of defile, and defilement, follows the second meaning rather than the first. A defilement is a line which takes off from the main body, thus leaving the body less than it was. In Buddhism this relates not to troops, but to energy, force or desire. Defilements allow energy to stream out rather than circulate.

One of the Buddhist terms for defilement is *asrava*, which means leak or outflow. *Anasrava-dhatu*, a term for nirvana, is then the 'non-streaming realm' – a state in which energy is constantly circulating and not streaming out. The primary error in Buddhist practice is then not the presence of thoughts, but the presence of defilements (whether or not thoughts are present). Anger, for instance, is non-circulating energy – it is a defilement because energy leaks out and cannot be used to create, sustain or increase the plateau of intensity. Other examples of non-circulating forces or leaks would be the problem states that arise during the Mild Deity Between: fear, pride, anger/aggression and envy.

3   *It has no preferential affective gaze but rather generates without*
    prejudice. That is, while in a negative sense it is not vectored, in a
    positive sense it is radiant. This radiance, though, is not passive
    but increases in magnitude. While in a negative sense it dissolves
    leaks or defilements, in a positive sense the dissolution of
    defilements adds to or increases the vitality of the field.

> Consciousness has become not only a phosphorescence internal to things but a fire in their heads, a light over each one and a 'soaring I'.
>
> (*Logic of Sense*, p. 312)

The world of all the ten directions is one luminous pearl.[11]

Field-oriented force is not passive but active. Its nature is to increase in strength or vitality. As conditioned qualities decrease in power, unconditioned qualities increase in power. 'With each level of progress in practice, the efflorescence of light increases in magnitude [...]'.[12] The term 'vitality' can be used to help distinguish between positive and negative plateaux: imagine plateaux becoming higher or lower, or perhaps deeper and shallower. A deep plateau is one full of vitality, whereas a shallow plateau is weak in vitality. In the same way that there are differences in warmth and light between a fifteen-watt bulb and a two hundred-watt bulb, there are differences in vitality between the plateau of the Buddhist student and that of the teacher. From one perspective, light is light and the two are the same. From another perspective, there are some things one is not aware of in a world illuminated by a fifteen-watt bulb.

As vitality increases, there are threshold points or passages where the nature or quality of desire changes and new possibilities present themselves. In Buddhism, the difference between the passions and the wisdoms is often compared to the difference between ice and water. A defilement is thus a 'frozen' wisdom – a change in the nature of energy is required before the wisdom manifests itself. The quality of desire or energy changes, much as ice changes to water and again as water changes to gas. It is then both correct and misleading to use the term 'desire' to refer to the energy of all three states. The move is from gross to subtle and refined. In Taoist practice one moves through three passes as the quality of desire is increasingly refined. One refines vitality into energy, energy into spirit, and spirit into openness. In a similar way, the *Tibetan Book of the Dead* lists three levels of the body-mind: gross, subtle and extremely subtle.[13] Through continued practice, one develops an increased awareness of progressively more subtle levels of energy.

4   *It is responsive rather than reactive. That is, the energy of a
    figure-dependent stimulus is received and transformed into a
    field-oriented response.*

> Stop the world. Becoming is about movement, but it begins with an inhibition. At least some of the automatic circuits between regularized stimuli and habitual responses must be disconnected, as if a crowbar had been inserted into the interlocking network of standardized actions and trajectories constituting the World As We Know It.[14]

Defilements are figure-dependent. In addressing them directly, one combats a figure-dependent problem with a figure-dependent response. In focusing on and being governed by the problem, one moves from bad reactions to good reactions, or from bad conditioned qualities to good conditioned qualities, but stays in (and affirms) the figure-dependent structure within which defilements exist – the world of the first light. Defilements need to be seen as 'unreal' (ghosts) in the first place. Anger is a good example. It is a force with an object – one is angry at something or at someone. In reacting to anger arising in oneself or in another, one reaffirms a figure-dependent perceptual and affective structure. It is this structure that is the problem: the defilements are simply a manifestation of the problem. A response from the second world not only breaks down the structure-other framework, but cultivates field-oriented sensitivities. The energy of the defilements is freed to increase the vitality of circulating energies.

The actions of the Buddhist teacher (dwelling in the second world) can be distinguished from the actions of the student (still in the first world) along two lines – as a response rather than a reaction and as vital rather than weak. For instance, the compassion of the student might still be figure-dependent. If so, this compassionate reaction would affirm the coding of his own defilements and allow energy to leak out rather than nourish and cultivate the plateau of intensity. The compassion of the teacher would presumably be field-oriented and further nourish the vitality of the plateau of intensity.

5 It is hyperdifferentiated rather than undifferentiated. That is, it
   is only undifferentiated from the perspective of differences in
   kind. While in a negative sense it is without differences in kind,
   in a positive sense it contains within itself differences of degree.

> The real distinction between orders is not 'identity versus undifferentiation' but *'identity-undifferentiation versus hyperdifferentiation'*. […] Hyperdifferentiation is conceptually indeterminate from the point of view of oppositional difference. But it is materially indeterminate in 'itself' – which is a teeming void (as opposed to a diacritical emptiness).
>
> (Massumi, p. 91)

In Buddhism, one of the challenges is to see and understand the logic of the absolute in a way distinctly different from the logic of the relative. To put it another way, real difference requires a shift in structures, or an epistemological break. The claim here is that each realm pivots on a different difference: in order to make the radical move to a 'world without others', one must be able to think difference without otherness.

In his work with Deleuze, Michael Hardt distinguishes between dialectical and nondialectical oppositions. Dialectical opposition is a difference without distinction. Real distinction requires an epistemological break, and this is only possible within nondialectical opposition.[15] While both these oppositions work with different differences, the dialectical difference is negative while the nondialectical difference is positive, an affirmation. This affirmation is not the binary or digital affirmation of staying the same, but rather an analogue affirmation that involves a transmutation.

A table and a chair are different in a negative sense, in that one exists independently of the other and the former is not tied to the production of the latter. A table is *not* a chair. Ice and water, however, are different in a positive sense, in that they do not exist independently of one another. There is a sense in which the ice *is* the water: frozen water when melted becomes unfrozen water. One cannot negate (reject or throw out) the ice without removing the possibility of the water that might come from it. We might say that negative differences are external or digital differences while positive differences are internal or analogue differences. As Anthony Wilden has put it:

> There are two kinds of differences involved, and the distinction between them is essential. Analog differences are differences of magnitude, frequency, distribution, pattern organization, and the like. Digital differences are those such as can be coded into distinctions and oppositions, and for this, there must be discrete elements with well-defined boundaries.[16]

These two differences correspond to two different understandings of affirmation. If there is oppositional and non-oppositional difference, then there is oppositional and nonoppositional affirmation. If one thinks within a system of oppositional or binary difference, then affirmation is robbed of any possibility of critique. The only option other than difference is sameness. Whether externally (in politics or social action) or internally (in Buddhist meditative practice) affirmation then serves the status quo. It keeps things the same but helps us feel better about it. Within this understanding, the goal of Buddhist practice is to help us become more of what we already are – Deleuze's becoming being rather than becoming becoming.

We are working here with both liberal and radical notions of difference. A liberal difference is a distinction between two objects or two states in the present framework or structure, whereas a radical difference requires a change in the present framework or structure. Feminist social action provides a clear example: liberal feminists work for change within the system, whereas radical feminists see the patriarchal system itself as the problem. From the radical perspective, meaningful change can only occur by changing the existing frame or structure, and those who work for liberal change only strengthen the problem.

Understandings of Buddhist practice can be differentiated in the same way. Liberal practice would be the move from one point to another within the present frame, whereas radical practice would involve a move outside the present frame. In a liberal sense, Buddhist practice involves a complete acceptance of what already is, of impermanence, of the present self. The practice involves an appreciation and enhancement of present coding. From a radical perspective, Buddhist practice involves the cultivation of an entirely new set of sensitivities – moving outside the present notion of what is possible into something entirely new.

Let me return to the question used to distinguish among practices of meditation: how does one relate to that which arises in the heart-mind? Two different Buddhist schools may each give the same answer: 'Absolute acceptance or affirmation of what arises. Always say Yes'. But we must distinguish here between reactive and responsive affirmations. While the former affirms the subject in its present state, the latter dissolves the frame of the subject, thus not allowing a return to the previous state. The affirmation that hot water offers ice is the affirmation that a vital field-sensitive force (without an object) offers a figure-dependent force (with an object). It is only in this way that one can understand Dogen's 'Whole being is the Buddha Nature'.[17] Buddha Nature is a vital, hyperdifferentiated and affirmative force. Within the second world, the issue is not the relationship between beings (a negative or binary difference) but the nature or quality of the force of the field which sustains beings.[18]

Each light is coded in its own way. Each has its own logic, its own difference, its own notion of affirmation, its own perceptual and affective fields, its own force, its own intensity, its own quality of energy. The goal of

Buddhist practice is to alter the coding of the present being so it harmonises more with the second world than with the first. With this comes a vision of a new world – what existed once only in the 'between' now comes forth with a positivity of its own. This positivity can be characterised in its own terms in five ways: it is field-sensitive rather than figure-dependent; it is oriented towards maintaining an affective plateau, rather than seeking a climax; it has no preferential affective 'gaze' but rather generates without prejudice; it is responsive rather than reactive; it is hyperdifferentiated rather than undifferentiated.

Notes

1   Francesca Freemantle and Chogyam Trungpa, *The Tibetan Book of the Dead: The Great Liberation through Hearing in the Bardo* (Boston: Shambhala, 1987) pp. 41–2.

2   *The Tibetan Book of the Dead: Liberation Through Understanding in the Between,* trans. Robert A. F. Thurman (New York: Bantam Books, 1994) pp. xx–xxi.

3   See appendix to Gilles Deleuze, *The Logic of Sense,* trans. Mark Lester and Charles Stivale (New York: Columbia University Press, 1990) pp. 301–22.

4   The essays of Oliver Sacks have been particularly helpful in clarifying this issue for me. In 'To see and not see', Sacks asks: 'Does blindness have a positivity of its own?' That is, what is the other side of blindness? Is it possible that an absence of sight opens into a positive presence of something else? See Oliver Sacks, *An Anthropologist on Mars* (New York: Random House, 1995) p. 142.

5   The phrase 'Mild Deity Reality Between' is from Robert Thurman's translation, *The Tibetan Book of the Dead: Liberation Through Understanding in the Between* (New York: Bantam Books, 1994) p. 131.

6   Sogyal Rinpoche, *The Tibetan Book of Living and Dying* (New York: Harper Collins, 1994) p. 167.

7   The Buddha Mind – the world of the second light – is empty of defilements but full of virtues. See, for instance, *The Awakening of Faith Attributed to Asvaghosha,* trans. Yoshito S. Hakeda (New York: Columbia University Press, 1967) pp. 34–6.

8   See Michel Tournier, *Friday,* trans. Norman Denny (New York: Pantheon Books, 1985).

9   For the essay 'November 28, 1947: how do you make yourself a body without organs?', see Gilles Deleuze and Félix Guattari, *A Thousand Plateaus: Capitalism and Schizophrenia,* trans. Brian Massumi (Minneapolis: University of Minnesota Press, 1987) pp. 149–66. Deleuze borrows the term 'plateau of intensity' from Gregory Bateson's account of his work on Bali. See Gregory Bateson, *Steps to an Ecology of Mind* (New York: Ballantine Books, 1972) pp. 112–13.

10   Miranda Shaw, *Passionate Enlightenment: Women in Tantric Buddhism* (Princeton: Princeton University Press, 1994) p. 188.

11   From the Ikka-Myoju fascicle of Dogen's *Shobogenzo.* See *Flowers of Emptiness: Selections from Dogen's Shobogenzo,* trans. Hee Jin Kim (Lewiston: Edwin Mellen Press, 1985) pp. 126–130.

12   Tung-pin Lu, *The Secret of the Golden Flower: The Classic Chinese Book of Life,* trans. Thomas Cleary (New York: Harper Collins, 1991) p. 40.

13   As Robert Thurman explains, the gross level is the body of flesh, blood and bone and the mind of the six senses – eyes, ears, nose, tongue, body and mental consciousness. The subtle level in the body corresponds to the central nervous system and a system of energy 'winds', and in the mind to three states of consciousness

known as luminance, radiance and imminence. The extremely subtle level of body-mind is a very small energy pattern existing in the heart complex. See Thurman's translation of the *Tibetan Book of the Dead* (New York: Bantam Books, 1994) pp. 35–7.

14 Brian Massumi, *A User's Guide to Capitalism and Schizophrenia: Deviations from Deleuze and Guattari* (Cambridge MA: MIT Press, 1996) p. 103.

15 Michael Hardt, *Gilles Deleuze: An Apprenticeship in Philosophy* (Minneapolis: University of Minnesota Press, 1993) pp. 52, 61.

16 Anthony Wilden, *System and Structure: Essays in Communication and Exchange* (London: Tavistock, 1972) p. 169.

17 'Dogen's Shobogenzo Buddha-nature part I', trans. Norman Waddell and Masao Abe, *Eastern Buddhist*, 8, 2 (summer 1975) pp. 94–112 (p. 97). The inability of some scholars to think more than one difference has led to a total re-reading of part of the Zen Buddhist scholarship. See Paul L. Swanson, ' "Zen is not Buddhism": recent Japanese critiques of Buddha Nature', *Numen*, 40 (1993) pp. 115–49. For a summary of the attempt to re-read Dogen's work, see Steven Heine, ' "Critical Buddhism" (*Hihan Bukkyo*) and the debate concerning the 75-fascicle and the 12-fascicle texts', *Japanese Religious Studies*, 21, 2 (1994) pp. 31–72. Put in the language of this paper, the argument is that, since Zen Buddhism is without binary difference, then it is without any kind of difference, and cannot support an ethical system. Buddhism is ethical, so this sort of Zen is not Buddhism. The contemporary re-reading addressed in Heine's article attempts to re-introduce 'otherness' into the work of Zen master Dogen Kigen (and thus re-introduce an ethics based on binary difference). To my mind, this is a classic example of attempting to read the second world using the logic, understanding and vision of the first.

18 As Peter Gregory puts it: 'It was the luminous quality of the enlightened mind that made possible the reflection of the harmonious interrelation of all phenomena on the surface of the Buddha's enlightened mind'. See his 'Tsung-mi and the problem of *Hongaku shiso*', *Komozawa Daigaku Zen Kenkyujo Nenpo*, 5 (March 1994) pp. 200–151 (p. 181).

6 Thinking difference

A comparative study of Gilles
Deleuze, Plotinus and Meister
Eckhart

Oliver Davies

In *Difference and Repetition*, Deleuze advances the thesis that Western
metaphysical thought is fatally ensnared in a fourfold structure of representational thinking which reduces difference to its relation with identity and
thus fails to grasp difference in its radical authenticity. He traces the
privileging of the 'model' and the 'copy' to Plato, who 'exorcises' simulacra
with their 'free oceanic differences', 'nomadic distributions' and 'crowned
anarchy'. This notion of sameness is in due course transposed to the
thinking subject and to the identity of the concept. Deleuze is thus able to
offer a critique of the Western metaphysical tradition as a system of
thinking, predicated always upon operations of identity, and underpinned by
a unified theory of the self, which obscures and tames the radical otherness
of difference. It thus effaces creativity or what he calls 'the genitality of
thinking'.[1] Extended reflection upon difference is not unique to Deleuze,
however, nor to the era of postmodernity, despite the prevalence of this
theme in contemporary texts.[2] Indeed, Deleuze himself is keen to locate his
study in the context of a thinking of being which extends back to the pre-
Socratic movement of ancient Greece. The purpose of the present essay,
then, is to compare Deleuze's engagement with the theme of difference and
ontology with that of two earlier thinkers, Plotinus and Meister Eckhart,
whose own philosophical systems found their central focus in the thinking of
a radical and unconditioned difference which resisted any kind of representational constraint. By placing Deleuze alongside such explicitly theological
thinkers, we hope to cast a new light on his philosophy, drawing out aspects
from it which may otherwise remain concealed from view.

The principle of difference under the aspect of the One first emerges in the
work of the Eleatic philosophers, but the classical engagement with it occurs
in the *Enneads* of Plotinus, who lived from 204/5 until 270 BCE. The
designation of sovereign difference as Oneness which – as Augustine wrote in
De Libero Arbitrio – entirely stands outside our sense experience of the world
as multiplicity, creates a distinctive structure of sublimity or transcendence in
Plotinus' thought.[3] On the one hand, he argues that the One, or the Good
(for Plotinus the two terms are interchangeable)[4] cannot be spoken of, since
it is 'in truth beyond all statement' (*Enneads*, V, 5, 13), and that to clothe it

in any name or image is to reduce it and to make of it a thing amongst other things. Even the term 'the Good' is only used since 'sheer negation does not signify' (*Enneads*, VI, 7, 38). But, on the other hand, Plotinus understands the One to be profoundly implicated in the domain of ontology, or the way things are. This is expressed as a twofold dialectic, the first form of which is purely logical and posits that absolute oneness must both include all that is (otherwise oneness is partial or impaired) and yet be distinct from it (since it is a characteristic only of oneness to include all that is). But it is the second form of the dialectic, which can be described as a cosmological outworking of the first, that truly engages Plotinus: the One is 'all things and no one of them; the source of all things is not all things; and yet it is all things in a transcendental sense' (*Enneads*, V, 2, 1). Similarly, the One is both 'everywhere and yet nowhere' and 'from none is that Principle absent yet from all' (*Enneads*, VI, 8, 16, and 9, 4).

Plotinus offers extensive reflections on the metaphysics of oneness as the cosmological principle of origination, governing all aspects of the multiple universe, focusing in particular upon the mechanisms of participation and the image. These indicate that each level of the universe is an imperfect copy of the higher, though one which includes a genuine participation or sharing in the higher level. Plotinus envisages a double function for each principle or level of being, one which is internal to it and another which represents its action upon the lower levels of being, though both functions are essential to the principle and do not imply its reduction or change (*Enneads*, V, 4, 2). And in consequence of his theory of the image, the Plotinian universe is one which is filled with beauty, as a reflection of the highest principles. Though only a copy, nothing has been omitted from the visible world 'which a beautiful representation within the physical order could include' (*Enneads*, II, 9, 8). But to the physical domain with its beauty as well as its fictions, Plotinus opposes a transcendental realm consisting of the One, Intellect and Soul. Soul, the lowest of the triad, both serves to mediate between the transcendental and the physical realm and itself constitutes the animating life of the universe. The true site of being and of representation, however, lies in Intellect, the second term, which contains the essence of all that is in pure, self-sufficient and unchanging being (*Enneads*, V, 1, 4). Intellect represents a divine reality in which the knower and the known exist in a unity, and it is here that being is formed: 'Intellect by its intellective act establishes being, which in turn, as the object of intellection, becomes the cause of intellection and of existence to the Intellect' (*Enneads*, V, 1, 4). The pluriform character of both being and intellection are mutually implicating, therefore.

The notion that being belongs irreducibly to the realm of multiplicity, as does knowledge, and that both are opposed to their own origin and source in the One, as primary difference, suggests that being (or representation) is itself a form of deficiency since the One itself 'has no need of being', and 'we use the term the Good to assert identity without the affirmation of being' (*Enneads*, VI, 7, 38). As in Plato, therefore, love derives from a sense of lack, and has cosmic proportions, since the Intellect turns back to the One, together with all the beings that it contains, as to the source of its own origin (*Enneads*, V, 1, 6). In the case of human beings, the project of a return to the principle of origination necessarily involves the recognition that the One escapes all human knowing. It is itself even beyond all self-knowing, for 'if we assume within it the distinction of knowing and known, we make it a manifold; and if we allow intellection in it, we make it at that point indigent' (*Enneads*, V, 3, 13). And yet, dialectically, the One or the Good, which so decisively escapes thought and language, is nevertheless powerfully present in the Plotinian universe, and our gaze is drawn constantly towards it. At times, Plotinus is optimistic that we can indeed come to know it in a certain way. He affirms: 'Cleared of all evil in our intention towards the Good, we must ascend to the Principle within ourselves; from many we must become one; only so do we attain to knowledge of that which is Principle and Unity' (*Enneads*, VI, 9, 3). Elsewhere, however, he is more cautious about the possibilities of knowledge, though he stresses that, even if we cannot know or state it in itself, we can paradoxically possess it by reflecting upon its effects:

> We do not, it is true, grasp it by knowledge, but that does not mean that we are utterly devoid of it; we hold it not so as to state it, but so as to be able to speak about it. And we can and do state what it is not, while we are silent as to what it is: we are, in fact, speaking of it in the light of its sequels; unable to state it, we may still possess it.
>
> (*Enneads*, V, 3, 14)

The root of the problem which underlies these passages is the nature of knowledge itself, as Plotinus repeatedly admits, for knowledge presupposes the manifold, a unity composed of the knower and the known (*Enneads*, V, 3, 10). Apprehension of the One, on the other hand, must simultaneously be access to a point beyond duality, and here lies the difficulty, since knowledge implies subjectivity and subjectivity difference, while unity, the supposed object of this transcendental knowledge, can admit of no duality or distinction in itself. Thus, in knowing unity, the mind 'is prevented by that very unification from recognising what it has found; it cannot distinguish itself from the object of the intuition' (*Enneads*, VI, 9, 3).

Plotinus attempted in various ways to get around this difficulty. In one passage, for instance, he ingeniously suggests that, in our vision of the One, the object of knowledge is the possibility of knowledge itself, such that the one who seeks 'is lifted and sees, never knowing how; the vision floods the eyes with light, but it is not a light showing some other object, the light is itself the vision. No longer is there thing seen and light to show it' (*Enneads*, VI, 7, 36). In others, he stresses that the knowledge by which we know the One is not a knowledge at all, since 'awareness of this Principle comes neither by knowing nor by the Intellection that discovers the Intellectual

Beings but by a presence overpassing all knowledge' (*Enneads*, VI, 9, 3–4); we know it by a 'direct intuition' (*Enneads*, III, 8, 9). But even though such strategies of meta-cognition avoid the more obvious duality of knower and known, the problem of subjectivity and the self remains.[5] Otherness is built into the human cognitive process and is constitutive of the very sense of self. Absolute unicity, the complete absence of otherness, is a concept that definitively stands outside human experience, therefore, and presents to thought the conceptual dialectic of an irreducible aporia.[6]

What we find in Plotinus, then, is a link between the One, which disrupts any possibility of knowledge or representation, and the Good, which is the desirable end of all human striving and activity. The One-Good is also the principle of origination, and is the source from which the universe emerged and to which it will return. Crucially for Plotinus, the cosmological dimension of the One that transcends language, representation, being and knowledge, guarantees our own participation in it, however problematic that concept might be. It is the cosmological dimension also which supports the self-communication of sublime difference as the mediation of the Beautiful which, although not itself to be identified with the One, communicates something of it to the beholder and thus reorders the human spirit back towards the source from which it came.

Some of these same themes return in the work of Meister Eckhart, where, however, absolute and unthinkable difference as dialectical unity is set in a new, Christian context. Eckhart was born in Gotha, near Erfurt, around 1260, and he died in Avignon in 1327/8.[7] The early educational influences upon him were those of the German Dominican School, centring upon Albert the Great at Cologne, in which neoplatonic sources played a key role.[8] Eckhart has come to be seen as a leading figure of the intellectual movement associated with the German Dominicans, and his own theological system represents a synthesis of classical – neoplatonist – thought with Christianity in a way that parallels the Aristotelian synthesis achieved by Thomas Aquinas.[9] But in the Eckhartian system, the theme of oneness is found in a new configuration with respect to both intellect and being. Whereas, for Plotinus, intellect was the site of being, and both were opposed to the One on account of their intrinsically pluriform character, intellect, for Eckhart, actually partakes of oneness and thus shares the unity of the divine nature.

In distinction from Plotinus' emanationism, Eckhart's metaphysics of the One, as primary difference, is located within his Christian philosophy of Creation as *creatio ex nihilo*, modelled upon the inner-Trinitarian process of the generation of the Son. In his *Commentary on John*, Eckhart combines the Trinitarian theology of Nicaea with neoplatonist notions to do with the relation of an image to its origin, and with a formal theory of analogy. Eckhart is primarily concerned at this point to map out the relations which obtain between the transcendentals and God the Creator. He argues firstly that if the Son is of one essence with the Father, though different in person, then the just man is the 'offspring' (*proles*) of justice, and is one essence with justice, though different in person. This serves to emphasise the extent to which the transcendentals, for Eckhart, remain within God. He explicitly rejects a Thomist understanding of analogy, whereby the creation is related to the Creator as an effect to a cause, and is ranked below the Creator, and advocates instead a form of analogy which maintains that the property of the first analogate does not properly belong to the second analogate but inheres in it only by imputation. This applies to every perfection, including existence.[10] Thus it seems that, for Eckhart, being is on loan to the creature, and never properly comes into its possession. This begs the further question of the sense in which the creature can be said to exist in itself, if those properties which define the essence of the creature can be said to remain within God, even to be God. On a number of occasions, Eckhart specifically equates the creature with 'pure nothingness' or the 'shadow of nothingness', and in a German sermon we read: 'All creatures are a pure nothingness. I do not say that they have some worth, or that they are anything at all. They are absolutely nothing. Whatever has no being is nothing'.[11] According to Eckhart's neoplatonist metaphysics, the creature is essentially distinguished from the Creator on the grounds that the mode of existence of creatures is pluriform, whereas God is perfect unicity. In other words, the properties which are still rooted in the divine coexist in the creature in a state of multiplicity, whereas in God they are wholly united within his divine unity.

As for Plotinus, therefore, the binary opposition of unity and multiplicity is the key metaphysical principle for Eckhart, which determines all else, God being specifically equated with 'the One'. In contrast to Plotinus, however, for whom the language of the One was ultimately a construct on the surface of the Ineffable (and wholly exchangeable with 'the Good'), Eckhart has a more positive evaluation of the signifying power of 'the One', which 'adds nothing' to God, unlike 'truth and goodness', which add something to him 'in thought'.[12] As a way of speaking about God, the term 'the One' remains entirely unfathomable and is thus a more adequate name of God than any other. While God is somehow present in the notion of the One, our knowledge of him as the One is set apart from any kind of ordinary knowing and is rather a knowing by participation, since the human *intellectus* (Middle High German: *vernünfticheit*), which is our own cognitive essence, is itself wholly dynamic and unified and thus shares in the divine nature itself. We can see this understanding at work in an important German sermon, where Eckhart tells his congregation that human 'intellect' is 'detached from here and now', that it is 'like nothing', which means to say, according to Eckhartian metaphysics, that it is 'like God' (*DW69*). It is like the divine nature too in that it is both 'pure and uncompounded' and is reflexive 'or ever inwardly seeking'. Further, 'intellect' is described as being 'an image', which is to say an image of the divine image, or Eternal Word. Under the influence of the Trinitarian theology of Nicaea, whereby the Son is the identical image of the Father, Eckhart posits an understanding of the image which radically emphasises – more even than Plotinus – the unity of the thing imaged with its source. The image and source are one, just as the Son and Father are one.[13] The human intellect and the divine nature exist one in the other, and show a dynamic symmetry which becomes a programme for the mystical knowledge of God:

> Intellect peeps in and ransacks every corner of the Godhead, and seizes on the Son in the Father's heart and in the ground, and sets him in its own ground. Intellect [...] bursts into the ground whence goodness and truth proceed, and seizes it *in principio*, in the beginning where goodness and truth are just coming out, before it has any name, before it burgeons forth, in a much higher ground than goodness and wisdom.
>
> (*DW69*)

In the case of Meister Eckhart, then, the One has set itself in intimate relation with the human creature, who is the *imago dei*. Eckhart lacks Plotinus' interest in cosmic mediations of the One, therefore, and does not share his opposition between intellect and unicity. As a wholly unified act, the process of *intelligere* is rather a participation in the divine unity than a descent from it. Its function as difference, with respect to all other forms of human knowing, both concrete and 'spiritual', is underlined by Eckhart's constant replication of metaphors for the knowledge of the One, showing how it disrupts and destabilises ordinary language use, and is more adequately spoken of through negation. But, despite the complete otherness of God as the One, the Wholly Other is again dialectically present within creation through the dynamic relation of image and source, which attains its fullest potency in the human mind itself as the site of transcendental cognition.

Deleuze clearly inhabits a very different philosophical world from that of Plotinus and Eckhart. There is in his thought no trace of cosmology, for instance, which played a central role in the systems of our earlier thinkers. It was this indeed which – more strongly in the case of Eckhart – allowed them to construct a symmetry between difference itself and human thought, which somehow participates in or holds a privileged relation to the principle of radical difference. Consequently the human person is drawn to the One, as the Good or as God, as to her own highest self-realisation. In his own engagement with difference, however, Deleuze is ostensibly concerned with the nature of philosophy itself and, in particular, with freeing the practice of philosophy from the constraints of the 'image of thought' which, he argues, has since Plato obscured the radical and generative potency of thinking and what he calls 'the art of forming, inventing and fabricating concepts'.[14] Conventionally, philosophy advances through propositions, whereas the true genesis of thought, 'the true philosophical beginning' lies in problems which crucially embody difference as a potentiality pointing beyond the terms of reference that are already known to something quite new.[15] Problems are 'the differential elements in thought, the genetic elements in the true' (*DR*, p. 162). In terms which Deleuze develops in *What is Philosophy?*, we can say that the 'fabrication' of concepts requires a kind of creative originality which is marked not by its continuity with previously held positions but rather by its disruptive difference: that is, by the opening up of a new and unimagined space of thought. The 'dogmatic image of thought' as representation, on the other hand, which is founded upon the consensus of the faculties, recognition and the logical stability of the ground of sufficient reason, denies the possibility of a radical or pure thinking of difference. Deleuze seeks to rethink philosophy therefore as 'a theory of thought without image', in parallel with the turn from representational to abstract art (*DR*, p. 276).

Although Deleuze is unequivocally operating within a purely philosophical space at this point, there is an undeniable sense that he is courting perspectives which link his thinking with that of earlier traditions which are exemplified in Plotinus and Eckhart. He is, after all, concerned with creativity, and the generation of new ideas which proceed not from the adaptation of previously existing material, but rather from difference as absence or negation: as a kind of *creatio ex nihilo*. It is inevitable, moreover, that, by removing difference entirely from the province of representation, or being, Deleuze renders it transcendental and aligns it precisely with the One of Plotinus and Eckhart's *unum indistinctum*. Much of *Difference and Repetition* is taken up with an exhaustive critique of 'the thinking of representation', which constrains difference by enclosing it within 'the four iron collars of representation': 'identity in the concept, opposition in the predicate, analogy in judgement and resemblance in perception' (*DR*, p. 262). He argues that the taming of 'the free oceanic differences' of simulacra is first undertaken by Plato, whose system of Forms selected out, on the grounds of purely moral criteria, certain images from free-floating simulacra that were henceforward to function as copies of transcendental models and to be constrained by *identity*.

In later tradition, the Kantian system similarly emasculated difference by making it that which distinguishes one concept from another: however, this is to confuse 'the concept of difference with a merely conceptual difference', which is still mediated by representation (*DR*, p. 27). Hegel and Leibniz proposed an orgiastic system by enclosing difference within the infinitely large in the former case, and the infinitely small in the latter. But again, difference remained ensnared within representation, with its assumption of identity, opposition or similarity (*DR*, pp. 45–9). Nor was it captured in the Hegelian notion of the negative, which is 'the inverted image of difference', since again this presupposes 'the requirements of representation which subordinate it to identity' (*DR*, p. 235). In general, then, difference evades thought, since it is cancelled by the very systems which explicate it. Its being, which is that more of the 'noumenon' than the 'phenomenon', is rather one of 'implication' (*DR*, pp. 228, 222).

The sense that, in his pursuit of difference, Deleuze is guided by more than a formal philosophical critique, and that something essential to do with the authenticity of the self and the nature of reality itself is at stake, is supported also by his reflections upon those points in the tradition at which a new kind of thinking of difference seemed to appear. In a typically subversive reading of Kant for instance, Deleuze discerns this possibility in Kant's description of the rupture of the consensus of the faculties, specifically imagination and thought, in the perception of the sublime (*DR*, p. 146). It is to Kant also that Deleuze attributes the important insight that time functions as the 'inner sense' of the self and so inaugurates the tradition of the 'fractured I', which dissolves the Cartesian subject and begins the tradition of the modern (*DR*, p. 86). But the dominant influence for Deleuze at this point is Nietzsche, whose theory of Eternal Return constitutes a turning point in the history of thought, and represents the summation of a thinking of difference and repetition. The Nietzschean turn of Deleuze's philosophy is evident in his identification of knowing as recognition and representation with ontology, and specifically with 'the sedentary distributions' of the categories and 'sedentary proportionality' of analogy (*DR*, pp. 284–5). Analogy is fundamentally the ontology of representation:

> The analogy of being implies both these two aspects at once: one by which being is distributed in determinable forms which necessarily distinguish and vary the sense; the other by which being so distributed is necessarily repartitioned among well-determined beings, each endowed with a unique sense. What is missed at the two extremities is the collective sense of being [*être*] and the play of individuating difference in being [*étant*]. Everything takes place between generic difference and specific difference. The genuine universal is missed no less than the true singular: the only common sense of being is distributive, and the only individual difference is general.
>
> (*DR*, p. 303)

Against analogy, therefore, Deleuze traces the tradition of ontological univocity, which is the 'one ontological proposition' there has ever been, noting it first in Duns Scotus (*DR*, p. 35). A second stage is reached with Spinoza, in whose work 'univocal being ceases to be neutralised and becomes expressive; it becomes a truly expressive and affirmative proposition' (*DR*, p. 40). In the ontology of analogy, difference ceases to be thought and 'is dissipated in non-being', while the ontology of univocity preserves the possibility of the thinkability of difference in a radically new way (*DR*, p. 262). That possibility only comes to fruition in Nietzsche's 'doctrine' of the Eternal Return, which 'is univocity of being, the effective realisation of that univocity', where univocity of being is not only thought and affirmed but actually realised (*DR*, pp. 41–2). Deleuze sees the Eternal Return as a form of eschatological purification that strips away the Identical with its 'quality and extension', and leaves only repetition and difference, as 'the intensive' (*DR*, p. 243; cf. p. 299). He declares:

It is because nothing is equal, because everything bathes in its difference, its dissimilarity and its inequality, even with itself, that everything returns – or rather, everything does not return. What does not return is that which denies eternal return, that which does not pass the test. It is quality and extensity that do not return, in so far as within them difference, the condition of eternal return is cancelled. So too the negative, in so far as difference is thereby inverted and cancelled. So too the identical, the similar and the equal, in so far as these constitute the forms of indifference.

(*DR*, p. 243)

The cosmic retrieval of pure difference, as what he calls 'chaosmos', and the eradication of representation as 'the image', outlines the possibility of a new and more creative way of doing philosophy. But Deleuze's Nietzschean inheritance lends this theme a much broader significance in his thought which can be more appropriately described as 'religious' or 'metaphysical', if we take into account the peculiarly Nietzschean inversions of these terms. Representation is error and 'is a site of transcendental illusion'.[16] The four expressions of that illusion – thought, sensibility, the Idea, and being – 'culminate in the position of an identical thinking subject, which functions as a principle of identity for concepts in general' (*DR*, p. 265). Intrinsic to the Eternal Return therefore – 'not a doctrine but the simulacrum of every doctrine [the highest irony]' (*DR*, p. 95), is the notion that both the self and 'God' are eradicated in the affirmation of pure difference. Like Nietzsche before him, Deleuze preaches the transformation of the self from within a parodic reversal of Christian metaphysics, whereby the openness and therefore meaning of history collapses into pure repetition, and being is banished in favour of 'dissemblance and disparateness, chance, multiplicity and becoming', which, as Deleuze would say, mark the excess of difference (*DR*, p. 300).

Deleuze's engagement with the Wholly Other turns out not to be so very different from that of Plotinus and Eckhart, therefore, but with one important reservation. The loss of cosmology, and thus of an organic relation between difference and the self understood in terms of creation, risks the positing of difference as a chimera or the shadow of normative human experience in a pluralistic world. In the absence of a mapping of the relation between difference and ourselves in the representational terms of creation (whether as emanation or *creatio ex nihilo*), difference retreats into itself and thus withdraws from thinkability. It is only the thinking of a relationality between difference and ourselves – most evident in a transcendentalist cosmology – that can offer a dialectic in which thinking as a thinking beyond thought becomes meaningful. Thus, paradoxically, it is only the *representation* of the relation between self and difference precisely as representation in conflict with itself that allows the emergence of a dialectic as a space in which the full radicality of Otherness can 'non-thinkingly' be thought, in negations and disruptions of language. Such a creationist dialectic leads not to the extinguishing of the self as such but rather to its radical problematicisation as the primary site in which – as the *imago dei* – the conflicts between representation and non-representation, relation and non-relation, thinking and non-thinking, are rehearsed and performed. But, unlike Derrida, Deleuze shows no awareness of the proximity of an apophatic God, who might lay claim to difference itself, nor indeed, of the affinities between his own pursuit of a trans-representational difference and Christian, or neoplatonist, negative theology.[17] And yet, in *Difference and Repetition*, we encounter the agon of a mind which is confronted with the absolute necessity of thinking difference on the one hand and with its radical unthinkability on the other. Outside a cosmological system which sets difference – as origin and oneness – into an intimate and even connatural relation with the human mind, this preoccupation might seem deluded or at best eccentric. It is Deleuze's conviction, therefore, that such a thinking of difference remains *possible*, in the face of all the evident incommensurabilities of the project, that lends his text a certain familiar tension which – despite the absence of any rhetoric of grace or participation – seems to this reader at least to be natively and ecstatically theological.

Notes

1 Gilles Deleuze, *Difference and Repetition*, trans. Paul Patton (London: Athlone Press, 1994) p. 266. Henceforth referred to as *DR*.

2 Deleuze himself points out that difference 'is in the air' (*DR*, p. xix).

3 *De Libero Arbitrio*, II, 8, 22.

4 Plotinus, *Enneads*, II, 9, 1. Quotations from Plotinus are taken from Stephen MacKenna's translation (Harmondsworth: Penguin, 1991) with occasional slight adaptations. But P. A. Meijer argues that the particular name for the One used by Plotinus is often not arbitrary but context-dependent: see *Plotinus on the Good or the One* (Amsterdam: J. C. Gieben, 1992) pp. 58–64.

5 Gerard J. P. O'Daly, *Plotinus' Philosophy of the Self* (Shannon: Irish University Press, 1973) pp. 82–94. Bernard McGinn surveys the discussion around the highest cognition of the self in his *The Presence of God, vol. 1: Foundations of Mysticism* (London: SCM, 1992) pp. 44–55.

6 Pierre Hadot offers a perceptive psychological comment on this spiritual state when he says: 'Here we have the whole paradox of the human self: we only are that of which we are aware, and yet we are aware of being more fully ourselves precisely in those moments when, raising ourselves to a higher level of inner simplicity, we lose our self-awareness': *Plotinus or the Simplicity of Vision*, trans. Michael Chase (Chicago: Chicago University Press, 1993) p. 32.

7 On the life of Eckhart, see my *Meister Eckhart: Mystical Theologian* (London: SPCK, 1991) pp. 22–50.

8 Other members of this school include Dietrich von Freiberg, Ulrich von Strasburg and Bertold von Moosberg. On the influence of Proclus' work *The Book of Causes*, and Avicenna's highly platonising way of reading Aristotle's *De Anima*, see Alain de Libera, *Introduction à la mystique rhénane* (Paris: OEIL, 1984) pp. 25–72.

9 On the political background to the condemnation of Meister Eckhart, see my 'Why were Meister Eckhart's propositions condemned?', *New Blackfriars*, no. 71

(October 1990) pp. 433–45; and *Meister Eckhart: Mystical Theologian* (London: SPCK, 1991) pp. 31–45.

10 Latin Works (= *LW*). *Meister Eckhart: Die deutschen und lateinischen Werke* (hereafter *ME*) hrsg, im Auftrage der deutschen Forschungsgemeinschaft (Stuttgart and Berlin: Kohlhammer Verlag, 1936–, vol. 2) p. 282. Translation in B. McGinn, F. Tobin and E. Borgstadt, *Meister Eckhart: Teacher and Preacher* (London: SPCK, 1986) p. 178.

11 German Sermon no. 4 (= *DW4*), in *ME*.

12 *DW21*. In *DW23* he deconstructs even the 'One' in favour of the term *nihtes niht*, or 'nothing of anything'.

13 Cf. *DW16a*, concerning the image of the soul: 'This image is the Son of the Father, and I myself am this image, and this image is wisdom'. On this important though fragmentary sermon, see Loris Sturlese, 'Mystik und Philosophie in der Bildlehre Meister Eckhart', in *Festschrift für Walter Haug und Burghart Wachinger* (Tübingen: Max Niemeyer Verlag, 1992) pp. 349–61.

14 Gilles Deleuze and Félix Guattari, *What is Philosophy?*, trans. Graham Burchell and Hugh Tomlinson (London and New York: Verso, 1994) p. 2. These themes were originally pursued in *Différence et Répétition* (1968).

15 Gilles Deleuze, *Difference and Repetition*, trans. Paul Patton (London: Athlone Press, 1994) p. 129. Hereafter referred to as *DR*.

16 *DR*, p. 301. Cp. 'The history of the long error is the history of representation, the history of the icons' (*DR*, p. 265).

17 See especially Jacques Derrida, 'Comment ne pas parler: dénégations' ('How to avoid speaking: denials'), originally published in Jacques Derrida, *Psyché: Inventions de l'autre* (Paris: Galilée, 1987) pp. 535–95. The English translation used here was published in Sanford Budick and Wolfgang Iser (eds) *Languages of the Unsayable: The Play of Negativity in Literature and Literary Theory* (New York: Columbia University Press, 1989) pp. 3–70.

7   Bodily organs and organisation

Maximilian de Gaynesford

> A disciplined body is the prerequisite of an efficient gesture.
>
> Michel Foucault[1]

I

Michel Foucault emphasised ways in which a 'subject' is that which is *subjected*. A precondition for describing the world as containing 'subjects' at all is the existence of methods of individuating entities as such. These methods evidently depend on the existence of principles of individuation and opportunities for their application. Foucault emphasised different principles at different times – principles for deciding who is or is not rational, guilty, safe for society, worthy of the interest of the social sciences, worthy of 'care', and so on.[2] These differences are not deep. What matters is what is true for each: that, in the very process of becoming a 'subject' or counting as such, an entity is made the victim of various types of violence, repression and/or political ordering.

In a similar way, Deleuze and Guattari regard an 'organism' as that which is *organised*. The principles of individuation on which the process depends are, for Deleuze and Guattari, directly related to theology: 'The judgement of God, the system of the judgement of God, the theological system, is precisely the operation of He who makes an organism, an organization of organs called the organism'.[3] Further: 'The first things to be distributed on the body without organs are races, cultures, and their gods'.[4]

By 'organs', Deleuze and Guattari mean objects that perform specific functions in relation to desire, its production and transference. An infant's eye or mouth counts as such, for example, in desire-producing connection with its mother's breast.[5] Thus a single organised collection of organs might, but need not, map onto a single corporeal object – such as a human or animal body.

The distinction between being a mere corporeal object and being an organism in Deleuze and Guattari's sense goes beyond, for example, Husserl's use of the distinction in German between *Leib* (the animated flesh of an animal or human being) and *Körper* (mere inanimate physical matter).[6] It is more closely connected to Maurice Merleau-Ponty's account of the human body in his *Phenomenology of Perception* (1945).[7] Merleau-Ponty rejects the notion that this body could be just 'one more among external objects' (*P*, p. 93). Indeed, he claims that one's body is not an object at all – if that means it must be reducible to a 'scientific object' (*P*, p. 174). It is not something which 'acknowledges between its parts, or between itself and other objects only external and mechanical relationships, whether in the narrow sense of motion received or transmitted, or in the wider sense of the relation of function to variable' (*P*, p. 73). This is precisely what an organism is not. And that definition is consistent with Merleau-Ponty's evocative suggestion that the body is properly comparable 'not to a physical object, but rather to a work of art' (*P*, p. 151). 'It is a nexus of living meanings, not the law for a certain number of covariant forms' (*P*, p. 152).

Organism-producing organisation occurs in the context of what Deleuze and Guattari, recalling Antonin Artaud, call the 'Body without Organs' (BwO) (*AO*, p. 9): 'It is in the BwO that the organs enter into the relations of composition called the organism' (*ATP*, p. 159).

What Deleuze and Guattari mean by 'the BwO' is complex and the subject of later discussion, but neatly summed up for present purposes by various definitions they offer: '[It is that which] serves as a surface for the recording of the entire process of production of desire' (*AO*, p. 11); '[It is] the field of the immanence of desire' (*ATP*, p. 154); 'The BwO is not "before" the organism; it is adjacent to it and is continually in the process of constructing itself' (*ATP*, p. 164).

This field is described as an 'enemy' to the organism. Deleuze and Guattari regard the process by which organs are organised as a violent struggle. This again has a theological explanation. The judgement of God organises organs

> because He cannot bear the BwO, because He pursues it and rips it apart so He can be first, and have the organism be first. [...] For the judgement of God weighs upon and is exercised against the BwO; it is the BwO that undergoes it.
>
> (*ATP*, p. 159)

Moreover, 'beneath its organs it [the BwO] senses there are larvae and loathsome worms, and a God at work messing it all up or strangling it by organizing it' (*AO*, p. 9). Thus, in the very process of becoming an 'organism' or counting as such, an entity is made the victim of the judgement of God – what Deleuze and Guattari equate with 'the theological system'.

These claims give rise to many questions; one is particularly striking. What, then, are we to make of the person of Christ? There is little doubt that Christ's person may be regarded as, in the relevant senses, 'organised' by the judgement of God/the theological system. This is so whether we consider as the organism in question the collection of organs that count as the historical Jesus, the second person of the Trinity, the Eucharist, the earthly and institutional Church, the Eternal Church, κερυγμα, relevant dogma, and so on.

Is the person of Christ, then, to be regarded as the site of conflict between various BwO's and the theological system? Using a series of examples, drawn mainly from post-Nicea debates, I want to show how this might be an illuminating way of approaching certain aspects of the development of Christology. The understanding of Christ's incarnation is of particular interest, given that 'the body without organs is not God, *quite the contrary*' (*AO*, p. 13; my emphasis). And, bearing in mind the definition of BwO, 'desire always remains in close touch with the conditions of objective existence; it embraces them and follows them, shifts when they shift, and does not outlive them' (*AO*, p. 27).

Christ's body was, after all, the operational context within which redemption was conceived as having occurred. The overall position and disposition of that body was a necessary condition of, and integral to, salvation. Thus Christ's body underwent both discipline and laying out at the hands of the fourth- to fifth-century 'theological system'. Each of the relations that it must have had with the bodies and other objects it manipulated (or was manipulated by) in order to achieve the redemptive goal had to be defined by theologians, established by councils and policed by imperial officials:

> Who because of us men and because of our salvation came down from the heavens, and was incarnate from the Holy Spirit and the Virgin Mary and became man, and was crucified for us under Pontius Pilate, and suffered and was buried, and rose again on the third day according to the Scriptures and ascended to heaven and sits on the right hand of the Father, and will come again with glory to judge living and dead.
>
> (Creed of Constantinople [381])[8]

In Section II, I briefly establish the main terms of debate.

II

After the council of Nicea (325), Christological debate centred no longer on Christ's relation to the Father, but on how the humanity of the incarnate Son was related to his divinity. The ensuing debate was structured around widespread agreement on the following points:

(i) 'The Word became flesh' (*John*, 1:14).

(ii) The Word 'for our salvation, was incarnate, and lived among men, and suffered, and rose again on the third day' (Nicene Creed).[9]

(iii) The Word was 'ομοουσιον τω πατρι (of one substance with the Father); 'εξ της 'ουσιας του πατρου (from the innermost being of the Father); and therefore Son by nature, not grace or adoption, etc.

(iv) The Word, as the Logos of God, was the revelation of God's nature, and thus immutable and impassible.

(v) The incarnation of the Word is the main point of our salvation.

Acceptance of (i)–(v) need not block differential emphasis or interpretation of those points. Thus a wide spectrum of opinion about human-divine union ('υποστασις) in the incarnation was still possible.

At one end of the spectrum, Christ is two persons, each with its own nature, one human, one divine. This makes talk of 'υποστασις mysterious or mundane, depending on how much significance is given to the 'became' in (i). Nestorius (c.381–c.452), for example, preferred to describe the union as συναφεια, the term used to describe the conjunction of man and wife; they become 'one flesh' while remaining two separate natures and persons.[10]

At the other end of the spectrum, Christ is one person with one nature. Post-Nicea, the only option is a wholly divine being inhabiting a phantasy-body[11] or mystically associated with a real body; a wholly human being could not satisfy (i)–(v). There is no true 'υποστασις to account for.

For these various reasons, the central position might be thought attractive: that Christ is one person with two natures. The significance of 'became' and the nature of the union have still to be explained. This is made complex by the fact that every person is by nature both active (as agent) and passive (as subject of experience). It is common to place emphasis on one or other of these – i.e. on our capacity to have things happen to us, or on our ability to make things happen. So the central position offers various further possibilities, depending on how Christ's experience and agency is related to his divine or human nature. The status of (v) is crucial here; if redemption is effected both in man through a human life and by God through divine agency, the 'υποστασις must be correctly conceived. It might be thought that (ii) offers a guide here, but, as baldly stated, it is consistent with each of the following possible views:

(a) *Disjunction*: Christ experiences the world and acts in it in virtue of his human nature, and experiences the divine and acts divinely in virtue of his divine nature.

(b) *Strong concurrence*: Christ only experiences and acts from the 'υποστασις of his human and divine natures.

(c) *Agency concurrence*: Christ experiences the world in virtue of his human nature and the divine in virtue of his divine nature, but only acts from the 'υποστασις of the two.

(d) *Experience concurrence*: Christ acts in the world in virtue of his human nature and acts divinely in virtue of his divine nature, but only experiences from the 'υποστασις of the two.

The problems with (a) are clear: it invites the charge of making Christ a hybrid compound neither wholly human nor divine under some uniting force that is either wholly supernatural or observes some physical law of mechanical combination. It is difficult to see how this could be compatible with (iv).

The problem with any form of concurrence, i.e. (b)–(d), is the difficulty of retaining proper significance for Christ's humanity. If his actions only ever proceed from the 'υποστασις, it is difficult to see them as in any sense the outcome of ordinary human moral effort. If his experiences are only ever enjoyed or suffered by the 'υποστασις, it is difficult to see them as in any sense contributing to ordinary human apprehension of truth. It is implied by (ii) that our salvation depends on Christ's actions and experiences being made the actual actions and experiences of God in a human embodiment. If this embodiment is made insignificant, then, if (v) is true, the reality of salvation is threatened.

III

Deleuze and Guattari identify various defining features of BwO's. Each illuminates the ways in which Christ's incarnation was handled by the fourth- to fifth-century theological system – by which I mean, primarily, theologians, councils, patriarchal (including papal) and imperial authority. In this essay, space forces me to illustrate the claim by reference to three major theologians and three essential features of BwO's.

Emptied bodies/κενωσις

'So what is this BwO? – But you're already on it […]. It is already under way the moment the body has had enough of organs and wants to slough them off, or loses them' (*ATP*, p. 150). Deleuze and Guattari describe ways in which bodies are emptied. The hypochondriac body is entirely dis-organised. The paranoid body contains organs that are under continual external threat. The schizophrenic body contains organs that struggle against each other internally. Christ's body is kenotic. In the description of Gregory of Nyssa (*c.*335–95): 'The godhead "empties itself" [*Philippians*, 2:7] in order that it may come within the capacity of the human nature; the humanity is renewed by becoming divine through commixture with the divine'.[12]

Deleuze and Guattari distinguish between ways of emptying oneself. The first is a 'wild destratifying' (*ATP*, p. 160), a mere emptying oneself of organs. This way, exemplified by hypochondriac, paranoid, schizophrenic, drugged and masochist bodies, they describe as 'dreary' and 'botching the BwO' (*ATP*, p. 160). The second way is patient and careful: a momentary dismantling of 'the organisation of organs we call the organism' (*ATP*, p. 161). Deleuze and Guattari go on to offer advice about entering on this second, successful way of 'making oneself a body without organs':

You have to keep enough of the organism for it to reform each dawn; and you have to keep small supplies of significance and subjectification, if only to turn them against their own systems when the circumstances demand it, when things, persons, even situations, force you to; and you have to keep small rations of subjectivity in sufficient quantity to enable you to respond to the dominant reality.

(*ATP*, p. 160)

This advice, and the very Greek myth it depends on, resonate in the way Gregory of Nyssa continues his account: the incarnation as fire from Heaven.

As fire that often lies hidden below the surface of wood is not observed by the senses of those who see or even touch the wood, but is manifest when it is kindled into flame; so [...] he who, because he is 'the Lord of Glory' [*Corinthians*, 2:8] thought nothing of that which men think shame, and concealed, as it were, the embers of his life beneath his bodily nature in fulfilling the divine plan by means of his death, kindled it to flame again by the power of his own Godhead, warming into life that which had been brought to death, pouring that limited first-fruit of our nature into the infinity of his divine power.

(*Against Eunomius*, p. 139)

Desire/ευδοκια

'The BwO is the field of immanence of desire, the plane of consistency specific to desire' (*ATP*, p. 154). Of crucial concern to Christology is the nature and extent of the 'indwelling' of God in Christ's incarnation. In a swift argument, Theodore of Mopsuestia (d. 428) proved it could not be a matter of essence ('ουσια) or activity ('ενεργεια) but of the good satisfaction of desire or pleasure ('ευδοκια). The argument proceeds by *modus tollens*. God's indwelling is not universal: God chooses some and not others to dwell in. Thus, if indwelling is to be defined as essence or activity, it could not be in God's essence to be present everywhere or in God's power to be active everywhere. Yet God's essence and activity are not constrained, even self-constrained, in these ways. So indwelling cannot be a matter of essence or activity. This leaves 'ευδοκια. And since God's 'ευδοκια is not universal, there is no reason to deny that it defines that indwelling by which Christ's nature is constituted as such:

It is obviously appropriate to speak of indwelling being a matter of 'ευδοκια. 'Ευδοκια is the name for that very good and excellent will of God which he exercises because pleased with those who are earnestly devoted to him; the word is derived from his 'good' and excellent 'pleasure' for them.[13]

It makes no sense to individuate desires and their satisfaction as one would physical objects. Thus Deleuze and Guattari focus on two features: intensity of desire and kind of desire. The first feature allows them to distinguish BwO's as 'pieces of immanence': 'A BwO is made in such a way that it can be occupied, populated only by intensities' (*ATP*, p. 153).

Deleuze and Guattari then categorise BwO's, according to intensity, using Gregory Bateson's term 'plateau'; they are 'continuous regions of intensity constituted in such a way that they do not allow themselves to be interrupted by any external termination' (*ATP*, p. 158).

Similarly, Theodore distinguishes persons by the intensity of God's indwelling-'ευδοκια. In the 'unworthy', the intensity is degree-zero; in Christ's case, it is absolute: 'It is an indwelling in which he united the one who was being assumed wholly to himself and prepared him to share all the honour which he, the indweller, who is a son by nature, shares' (*On the Incarnation*, p. 1296).

With regard to the second feature of BwO's by which they are categorised, kind of desire, Deleuze and Guattari suggest that, for each type of BwO, we ask: '(1) What type is it, how is it fabricated, by what procedures and means (predetermining what will come to pass)? (2) What are its modes, what comes to pass, and with what variants and what surprises, what is unexpected and what expected?' (*ATP*, p. 152).

Theodore establishes the same criterion and employs it as follows:

> Just as the indwelling is a matter of 'ευδοκια, so also in precisely the same way the 'ευδοκια varies the mode of indwelling. That which effects God's indwelling and explains how the one who is universally present in his essence can indwell only some – indeed only a very small proportion – of the whole of mankind is, as I have said, 'ευδοκια; and this 'ευδοκια also qualifies the particular mode of indwelling in every case. […] Thus when [God] is said to indwell the apostles, or more generally the righteous, then it is an indwelling as being well pleased with the righteous, according to the mode of pleasure he has in the virtuous. But we would never describe the indwelling in [Christ's] case as of that kind – that would be sheer madness; in his case it is as in a son; that is the form of 'ευδοκια by which the indwelling took place.
>
> (*On the Incarnation*, p. 1295)

Apophaticism/αναθεμα

'The BwO is what remains when you take everything away. What you take away is precisely the phantasy, and signifiances and subjectifications as a whole' (*ATP*, p. 151). Thus the BwO is defined apophatically, in relation to that which it is not. The same tendency informs the attempts by various theologians to define Christ's incarnation. Thus what has often been described as a 'summary' of the Christology of Cyril of Alexandria (412–44) is in fact a list of negatives the declaration of which makes the holder suitable for anathematisation (cf. Kelly, *Doctrines*, 324):

> If anyone in the one Christ divides the personalities [...], let him be anathema. [...] If anyone dares to say that Christ is a man who carries God (within him) and not rather that he is God in truth [...], let him be anathema. [...] If anyone says that Jesus as man was actuated by God the Word, as being other than he, let him be anathema. If anyone dares to say that the man who was assumed ought to be worshipped jointly with God the Word [...], let him be anathema. If anyone says that the one Lord, Jesus Christ, was glorified by the Spirit, as though the power he exercised was another's received through the Spirit [...], let him be anathema.[14]

IV

If Christ's body is the site of various BwO's, and given what Deleuze and Guattari claim, we would expect conflict with the theologically imposed organisation of organs called the 'organism'. Evidence from the fourth to fifth centuries is widespread.

Consider, first, the language of theologians. The following passage is from a letter of Gregory of Nazianzus (*c.*330–*c.*390); its main target is Apollinarianism:

> If anyone does not believe that holy Mary is Θεοτοκος [God-bearer], he is severed from the Godhead. If anyone should assert that [Christ] passed through the Virgin as through a channel, and was not at once divinely and humanly formed in her (divinely, because without the intervention of a man; humanly, because in accordance with the laws of gestation), he is in like manner godless. If any assert that the manhood was formed, and that afterwards God insinuated himself into the manhood, he is to be condemned. For this is not a generation of God, but a shirking of generation. If any introduce the notion of two sons, one of God the Father, the other of the mother, and discredits the unity and identity, may he lose his part in the adoption promised to those who believe aright. For God and man are two natures, as also soul and body are; but there are not two Sons or two Gods. [...] If any should say that the Godhead was wrought in him by grace as in a prophet, but was not and is not united with him in essence, let him be empty of the higher energy, or rather full of the opposite. If any does not worship the Crucified, let him be anathema and be numbered among the deicides. If any assert that he was made perfect by works, or that, after his baptism, or after his resurrection from the dead, he was counted worthy of an adoptive Sonship, like those gods whom the Greeks call 'the interpolated', as added to the ranks of the gods, let him be anathema.[15]

The passage presents theology as an aggressive code of discipline, a syntax of doctrinal manoeuvres necessary for determining the canonical ordering of Christ's body, its movements and proper significance. Particularly noteworthy is the way it calls for justice and the way it would have that justice administered. Each punishment must fit its crime; it is that symmetry which gives the passage the tone of a manual for the effective policing of Christ's body.

Theological disputation was often insufficient for the purpose. The Patriarch of Constantinople in 428, Nestorius, turned to secular authority: 'Give me, O Emperor, the earth purged of heretics, and I will give you heaven as a recompense. Assist me in destroying heretics, and I will assist you in vanquishing the Persians'.[16]

Signs of conflict with the theological system are not restricted to educated and imperial circles; Nestorius' call for discipline met a widespread demand. The historian Socrates noted that it was 'extremely gratifying to some of the multitude, who cherished a senseless antipathy to the very name of heretic' (*Historia Ecclesiastica*, 29). Even emperors were keen to meet the demand: Marcian's Edict of 7 February 491 makes clear that, if 'controversy about the orthodox religion [lex] of Christians has been put away; remedies at length have been found for culpable error, and diversity of opinion among the peoples has issued in common consent and concord',[17] that was because a Church council had occurred 'in accordance with our commands' (Marcian, p. 301). The purpose of the council was

> [to teach] by clear definition what ought to be observed in the matter of religion. [...] He is a truly impious and sacrilegious person who, after the sentence of so many bishops, reserves anything to be decided by his own opinion. It is the mark of utter madness to search, in the full light of noon day, for counterfeit illumination.
>
> (Marcian, p. 301)[18]

The role of the emperor is to ensure that 'profane wrangling' now ceases:

> For whoever, after this finding of the truth, enter upon any further debate, searches for falsehood. No one, therefore, whether cleric, or official, or of any other estate whatsoever, shall henceforth collect a crowd of listeners and publicly try to discuss the Christian faith, devising occasion of riot and treachery thereby. [...] Take heed, therefore, to this edict of our Serenity, and abstain from profane words, and cease all further discussion of religion, which is forbidden. This sin, as we believe, will be punished by the judgement of God; but it will also be restrained by the authority of the laws and judges.
>
> (Marcian, p. 302)

V

All of this might be thought to give rise to significant feedback problems. One is of particular interest since it threatens the conclusions drawn so far with a charge of internal inconsistency.

One's BwO is said to be 'desire', 'that which one desires and by which one desires'; 'there is desire whenever there is the constitution of a BwO under one relation or another' (*ATP*, p. 165). (1) and (2) follow from this:

1   To be properly constituted as a BwO among other such in the world, Christ's BwO must be an object of his desire.[19]
2   Christ's BwO is the means by which Christ desires; it is the vehicle of his desiring, his general medium for experiencing desire.

Now it is plausible to suppose that:

3   Since, and in so far as, it is that by which other objects are desired, Christ's body cannot itself be the object of his desire.

Given (1)–(3), it follows that

4   Christ's BwO cannot be properly constituted as such; it is not a BwO among other such in the world.

The intuition behind (3) is this. If Christ's BwO is the means by which he desires objects in the world, then desiring something is precisely to bring BwO-dependent desire to bear on it. This presumably applies to desiring the BwO also. But the BwO cannot be desired as an object *of* BwO-dependent desire if it is the BwO that *provides for* that desire. For we may bring into being the kind of intensity proper to desiring an object. But only because we have, in so doing and by definition, exercised BwO-dependent desire – the BwO is that by which one desires. And to grasp the BwO providing for *that* desire, we must bring deeper possibilities of intensity into being-possibilities which are in turn made actual by deeper and as-yet ungrasped features of the BwO. If it is possible to desire some BwO, the possibility must be underwritten by an as-yet unexercised intensity of BwO-dependent desire. And so on in infinite regress. In short, something (i.e. Christ's BwO) cannot be the object of a desire for which it provides. Thus Christ desires things with his BwO, but his BwO itself is a thing he cannot desire; in order to do so, he would need the use of a second BwO which would itself desire and be desirable; and so on.[20]

However, the intuition behind (3) is false: things *can* be the object of a desire for which they provide. It may be that what, in the relevant sense, 'provides for' A's desire to go fishing (necessarily, if not sufficiently) are the existence of a well stocked river, an available fishing rod, and happy memories of former trips. But those very entities can become the object of

A's desires – A wishes *that* such a river should exist, *that* her rod be ready to hand, *that* she could remember successful fishing trips, and so on.

If (3) is false, we have no reason to conclude with (4). So there is no challenge to the internal consistency of the claim that Christ's nature may fruitfully be investigated in terms of BwO's.

VI

This essay has been concerned to identify certain connections between Deleuze and Guattari on BwO's and fourth- to fifth-century accounts of Christ's nature – in particular to deepen, with their aid, the kind of approach to the incarnation made by various recent authors, including Don Cupitt.[21] Naturally, it raises far more questions than it could possibly deal with. So it is in keeping to conclude with two significant feedback problems which bear further inquiry.

(a) The person of Christ is organised by the judgement of God. But that person is also to be considered, post-Nicea (325), as 'ομοουσιος in relation to the Father, and thus integral to that judgement. Thus, in whatever way Christ is organised as the output of the theological system, that person returns immediately to the system as part of its input.

(b) Given (a), whatever *understanding* of the person of Christ is made available as the output of the theological system, that information must return immediately to the system as part of its input.

Notes

1 Michel Foucault, *Discipline and Punish: The Birth of the Prison*, trans. A. Sheridan (Harmondsworth: Penguin, 1975) p. 152.
2 See, in particular, Michel Foucault, *Madness and Civilisation*, trans. R. Howard (New York: Random House, 1965); *The Order of Things*, unidentified collective translation (London: Tavistock Publications, 1970); *Discipline and Punish*, trans. A. Sheridan (Harmondsworth: Penguin, 1975); *The Care of the Self: The History of Sexuality vol. III*, trans. R. Hurley (New York: Pantheon, 1988).
3 Gilles Deleuze and Félix Guattari, *A Thousand Plateaus: Capitalism and Schizophrenia*, trans. Brian Massumi (London: Athlone Press, 1988) p. 158. Hereafter referred to as *ATP*.
4 Gilles Deleuze and Félix Guattari, *Anti-Oedipus: Capitalism and Schizophrenia*, trans. Robert Hurley, Mark Seem and Helen R. Lane (London: Athlone Press, 1984) p. 85. Hereafter referred to as *AO*.
5 See Eugene W. Holland, *Deleuze and Guattari's 'Anti-Oedipus': Introduction to Schizoanalysis* (London: Routledge, 1999) p. 26.
6 Edmund Husserl, *Ideas pertaining to a Pure Phenomenology and to a Phenomenological Philosophy, Second Book: Studies in the Phenomenology of Constitution*, trans. R. Rojcewicz and A. Schuwer (Dordrecht: Kluwer, 1989). See Editors' Introduction, xiv.
7 Maurice Merleau-Ponty, *Phenomenology of Perception*, trans. C. Smith (Bury St Edmunds: Routledge and Kegan Paul, 1962). Hereafter referred to as *P*.
8 J. N .D. Kelly, *Early Christian Creeds* (London: Longmans, Green, 1972) pp. 297–8.

9 *A New Eusebius*, ed. J Stevenson (London: SPCK, 1987) p. 344.
10 Nestorius, *Dialogues*, in Migne, *Patrologia Graeca*, VI (Paris: Vives, 1857–66) p. 75.
11 Compare

> Such exaltation of thought, while it let adrift the spirit, and gave it licence in strange airs, lost it the old patient rule over the body. The body was too coarse to feel the utmost of our sorrows and of our joys. Therefore we abandoned it as rubbish; we left it below us to march forward, a breathing simulacrum, on its own unaided level, subject to influences from which in normal times our instincts would have shrunk.
>
> (T. E. Lawrence, *Seven Pillars of Wisdom* (London: Penguin, 1962) p. 28)

12 Gregory of Nyssa, *Against Eunomius*, v. 5, trans. and ed. H. Bettenson, in *The Later Christian Fathers* (Oxford: Oxford University Press, 1970) p. 138.
13 Theodore of Mopsuestia, *On the Incarnation*, VII, trans. and ed. H. B. Swete, *Minor Epistles of St Paul*, 2 (Cambridge: Cambridge University Press, 1880–2) p. 1294.
14 Cyril of Alexandria, *Epistola XVII*, in Migne, *Patrologia Graeca*, LXXVII (Paris: Vives, 1857–66) pp. 105–22; trans. in J. Stevenson, *Creeds, Councils and Controversies* (London: SPCK, 1989) pp. 307–8.
15 Gregory of Nazianzus, *Epistola CI*, 177B–189B, in Migne, *Patrologia Graeca*, XXXVII (Paris: Vives, 1857–66); trans. in J. Stevenson, *Creeds, Councils and Controversies* (London: SPCK, 1989) p. 89.
16 Socrates, *Historia Ecclesiastica*, VII, 29; trans. in J. Stevenson, *Creeds, Councils and Controversies* (London: SPCK, 1989) p. 287.
17 Marcian, in B. J. Kidd, *Documents Illustrative of the History of the Church*, vol. II (London: SPCK, 1923) p. 301.
18 The resonance is with Friedrich Nietzsche, *The Gay Science*, 125, trans. W. Kaufmann (New York: Random House, 1974) p. 181.
19 I use 'Christ's BwO' in this section for simplicity's sake as a locution for the various BwO's intimately associated with or sited on Christ.
20 There is some evidence that Deleuze and Guattari would be content with this conclusion:

> If the BwO is a limit, if one is forever attaining it, it is because behind each stratum, encasted in it, there is always another stratum. For many a stratum, and not only an organism, is necessary to make the judgement of God.
>
> (*ATP*, p. 159)

My point in what follows is that Deleuze and Guattari are not susceptible to a charge of internal inconsistency here – maintaining that Christ's BwO is properly constituted as such when, according to their account, it cannot be.

21

> Picturesquely, we may think of the surface of the human body as the primal surface, a living paper on which signs move. On the body-surface desire and culture meet, as the body's feeling-expression is converted by culture into the common world of signs.
>
> (Don Cupitt, *The Long-Legged Fly* [London: SCM Press, 1987], p. 11)

Part III

Literature and religion

8 Nietzsche's arrow

Deleuze on D. H. Lawrence's *Apocalypse*

Mary Bryden

Les mineurs s'y connaissent en strates [Miners are well up on strata].
(Gilles Deleuze on D. H. Lawrence's *Apocalypse*)[1]

Deleuze's witty comment upon Lawrence's *Apocalypse* is an appropriate one from a writer who, with Guattari, makes full use of the image of stratification in his own writing.[2] The Nottinghamshire mining community in which Lawrence grew up depended upon the exploitation of carboniferous strata and substrata beneath their feet. Their Christ, in Deleuze's reading, is a man of coal: 'C'est du charbon, c'est du Christ' [It's coal, it's Christ] (*PR*, p. 21). Christ is thus rendered, like coal, a common good to be brought forth, made serviceable, and distributed to all. Moreover, in their responsiveness to the *Book of Revelation* can be seen an attachment to 'un sédiment secret' (*PR*, p. 20), a hidden seam of revelation with the potential, once uncovered, to transform the spiritual and material landscape.

This triumphal outreach of the *Book of Revelation* is, however, at odds with Lawrence's own response to it. Antagonistic to its liturgical use as allegory for the dispersal of wrongdoers and justification of the righteous in the Final Judgement, he places the emphasis upon excavating the multiple strata of a book whose genesis remains, and is likely to remain, mysterious. The *Book of Revelation* is a composite of layerings, echoings and transformations. It declaims, suggests, and occludes in turns, or simultaneously. As Lawrence affirms elsewhere: 'An Apocalypse has, must have, is intended to have various levels or layers or strata of meaning'.[3] Resisting the world of closed hermeneutics, he aims to peel back some of those layers, to rediscover the pagan strata denied by some Christian apologists.

A stratiform perspective will be similarly apparent at each stage of this essay, which will consider Deleuze's preface to the translation into French (by Fanny Deleuze) of Lawrence's own commentary upon the *Book of Revelation*. Given the fact that Deleuze reads Lawrence through the filter of Nietzsche, the layerings are already complex enough. Further, however, the focus text – the *Book of Revelation* – is one whose authorship is not attributable to a single and identifiable individual. Despite a widespread consensus until the sixteenth century about the self-proclaimed 'John' of

Revelation being also the author of the Johannine Gospel and epistles, there were on this score recurrently dissenting voices, even before those of Erasmus and Luther. While convincing arguments have been advanced for the presence of at least three distinct redactional strata, the text is not devoid of internal coherence, and there are some significant similarities to be found between *Revelation* and the fourth Gospel which might at least suggest the influence of a shared source.[4]

Among these stances, Lawrence opts strongly for contrasting the two texts rather than for seeking similarity, taking the author's reference to the island of Patmos in Chapter 1 as justification for the usage 'John of Patmos'. Deleuze supports this view, declaring in a footnote: 'Les raisons savantes d'assimiler les deux auteurs semblent très faibles' [The scholarly justification for merging the two authors seems very weak] (*PR*, p. 7).

In accordance with apocalyptic tradition, the *Book of Revelation* situates itself within an unfolding of history in which two opposing tendencies have confronted one another over several distinct epochs. It differs from other apocalyptic forebears in looking ahead, within a Christological and eschatological perspective, to an era of final victory. However, it is this vision of ultimate strength which, for Lawrence, constitutes the text's ultimate weakness, for its meaning and application are embedded for him in his memories of hearing it read aloud in the chapels of his boyhood.

What emerges from the early chapters of Lawrence's *Apocalpyse* is a strong distaste for a spiritual force-feeding in which the Bible was 'verbally trodden into the consciousness'.[5] In Deleuzian terms, its entity was molar, for 'the interpretation was always the same' (*AP*, p. 59), and the delivery always loud and portentous. What Lawrence dubs the 'parson voice' was, he recalls, 'always at its worst when mouthing out some portion of Revelation' (*AP*, p. 61). For him, the text had been institutionalised, its meaning allegedly explicated and despatched. As such, it was dead: 'A book lives as long as it is unfathomed. Once it is fathomed, it dies at once' (*AP*, p. 60).

Books may, however, be resurrected in different circumstances. Decades after that boyhood revulsion, Lawrence writes in his introduction to Frederick Carter's *The Dragon of the Apocalypse* that: 'Nothing delights me more than to escape from the all-too-moral chapel meaning of the [Apocalypse], to another wider, older, more magnificent meaning. In fact, one of the real joys of middle age is in coming back to the Bible'.[6] Deleuze confirms this instinct when he advises treating Lawrence's text as a postlude rather than a prelude: 'Le texte de Lawrence, il vaut mieux le lire après avoir lu ou relu le texte de l'Apocalypse' [It is better to read Lawrence's text after having read or re-read the text of the Apocalypse] (*PR*, p. 8).

Lawrence's text details the manner in which 'strong-voiced colliers' (*AP*, p. 64) harnessed *Revelation* as an allegory of their own future apotheosis: 'The weak and pseudo-humble are going to wipe all worldly power, glory and riches off the face of the earth, and then they, the truly weak, are going to reign. It will be a millennium of pseudo-humble saints, and gruesome to contemplate' (*AP*, p. 65).

Indeed, Apocalypse is a millenarian text. It is a vision of a world in which powers are uprooted and replaced with others. As such, it provides a paradigm for a variety of circumstances. Lawrence, alienated by a remembered timbre of declaimed Revelation, scarcely acknowledges the power of its message when addressed by John of Patmos to those Christians whose own torture and death, staged as public entertainment, was a very real prospect to them, and constituted, as Peter Brown puts it, 'a peculiarly chilling aspect of the Roman order'.[7] On this point, Deleuze is more expansive in his application, and yet more succinct in his description, than Lawrence:

> Si nous baignons dans l'Apocalypse, c'est plutôt parce qu'elle inspire en chacun de nous des manières de vivre, de survivre, et de juger. C'est le livre de chacun de ceux qui se pensent survivants. C'est le livre des Zombies [If we revel in Apocalypse, it is, rather, because it inspires each of us with ways of living, surviving, and assessing. It's the book of everyone who thinks of themselves as survivors. It's the book of Zombies].
>
> (*PR*, p. 8)

Deleuze succeeds here in broadening *Revelation* out into a book not for mere power-seekers, but for those of optimistic kidney, for would-be livers.

It is at this point that Deleuze dons his Nietzschean glasses. Indeed, he goes so far as to assert that Lawrence would probably not have written his *Apocalypse* if Nietzsche's *The Anti-Christ* had not existed. In this, he overstates his point. Lawrence had indeed immersed himself in reading Nietzsche at earlier points in his life, and it is not difficult to establish Nietzschean affinities within his writing,[8] not least in his dislike of renunciation and asceticism when preached as positive values on the path towards religious enlightenment.[9] Yet Lawrence's project differs in important respects from that of Nietzsche. *Apocalypse* does demonstrate a disaffection with organised religion, and that in a particular and localised form. It is not, however, a dismissal of theism. In some respects, as with other parts of Lawrence's oeuvre, it is a profoundly religious text.

Nietzsche vents his spleen upon the whole range of Judaeo-Christian literatures which form the composite called 'The Bible'. Lawrence appears to be inheriting his mantle when he declares, with the most Nietzschean of emphases: 'My very instincts *resent* the Bible' (*AP*, p. 59). He goes on to analyse and situate this resentment within that particular life-experience of childhood attendance at nonconformist chapels. Nietzsche distances himself from any biographical underpinning in *The Anti-Christ* (though the fact that the author, son of a Lutheran clergyman, reserves his concluding venom for Luther himself gives cause for reflection). Although Nietzsche had a good knowledge of the differing Judaeo-Christian literatures whose import he rejected, it is convenient for him to issue a blanket condemnation of all biblical texts, since his primary target (as in *On the Genealogy of Morals*) is the priestly caste who use them for self-licensing purposes. Lawrence, however, having discharged his dislike of biblical proclamation, then proceeds to a careful analysis of his chosen text before incorporating it within his own visionary perspective: that of the advocated recuperation of the cosmos.

Deleuze's biographical input is to remind the reader that both men wrote their texts as they began their respective descents, towards death from pulmonary tuberculosis in the case of Lawrence, and towards dementia and death in the case of Nietzsche. Despite his view of *The Anti-Christ* as a prompt-text for *Apocalypse*, Deleuze is nevertheless at pains to distinguish between Nietzsche and Lawrence in terms of the contrasts they propound. Whereas Nietzsche sets Christ against St Paul, Lawrence sets Christ against John of Patmos. Hence Lawrence sidesteps Nietzsche. To use Deleuze's image, Lawrence picks up Nietzsche's arrow and shoots it in another direction: 'Il ramasse une flèche, celle de Nietzsche, et la relance ailleurs, autrement tendue, sur une autre comète, dans un autre public' [He picks up an arrow, that of Nietzsche, and redirects it, set for another target, another comet, another audience] (*PR*, p. 9). Deleuze is here borrowing Nietzsche's own image (in his *Schopenhauer as Educator*[10]) of the philosopher being projected into the body of humanity like a random arrow, and he returns to the image later in the essay.[11] On this occasion, however, the eschatological panorama is laid out in ironic fashion as the two archers share hell while their targets commandeer heaven:

> Ils se retrouvent tous deux dans le même enfer, démence et hémoptysie, saint Paul et Jean de Patmos occupant tout le ciel [They are both re-united in the same hell, madness and blood-spitting, with Saint Paul and John of Patmos occupying the entire heavens].
>
> (*PR*, p. 22)

It is notable that Deleuze effaces Christ from the scenario in this instance. It is, however, necessary to examine more closely the Christ-figure with which both Paul and the author of *Revelation* are said to be at odds. Deleuze sees Nietzsche's Christ as being 'le plus doux, le plus amoureux des décadents' [the gentlest and most loving of the decadents] (*PR*, p. 9). Nietzsche in fact goes further: his paragraph 35 reads as a grudging tribute to a Christ who was all-of-a-piece, whose death process uncovered no inconsistency, and whose importance lies in orthopraxis rather than in orthodoxy. Nietzsche's overwhelming grievance is directed towards those who turned the end of Jesus's life into the beginning of a system. St Paul is here characterised as the appropriator, the inexorable sacerdotalist who keeps Christ nailed to his cross, the better to propagate that '*lie* of the "resurrected" Jesus'[12] which will gather authority for Christian teaching. For

Nietzsche, it is to the seductive but erroneous doctrine of personal immortality, as preached by Paul, that Christianity owes its influence.

In approaching Lawrence's treatment of Christ in relation to John of Patmos, Deleuze highlights the coincident contrast between individual and collectivity. It is a recurrent feature of human organisations that a charismatic figure is succeeded by a bureaucracy, and the development of Christianity is no exception to this tendency. For Lawrence, 'Jesus took up the position of the pure individual, even with his disciples. He did not *really* mix with them, or even really work or act with them' (*AP*, p. 69). Thwarting the desire of his followers to be their collective king, he attracted the penalty of betrayal. It was John of Patmos, in Lawrence's view, who re-invented Christ as lord of the cosmos. In doing so, he was not only responding to a present political necessity, but inserting Christ into a great sweep of salvation history, stretching back into pagan times, and forward into the vengeful future of 'the Logos which will smite the world (and in the end destroy it)' (*AP*, p. 74).

It is, however, surprising that Deleuze appears to build a contrast here between what are in facts points of communality between Nietzsche and Lawrence. Though engaged with different figures (respectively, Paul, and John of Patmos), they are united in taking issue with two consummate proselytisers, both similarly engaged in transforming an individual into an icon, in drawing Christ into the machinery of transmission to the masses. In their different ways, Lawrence and Nietzsche are both elitists. They romanticise the individual and disparage the populariser. They advocate the reassessment of values, but only from a position of strength.

In his preface to Verga's *Cavalleria Rusticana*, Lawrence writes: 'The peasant mass is the ugliest of all human masses, most greedily selfish and brutal of all. [...] If we have to trust to a *mass*, then better trust the upper or middle-class mass, all masses being odious'.[13] Further, the Christ of Lawrence's *Apocalypse* 'was an aristocrat [...]. It takes a great aristocrat to be capable of great tenderness and gentleness and unselfishness: the tenderness and gentleness of *strength*' (*AP*, p. 65). What neither Lawrence nor Nietzsche can tolerate is the idea of egalitarianism as doctrine. The notion of Christianity as representing (at least potentially) the empowerment of the poor and weak is odious to them. Hence Nietzsche intones: 'The aristocratic outlook has been undermined most deeply by the lie of equality of souls. [...] Christianity is a revolt of everything that crawls along the ground directed against that which is *elevated*' (*AC*, pp. 156–7). More particularly, for Lawrence, it is the *Book of Revelation* which supplies the biblical warrant for the unappetising cry of the weak: '*Down with the strong!*' (*AP*, p. 65).

Nevertheless, Deleuze writes astutely of a fascination which may co-exist with hostility. Citing the interest frequently manifested by Nietzsche in that which also disgusted him, he diagnoses a similar tendency in Lawrence:

> Voilà que Lawrence, avec toute son horreur de l'Apocalypse, à travers cette horreur, éprouve une obscure sympathie, même une espèce d'admiration pour ce livre [And here is Lawrence, with all his horror of the Apocalypse, through this horror, feeling a vague sympathy, even a kind of admiration for this book].
>
> (*PR*, p. 20)

This is, I would suggest, the most profound distinction between the respective projects of Nietzsche and Lawrence. Both are works of conviction, in more than one sense. They ably convict (incriminate) their targets, and they evince the strongly held convictions of their propagators. (Nietzsche may assert in *The Anti-Christ* that: 'Convictions are prisons' [*AC*, p. 172], but he refers here to principles of conduct. His own dictum that scepticism is the only proper stance for a great intellect is itself a conviction). Nietzsche's concern, however, is primarily with the *effects* of evangelisation, rather than with close textual analysis of one text rather than another. Lawrence, on the other hand, lingers among the resonance, mystery and colour of his chosen text. Moreover, he allows it to act as a springboard for further reflections of his own.

Revelation is, after all, a text full not only of ringing phrases, but also of strong images. Deleuze is humorously responsive to the gaudy menu set out therein:

> L'Apocalypse est sans doute le premier grand livre-programme, à grand spectacle. [...] Une espèce de Folies-Bergère, avec cité céleste, et lac infernal de soufre [The Apocalypse is surely the first great spectacular book-agenda. [...] A kind of Folies-Bergère, complete with heavenly city, and infernal lake of sulphur].
>
> (*PR*, pp. 15–16)

Such scenes may provide a Disney-style *frisson*, a passing encounter with wonderment or dread. They are much more sinister when seen as matter for gloating prophecy. Any programme incorporating a Radiant City, Deleuze later points out, is one with a bent for extermination: 'Chaque fois que l'on programme une cité radieuse, nous savons bien que c'est une manière de détruire le monde' [Every time plans are advanced for a Radiant City, we know perfectly well that it will involve the destruction of the world] (*PR*, p. 24). The new Jerusalem, with its glittering jewelled walls, is, for both Deleuze and Lawrence, a profoundly disquieting place: 'Chaque lecteur un peu sain de l'Apocalypse se sent déjà dans le lac sulfureux' [Every half-sane reader of the Apocalypse feels already plunged into the lake of sulphur] (*PR*, p. 25).

Nevertheless, the drama – 'a string of cosmic calamities' (*AP*, p. 105) – unfolds remorselessly. Across the apocalyptic stage strut all manner of beings: the angels, the cosmic beasts, the four horsemen. In place of the announced lion there bounds in a lamb with a disconcertingly assertive manner. Lawrence dubs it a 'good old lion in sheep's clothing' (*AP*, p. 99), and Deleuze picks up the incongruity by calling the creature 'l'agneau carnivore – l'agneau qui mord' [the carnivorous lamb, the lamb which bites] (*PR*, p. 12). The Lamb is the principal title for Christ throughout the *Book of Revelation*. On one level, it denotes the sacrificial victim, Christ put to death like the paschal lamb. However, after its immolation, the Lamb receives in the *Book of Revelation* the attributes of victory and dominion, taking the scroll as a sign of its enthronement.

Although Deleuze speaks highly of Lawrence's analysis of the Lamb, he appears to reserve his greatest admiration for his exposition of the pagan substratum which the *Book of Revelation* merely perverts rather than eliminates. When Lawrence declares: 'Perhaps the greatest difference between us and the pagans lies in our different relation to the cosmos' (*AP*, p. 76), he is pointing to a vital connection with the natural and astronomical landscape which has been lost to the modern world. More particularly, he deems the *Book of Revelation* to be an example of the severance, by a kind of remedial theology, of the link with that earlier elemental world.

An instance of this is the puzzling episode of the 'two witnesses' in *Revelation*, 11, who are given power over the waters. Conventionally, these two witnesses have been identified with Moses and Elijah. Yet Lawrence suggests that, in adjusting these figures to fit Judaeo-Christian tradition, the ancient myth of the heavenly twins has been suppressed. Citing examples from a range of cults and cultures, including pre-Olympian, Samothracian, Etruscan, Babylonian and Aegean, Lawrence demonstrates how the mysterious twins reappear as figures of transition, gods of gateposts and lords of the changing winds. As twins, they are sundered, 'each forever jealous of the other, keeping the other in bounds' (*AP*, p. 117). Yet they are also indissolubly linked. Thus they may represent not only division but also balance between two halves. They are also, suggests Lawrence, 'the secret lords of sex, for it was early recognised that sex is a holding of two things asunder, that birth may come through between them' (*AP*, p. 116).

Lawrence uses the twin motif to illustrate notions of dualism within human beings which is related to that which he explores elsewhere. In his essay 'The two principles', he envisages birth and creation as issuing from a succession of dualisms, including water and fire, and male and female: 'This dualism extends through everything, even through the *soul* or *self* or *being* of any living creature'.[14] He goes on to divide the human person into 'the spiritual and sensual being' ('The two principles', p. 235), aligning these somewhat crudely with the upper and lower halves of the body respectively.

Lawrence reiterates this theme in *Fantasia of the Unconscious*, where, in a (most un-Deleuzian) chapter entitled 'Trees and babies and papas and mammas', he asserts: 'There are two planes of being and consciousness and two models of relation and of function. We will call the lower plane the sensual, the upper the spiritual'.[15] This prompts him to describe the human body as a bicycle, and 'our individual and incomprehensible self is the rider' (*FT*, p. 53).

Lawrence's attachment to dualities is particularly noticeable in his discussion of gender, when his rhetoric frequently takes on a Nietzschean ring. In *The Anti-Christ*, Nietzsche presents 'the person of weaker will, women especially' (*AC*, p. 172) as being particularly drawn to systems of external regulation such as religious doctrine. In *Fantasia of the Unconscious*, Lawrence also associates 'the volitional centres' (*FT*, p. 44) with the male, enjoining the father to supply equilibrium to a child whose mother is concentrating too exclusively upon 'pure or spiritual love' (*FT*, p. 44). Although Lawrence has earlier signalled his qualified response to Freud in the phrase: 'What Freud says is always partly true' (*FT*, p. 11), he here relies upon that triangular libidinal economy which Deleuze and Guattari resist so explosively in *L'Anti-Oedipe*. Moreover, just as the physical domination of women is advocated in *Thus Spake Zarathustra*,[16] Lawrence writes: 'Combat her in her cock-sure belief that she "knows" and that she is "right". Take it all out of her. Make her yield once more to the male leadership' (*FT*, p. 189). This imposition of male will upon female is, in Lawrence's view, a restoration to woman of 'her own true unconscious' (*FT*, p. 188). If women appear to be appropriating 'male' ground, they must be resisted: 'The great flow of female consciousness is downwards, down to the weight of the loins and round the circuit of the feet. Pervert this, and make a false flow upwards, to the breast and head, and you get a race of "intelligent" women' (*FT*, p. 186).

In *Apocalypse*, Lawrence uses the imagery of the *Book of Revelation* to underline his antagonism to what he sees as the misdirection of the energy attaching to the woman figure. At the opening of *Revelation*, 12, there appears a 'woman clothed with the sun, and the moon under her feet, and upon her head a crown of twelve stars'.[17] Lawrence refers to her as 'the great cosmic Mother' (*AP*, p. 121), and indeed she is seen to be in the act of giving birth. Just a few verses later, however, she has been driven into the desert by the red dragon, incarnation of the energy of the cosmos in its malefic aspect.

It is Lawrence's contention that the cosmic, creative force of women has been in the desert ever since, having been supplanted by the imposition of the Logos, and this gives him the opportunity of returning to his plea for the restoration of woman's 'true' nature:

> Today, the best part of womanhood is wrapped tight and tense in the folds of the Logos, she is bodiless, abstract, and driven by a self-determination terrible to behold. A strange, 'spiritual' creature is woman today. [...] All women today have a large streak of the police-woman in them.
>
> (*AP*, pp. 126–7)

Deleuze includes a summary of Lawrence's presentation of both the cosmic mother and the twins in his preface. He also touches upon the 'police-woman' theme, although apparently acknowledging its somewhat digressionary nature, since he encloses it within parentheses. As one would expect, the strongly dualist foundation underlying many of Lawrence's analyses sits somewhat awkwardly with Deleuzian concepts of multiplicity and flux. This is not to overlook the fact that dualisms are also, of course, plentiful within Deleuzian analysis. However, they are based not upon psychological 'identities' or functions, but upon flows and processes which are themselves provisional. As Alan D. Shrift aptly states: 'Deleuze engages in a project that reformulates traditional binary disjunctions between given alternatives in terms of a pluralistic continuum in which choices are always local and relative rather than global and absolute'.[18]

Hence, it is interesting to note that, in his analysis of the twin figures, Deleuze sidelines the notion of polarity in order to concentrate much more emphatically than does Lawrence upon the status of the in-between, the transitional, and the transient:

> Le monde païen n'était pas seulement fait de conjonctions vivantes, il comportait des frontières, des seuils et des portes, des disjonctions, pour que quelque chose passe entre deux choses [...]. Les jumeaux sont donc les maîtres des flux, de leur passage, de leur alternance et de leur disjonction [The pagan world was not made up solely of living connections; it included frontiers, thresholds and gateways, separations, to allow passage between two things [...]. So the twins are the masters of flows, their passage, their alternation and their disjunction].
>
> (*PR*, pp. 28–9)

It is against this background that Deleuze sets the distinction between symbol and allegory. Lawrence rails repeatedly against what he sees as *Revelation*'s entrapment of pagan symbolism within the normalising activity of allegory. In this process, the mobility of symbol is arrested, mediated, and 'explained' by reference to another reality (here, a Christian reality) outside itself: 'Symbols mean something: yet they mean something different to every man. Fix the meaning of a symbol, and you have fallen into the commonplace of allegory' (*AP*, p. 101). Deleuze develops this contrast rather differently from Lawrence. Whereas the latter links symbols with polysemy, or with proliferation of meaning, Deleuze highlights much more the circuitry of meaning which symbols can provide: 'Car le symbole est la pensée des flux, contrairement au processus intellectuel et linéaire de la pensée allégorique' [For the symbol is the flow-thought, as opposed to the intellectual and linear process of allegorical thought] (*PR*, p. 31). An allegory is destination-bound, whereas a symbol may remain travelling in between positions:

> Le symbole rotatif [...] n'a ni début ni fin, il ne nous mène nulle part, il n'arrive nulle part, il n'a surtout pas de point final, ni même d'étapes. Il est toujours au milieu, au milieu des choses, entre les choses [The

rotational symbol [...] has neither beginning nor end, it leads us nowhere, it arrives nowhere; in particular, it has no final point, nor even
stages on the way. It is always in the middle, amid things, between things].

(*PR*, p. 30)

Lawrence's often dualist perspective is not overlooked in Deleuze's rendering, but it is in effect diluted by the much more fluid potentialities which
Deleuze allows to develop. Hence, it is not surprising that Deleuze should
choose to refer in his preface to another of the last texts Lawrence wrote,
'We need one another', written on 5 October 1929. In this text, Lawrence
again demonstrates his need to rehearse his grammar of sexual differentiation. In this case, however, there are important distinctions. In *Apocalypse*,
his diatribe against the 'police-woman' prompted his friend and ex-colleague
Helen Corke to retort in 1933: 'The male and female principles are not
sundered completely and housed in separate bodies. They occur together, in
the man and in the woman'.[19] In 'We need one another', Lawrence pictures
male and female not as watertight categories, but as 'the flowing of two
rivers side by side, sometimes even mingling, then separating again, and
travelling on'.[20] The hymn to individuality which had been such an emphatic
feature of, for example, *Fantasia of the Unconscious* and of *Psychoanalysis
and the Unconscious* here cedes to a journey towards inclusivity rather than
polarity. In *Fantasia of the Unconscious*, Lawrence writes: 'Life is individual,
always was individual and always will be' (*FT*, p. 147). 'We need one another'
does not abolish individuality, but attacks individualism, on the part of
either male or female: 'Reduce any individual, man or woman, to his
elements, or her elements, and what is he? what is she? Extremely little!'
(*WNOA*, p. 189). Rather: 'Everything, even individuality itself, depends on
relationship' (*WNOA*, p. 190). Moreover, Lawrence makes clear that
'relationship' here is not reducible to sex, although it may include it; where it
occurs, sex is 'the symbol of the relation' (*WNOA*, p. 193).

In 'We need one another', Lawrence travels noticeably further than before
towards a machinery of desire in which circuitry and flow are much more
prominent than polarities and insulations: 'The light shines only when the
circuit is completed' (*WNOA*, p. 190). It is not difficult to see why Deleuze
should have responded readily to the more fluid dynamic of this essay, which
was, after all, contemporary with Lawrence's completion of *Apocalypse*.
Further, it explains why Deleuze's treatment of the theme of shift, transition
and flux is more lengthily developed than the evidence of Lawrence's *Apocalypse* alone would seem to prompt. Indeed, the seamlessness of Deleuze's move,
towards the close of the preface, towards adept summarising of the 'individual-
is-relation' argument from 'We need one another' itself demonstrates Deleuze's
innovative use of conjunction and dialectic. Having discussed the relationship
between individual and collectivity, Deleuze forms a bridge between *Apocalypse* and essay, including a footnoted reference to the latter:

Ce qui est individuel, c'est la relation, non pas le moi. Cesser de se pen-
ser comme un moi, pour se vivre comme un flux, [...] hors de soi et en
soi. [...] 'Sexuel', et 'symbolique', (c'est pareil en effet) n'ont jamais
voulu dire autre chose: la vie des flux [What is individual is relationship,
not the self. Ceasing to think 'self' in order to live as a flow, [...] beyond
oneself and in oneself. [...] 'Sexual', and 'symbolic', (which come to the
same thing), have never meant anything but that: flow-life]

(*PR*, p. 35)

Notably, when he later returns to his preface in order to include it as a
chapter in *Critique et Clinique*, Deleuze introduces the word 'âme' [soul]
much earlier in the above analysis, such that the concept of soul is
unmistakably linked with that of cosmos: 'Ce qui est individuel, c'est la
relation, *c'est l'âme*, non pas le moi' [What is individual is relationship, *the
soul*, not the self] [my italics].[21] The modifications applied to this essay
between its 1978 and its 1993 versions are for the most part minor,
concerning italicisation, punctuation and paragraph division. At this
concluding stage of the argument, however, a supplementary passage is
inserted. Significantly, it concerns the identification of the 'soul' with an
organic life-struggle:

L'âme comme vie des flux est vouloir-vivre, lutte et combat. Ce n'est pas
seulement la disjonction, mais la conjonction des flux qui est lutte et
combat, étreinte. Tout accord est dissonant [The soul as flow-life is the
will-to-live, struggle and combat. It is not merely the disruption, but the
conjunction of flows which constitutes struggle, combat, embrace. All
harmony is discordant].

(*CC*, p. 69)

In this context of combat, Deleuze is also enabled to add here a further
reference to the abnegatory, pacifist principle, to be found in both Christianity and Buddhism, which he sees Lawrence and Nietzsche as being united in
resisting.[22]

A final link which can be made between Lawrence and Nietzsche in this
context concerns their Janus-like stance between past and future. In a sense,
both are in mourning for what they see as a lost culture. For Nietzsche, it is
the Graeco-Roman world and the Renaissance.[23] For Lawrence, it is the
pagan world and its cosmic and elemental connectedness. These purely
selective attachments permit, however, an equally selective iconoclasm. As
Deleuze notes, neither Nietzsche nor Lawrence could abide the notion of
deferred gratification, of paradise postponed:

On se trouve alors devant la tâche d'avoir à remplir un temps monstrueux, étiré, entre la Mort *et* la Fin, la Mort *et* l'Eternité [You then

find yourself facing the task of having to fill up a monstrous, long-drawn-out period between Death *and* The End, Death *and* Eternity].

(*PR*, p. 17)

By letting go of the crutches of convention and allegory, and by jettisoning any reliance upon eternal life assurance, both Nietzsche and Lawrence are enabled to revalorise the present.

Finally, it is useful to compare the concluding passages of Nietzsche, Lawrence and Deleuze respectively. While Nietzsche's arrows are here fired in searing volleys, towards multiple targets, Lawrence (whom Deleuze dubs 'adorateur du soleil' [sun-worshipper] [*PR*, p. 35]) fires a single arrow into the sky. In what might be seen as an adaptation of St Irenaeus' resonant dictum, 'For the glory of God is a living man',[24] Lawrence proclaims his anthropocentric version: 'For man, the vast marvel is to be alive' (*AP*, p. 149). Yet Lawrence's arrow is aimed at illuminating the cosmos rather than at puncturing the gods. It is more firework than missile. And while Nietzsche continues his heroic graffiti at the close of *The Anti-Christ* – 'I can write in letters which make even the blind see' (*AC*, p. 186), Lawrence slips quietly away: 'There is nothing of me that is alone and absolute except my mind, and we shall find that the mind has no existence by itself, it is only the glitter of the sun on the surface of the waters' (*AP*, p. 149). In the last words of his preface, Deleuze applauds Lawrence's recollected death:

> Comme ceux qui ont du génie, Lawrence meurt en repliant soigneusement ses bandelettes, en les rangeant soigneusement (il supposait que le Christ avait fait ainsi), et en tournant autour de cette idée, dans cette idée .. [Like a genius, Lawrence dies carefully folding up his binding-cloths and carefully putting them aside (as he fancied Christ did), while turning over that idea, within that idea ..]

(*PR*, p. 37)

Lawrence's text ends in forward-bound, visionary style. It is a text full of 'devenirs'. Deleuze's concluding text is resolutely human-centred, almost domestic, in its depiction of a man performing his last material task. Ingeniously, he chooses to end the sentence (and the Preface) with the word 'idea'. The dots of ellipsis which follow seem to indicate an ongoing intellectual programme of evaluation, of which Nietzsche would surely have most heartily approved.

Notes

1 My references are to the original version of this essay, published as a Preface to Fanny Deleuze's translation into French of Lawrence's *Apocalypse* (Paris: Editions Balland, 1978) pp. 7–37 (p. 21). Hereafter referred to as *PR*. The Preface appears in slightly modified form as Chapter 6 of Gilles Deleuze, *Critique et Clinique* (Paris: Editions de Minuit, 1993) pp. 50–70. The original Preface was

attributed jointly to Fanny and Gilles Deleuze. All translations from the French are my own.

2 See, for example, Gilles Deleuze and Félix Guattari, *Mille plateaux* (Paris: Editions de Minuit, 1980).

3 D. H. Lawrence, review of John Oman, *The Book of Revelation*, in D. H. Lawrence, *'Apocalypse' and the Writings on Revelation*, ed. Mara Kalnins (Cambridge: Cambridge University Press, 1980) pp. 41–2 (p. 41).

4 See, for example, Jean-Louis D'Aragon, 'The Apocalypse', §11, in *The Jerome Biblical Commentary*, ed. Raymond E. Brown, Joseph A. Fitzmyer and Roland E. Murphy (London: Geoffrey Chapman, 1970) vol. 2, pp. 467–93 (p. 469).

5 D. H. Lawrence, *Apocalypse*, in *'Apocalypse' and the Writings on Revelation*, ed. by Mara Kalnins (Cambridge: Cambridge University Press, 1980), pp. 57–149 [p. 59]. Hereafter referred to as *AP*.

6 D. H. Lawrence, introduction to Frederick Carter, *The Dragon of the Apocalypse*, in D. H. Lawrence, *'Apocalypse' and the Writings on Revelation*, ed. Mara Kalnins (Cambridge: Cambridge University Press, 1980) pp. 45–56 (p. 55).

7 Peter Brown, *The Body and Society: Men, Women and Sexual Renunciation in Early Christianity* (London: Faber, 1990) p. 75.

8 See, in respect to biblical issues, 'Two types of messianism: Nietzsche and Lawrence', in Bernd Magnus, Stanley Stewart and Jean-Pierre Mileur, *Nietzsche's Case: Philosophy as/and Literature* (New York: Routledge, 1993) pp. 119–32.

9 See, in this connection, Jörg Salaquarda, 'Nietzsche and the Judaeo-Christian tradition', in Bernd Magnus and Kathleen M. Higgins (eds) *The Cambridge Companion to Nietzsche* (Cambridge: Cambridge University Press, 1996) pp. 90–118.

10 See *Schopenhauer as Educator*, in Friedrich Nietzsche, *Untimely Meditations*, trans. R. J. Hollingdale, ed. J. P. Stern (Cambridge: Cambridge University Press, 1983) pp. 125–94: 'Nature propels the philosopher into mankind like an arrow; it takes no aim but hopes the arrow will stick somewhere' (p. 177).

11 There is something of a parallel to be found in Lawrence's caustic advice to Bertrand Russell: 'One must be an outlaw these days, not a teacher or preacher. One must retire out of the herd and then fire bombs into it' (letter of 19 February 1916). Letter 22, in *D. H. Lawrence's Letters to Bertrand Russell*, ed. Harry T Moore (New York: Gotham Book Mart, 1948) p. 70.

12 Friedrich Nietzsche, *The Anti-Christ* (published with *Twilight of the Idols*) trans. and ed. R. J. Hollingdale (Harmondsworth: Penguin, 1968) pp. 114–87 (p. 155). Hereafter referred to as *AC*.

13 D. H. Lawrence, preface to Giovanni Verga, *Cavalleria Rusticana*, in *Phoenix: The Posthumous Papers of D. H. Lawrence*, ed. Edward D. McDonald (London: Heinemann, 1936) pp. 240–50 (p. 246).

14 D. H. Lawrence, 'The two principles', in *Phoenix II*, eds Warren Roberts and Harry T. Moore (London: Heinemann, 1968) pp. 227–37 (p. 233).

15 D. H. Lawrence, *Fantasia of the Unconscious* (published with *Psychoanalysis and the Unconscious*) (London: Heinemann, 1961) pp. 11–192 (p. 41). Hereafter referred to as *FT*.

16 See, for example, ' "Thou goest to women? Remember thy whip!" ', in Friedrich Nietzsche, *Thus Spake Zarathustra*, trans. Alexander Tille (London: T. Fisher Unwin, 1899) p. 91.

17 Quotations from the *Book of Revelation* are from the translation familiar to Lawrence from his childhood: the King James Bible.

18 Alan D. Shrift, 'Putting Nietzsche to work: the case of Gilles Deleuze', in *Nietzsche: A Critical Reader*, ed. Peter R. Sedgwick (Oxford: Blackwell, 1995) pp. 250–75 (p. 258).

19 Helen Corke, *Lawrence and 'Apocalypse'* (London: Heinemann, 1933) p. 92.

20 D. H. Lawrence, 'We need one another', in *Phoenix: The Posthumous Papers of D. H. Lawrence*, ed. Edward D. McDonald (London: Heinemann, 1936) pp. 188–95 (p. 194). Hereafter referred to as *WNOA*.

21 Gilles Deleuze, 'Nietzsche et Saint Paul, Lawrence et Jean de Patmos', in *Critique et Clinique* (Paris: Editions de Minuit, 1993) pp. 50–70 (p. 68). Hereafter referred to as *CC*.

22 Deleuze returns to this linkage in 'Pour en finir avec le jugement', in *Critique et Clinique* (Paris: Editions de Minuit) pp. 158–69 (pp. 166–7), again footnoting Lawrence's 'We need one another' in its French translation.

23 See, notably, *AC*, pp. 182–5.

24 'Gloria Dei vivens homo', in Saint Irenaeus, *Adversus Haereses*, IV, 20, 7.

9   The future of an illusion

Melville's deconstruction of Deleuze's a/theology[1]

Thomas Cousineau

The literary criticism of Gilles Deleuze is clearly inspired by the Nietzschean project, which he sets forth in his *Nietzsche et la Philosophie*,[2] of following to its furthest consequences the discovery of 'the death of God'. His critics, however, have noted that in the midst of this effort at demystification, Deleuze remains faithful to certain terms and concepts that retain a distinctively theological flavour. Alberto Gualandi, for example, while generally sympathetic to Deleuze's project, detects in it the guiding spirit of religious nostalgia:

> Selon nous, en somme, la philosophie de Deleuze est une expression radicale du désir de reconduire la conscience déchirée de l'homme contemporain au moment initial de son histoire sans pourtant la priver de ce désir d'éternel que les religions du salut étaient appelées à satisfaire. Comme pour certains poètes romantiques, pour Deleuze aussi, c'est en traçant une 'ligne de fuite cosmique', en 'devenant plante ou animal', en 'devenant molécule', en 'devenant Sahara', bref, en retournant à la Nature infinie, que l'homme moderne peut retrouver la liberté et le bonheur qui préludent à l'éternel.[3]

Gualandi concludes, regretfully, that Deleuze's endeavour ultimately fails because 'il n'a pu s'affirmer jusqu'au bout en tant que système philosophique car son acte de pensée n'a pas su se démarquer de la *croyance* et de la *foi* qui sont les figures subjectives de *l'opinion* et de la *religion*' (Gualandi, p. 140).

Similarly, Alain Badiou has expressed reservations regarding Deleuze's attachment to 'la métaphysique de l'Un',[4] and René Girard, in his review of *l'Anti-Oedipe*, observed that Deleuze's conceptual scheme is fundamentally theological in its dependence on terms – 'psychosis', 'flux', 'deterritorialisation', 'lignes de fuite', etc. – whose purpose is to satisfy the need to believe in the possibility of transcendence. Indeed, the absolute division that Deleuze repeatedly maintains between the figures of the psychotic and the merely neurotic, or between oedipal repression and the 'lignes de fuite' – as well as his readiness to attribute to madness a completely transcendent status –

revisit traditionally theological dichotomies, although in an ostensibly demythologised way.

Girard attributes Deleuze's attachment to the vocabulary of transcendent originality to his reluctance to recognise the fundamentally imitative nature of human desire and the potentially tragic rivalries to which this can lead. He concludes that Deleuze's system amounts to a massive effort simply to ignore a seemingly intractable reality: 'Les excursions dans les flux ne sont qu'un coup pour rien. Le chant du désir ne peut jamais être qu'une ouverture lyrique. Une fois plaqué le dernier accord, il faut bien revenir aux problèmes qui nous obsèdent'.[5] For Girard, Deleuze's Nietzschean determination to establish the 'will to power' and the 'master' who is its agent as the absolutely original point of departure for his philosophy, is demystified in its own turn by the recognition that this master must in fact look to the example of other desiring subjects in order to learn what is desirable:

> Mais cette volonté s'exercera nécessairement sur des objets valorisés par les désirs des autres. C'est dans la rivalité avec l'autre que la puissance se révèle, dans une concurrence volontairement assumée cette fois-ci. [...] La volonté de puissance mettra toujours au centre du monde tout ce qui ne reconnaît pas en elle le centre du monde, et elle lui portera un culte secret. Elle ne manquera jamais, en somme, de virer au ressentiment.
>
> (Girard, p. 169)

Thus, according to Girard, the radical distinction that Deleuze would make between the psychotic and the neurotic, and between active and reactive forces, proves to be untenable. The psychotic will at some point in his career as a desiring subject reveal his dependence upon those models that have now become his rivals.

In the chapter of *Critique et Clinique* that he devotes to Herman Melville, entitled 'Bartleby, ou la formule', Deleuze, undoubtedly with Girard in mind, completely rejects mimetic desire as a useful hypothesis for the discussion of Melville.[6] Such a concept, he argues, merely reinforces the authority of the father, since the paternal figure is preeminently the model proposed for filial imitation: 'La rivalité mimétique [...] mobilise une fonction paternelle en général: l'image est par excellence une image du père, et le sujet est un fils, même si les déterminations s'échangent' (Bartleby, p. 99). While admitting that traditional novels of initiation do, indeed, furnish numerous examples of this pattern, Deleuze insists upon its subversion in Melville's novels, which he credits with staging the abolition of the paternal figure and the emergence of an entirely original subject:

> Il est certain que beaucoup de romans de Melville commencent par des images ou portraits, et semblent raconter l'histoire d'une formation sous une fonction paternelle. [...] Mais quelque chose d'étrange se produit

chaque fois, qui brouille l'image, la frappe d'une incertitude essentielle, empêche la forme de 'prendre', mais aussi défait le sujet, le jette à la dérive et abolit toute fonction paternelle. C'est là seulement que les choses commencent à devenir intéressantes.

(Bartleby, p. 99)

Adopting a metaphor that is presumably both geographical and linguistic, he concludes that, in Melville's novels, 'tout commençait à l'anglaise mais on continue à l'américaine' (Bartleby, p. 99).

Alluding to, although without actually engaging, Freud's description of the origins of religion in *Totem and Taboo*, Deleuze then elaborates, in Melville's name, a refurbished version of the sacrificial act through which the primal horde destroys the patriarchal father and creates new forms of social arrangements based upon the fraternal bond: 'La psychose poursuit son rêve, asseoir une *fonction d'universelle fraternité* qui ne passe plus par le père, qui se construit sur les ruines de la fonction paternelle, suppose la dissolution de toute image de père' (Bartleby, p. 101). Freud, of course, offered a quite different description of the aftermath to the murder of the primal father. He recognised that the fraternal bond could not, on its own, be trusted to serve as the foundation of a stable society since, according to his lapidary formulation, 'sexual desires do not unite men but divide them'. Hence, achievement of social unity required the elaboration of a system of prohibitions that would diminish the likelihood of the society's being destroyed by internecine rivalries: 'Thus the brothers had no alternative, if they were to live together, but – not, perhaps, until they had passed through many dangerous crises – to institute the law against incest. [...] In this way they rescued the organization that had made them strong'.[7]

Echoing Freud, Bernard Sichère, in *Le Moment Lacanien*, argues that Deleuze's self-limiting attachment to 'la révolte comme contestation de la loi dominante' requires that he ignore 'l'autre versant de d'éthique de la révolte, celui de la re-subjectivation, de *l'invocation d'une autre loi*'.[8] According to Sichère, Deleuze's decision to take sides with Nietzsche in the 'vieux débat' between Nietzsche and Freud leads him ineluctably to the 'répétition d'une impasse qui est celle de l'athéologie nietzschéenne, de la métaphysique de la volonté de puissance, malgré l'enseignement désormais implacable de l'horreur nazie' (Sichère, p. 151). Freud had himself issued a similar warning in *The Future of an Illusion* against the assumption that a life freed from the constraints imposed by an inherited civilisation would necessarily be more desirable:

But how ungrateful, how short-sighted after all, to strive for the aboli-tion of civilization! What would then remain would be a state of nature, and that would be far harder to bear. It is true that nature would not demand any restrictions of instinct from us, she would let us do as we liked; but she has her own particularly effective method of restricting us.

> She destroys us – coldly, cruelly, relentlessly, as it seems to us, and possibly through the very things that occasioned our satisfaction.[9]

Deleuze's unproblematically lyrical invocation of a community that has been freed from the tyranny of the paternal figure prevents his achieving Freud's lucidity on this point. It also requires, as we shall see, that in his reading of 'Bartleby' he largely miss the complexity of a story whose fundamentally biblical inspiration allows it to present a much more disabused portrayal of human nature than the 'mystical optimism' that Gualandi attributes to Deleuze would allow.

Throughout his essay on 'Bartleby', Deleuze systematically ignores the several biblical references through which Melville has created an implicit yet insistent subtext for his story.[10] He replaces these with a kind of alternative theological vocabulary in which the religious inspiration has been dissociated from any biblical provenance.[11] He echoes mystical terminology, for example, when he associates the formula 'I would prefer not to' with a 'souffle psychotique' (Bartleby, p. 93) and when he describes the effect produced by this formula: 'Comme si l'on avait entendu l'Indicible ou l'Imparable' (Bartleby, p. 91). Similarly, he accords a quasi-religious role to psychosis in his assertion that 'il appartient à la psychose de mettre en jeu un procédé [qui aboutirait à] une langue originale inconnue qui serait peut-être une projection de la langue de Dieu, et qui emporterait tout le langage' (Bartleby, p. 93). He creates his own version of the biblical distinction between heaven and hell when he praises the 'vocation schizophrénique de la littérature américaine' which he contrasts invidiously with 'la névrose anglaise' (Bartleby, p. 93). He later returns to this distinction in his twofold classification of the characters in Melville's fiction as either 'angels' or 'devils': the devils are 'pères monstrueux qui dévorent leurs enfants' while the angels are 'fils abandonnés sans pères' (Bartleby, p. 103). The fundamentally religious nature of Deleuze's reading of 'Bartleby' is likewise to be noticed in his casting Bartleby as a quasi-divine figure, 'le nouveau Christ' (Bartleby, p. 114).

Deleuze's readiness to believe in Bartleby's prophetic originality – his absolute freedom from any trace of imitative tendencies – is obvious from the beginning of his essay in the lengthy analysis that he offers of the celebrated formula, 'I would prefer not to'. While granting that this expression is not in itself ungrammatical, he claims that it nonetheless acquires something like ungrammaticality through its repeated use. He then imputes to it a radical dissimilarity from the more common expression, 'I had rather not'. Finally, following Maurice Blanchot, he translates the formula into French as the undeniably anomalous 'Je préférerais ne pas' (Bartleby, p. 90). Throughout this analysis of the expression's presumed unconventionality, Deleuze fails to recognise the simple fact that Bartleby's words are precisely the kind of excessively formal, high-toned expression that would be used by a person who wanted his superiority within an already established social hierarchy to be recognised. Far from expressing Bartleby's radical originality and the 'souffle psychotique' that Deleuze would attribute to it, the expression actually reveals his desire to model his language on received values. He is, in effect, speaking the words that the lawyer conveys implicitly every time he gives an order to one of his subordinates. Thanks to the position that he already occupies within the social hierarchy, the lawyer need not, of course, bother saying 'I would prefer not to'.

The imitative aspect that we detect in Bartleby's formula also appears in other details of his behaviour, as Melville underlines when he has the lawyer notice the copyist's 'cadaverously gentlemanly *nonchalance*'[12] as well as his 'pallid haughtiness, say, or rather an austere reserve about him' (*B*, p. 21). These attributes alert us once again to the fact that Bartleby is not, as Deleuze would maintain, a blessedly psychotic character who brings into the world of the law-office an absolutely transcendent originality. His demeanour assembles precisely the kind of qualities that aspirants to social distinction acquire by imitating admired models. Melville gives a comical twist to his portrayal of mimetic desire by showing the lawyer as irresistibly drawn into modelling his own behaviour on that of his presumed subordinate: 'Somehow, of late, I had got into the way of involuntarily using this word "prefer" upon all sorts of not exactly suitable occasions' (*B*, p. 24). This verbal tic, far from implying any originality on the part of the lawyer, reveals his subservience to the same mimetic principle as had previously inspired his rival. His fear of the 'deeper aberration' (*B*, p. 24) to which contact with Bartleby might lead reminds us of the potentially tragic consequences of mimeticism that Deleuze's devotion to the cult of originality habitually occludes.

Melville further points to the imitative nature of the bond between the lawyer and Bartleby by making both of them victims of exclusion. Bartleby is twice expelled from communities into which he had gained only temporary entry. Not only will he be removed to the Tombs at the end of the novella; as we will discover on the final page, this expulsion repeats the earlier loss of his position as a clerk in the 'Dead Letter Office at Washington, from which he had been suddenly removed by a change in the administration' (*B*, p. 41). In parallel with this, the lawyer, as he informs us at the beginning of the story, had served as Master in Chancery, a virtual sinecure that he lost when this position was abolished. Melville reinforces this surprising parallel between the narrator and Bartleby when he has the former express his outrage: 'I must be permitted to be rash here and declare, that I consider the sudden and violent abrogation of the office of Master in Chancery, by the new Constitution, as a – premature act' (*B*, p. 4). This characterisation of the loss of a political appointment as 'sudden and violent' both allows the narrator to indulge in a bit of therapeutic hyperbole and provides Melville with the opportunity to highlight the fundamentally mimetic relationship between his two principal characters.

Deleuze's commitment to the notion of Bartleby's uncompromising originality leads him, with perfect consistency, to offer an account of the plot of the story which, in its turn, seems deeply at variance with Melville's intention. Deleuze envisions this plot as involving three stages that revisit, but with a specifically Deleuzian twist, the theme of religious conversion. In the first, Bartleby's repetition of his formula produces general stupefaction, which Deleuze invests with a sacred significance: 'A chaque occurrence, c'est la stupeur autour de Bartleby, comme si l'on avait entendu l'Indicible ou l'Imparable. Et c'est le silence de Bartleby, comme s'il avait tout dit et épuisé du coup le langage' (Bartleby, p. 91).

In a second phase, the lawyer shows himself to be blessed with a clairvoyance, denied to lesser characters, that permits him 'à saisir et à comprendre, autant qu'on peut le faire, les êtres de la Nature première' (Bartleby, p. 103). This sacred encounter raises for the lawyer the prospect of discovering his own capacity to live an unalienated life: 'Dans le cas de Bartleby, se peut-il que le rapport avec l'avoué soit aussi mystérieux, et marque à son tour la possibilité d'un devenir, d'un nouvel homme?' (Bartleby, p. 96). Finally, however, the lawyer fails to respond to this challenge because his perspective is too contaminated by the residue of the paternal principle:

> Et Bartleby, qu'est-ce qu'il demandait, sinon un peu de confiance, à l'avoué qui lui répond par la charité, la philanthropie, tous les masques de la fonction paternelle? La seule excuse de l'avoué, c'est qu'il recule devant le devenir où Bartleby, par sa seule existence, risque de l'entraîner.
>
> (Bartleby, pp. 112–13)

Attention to the underlying pattern of mimetic rivalry, however, reveals that the plot of 'Bartleby' centres, not on the lawyer's potentially liberating encounter with Bartleby himself, but on his ambivalent response – a mixture of hostility and accommodation – to those threats to his equanimity directed at him by a succession of antagonists. The priority of this alternating rhythm of disturbances and resolutions over any of the individual characters – its independence, in particular, from Bartleby himself – is demonstrated by the fact that its emergence in the story does not await the arrival of the eponymous hero. Even in the pre-Bartleby phase of his life, the lawyer feels threatened by Turkey and Nippers. Turkey has 'a flighty recklessness of activity about him' which leads him to perform his tasks 'in a most indecorous manner' (*B*, p. 5). Likewise, Nippers is a 'rather piratical-looking man' who is guilty of 'an unwarrantable usurpation of strictly professional affairs' (*B*, p. 6).

In each of these preparatory trials, however, the attorney is able to achieve a compromise by discovering a utilitarian motive for keeping the potentially offensive worker in his employ. Thus he maintains a peaceful working relationship with Turkey through the expedient of overlooking the latter's eccentricities; similarly, he achieves an accommodation with Nippers because he recognises that 'he was a very useful man to me' (*B*, p. 8).

Bartleby's arrival greatly intensifies the threat that the lawyer had felt in the presence of his other copyists without, however, altering its essential nature. Thus he is 'turned into a pillar of salt' (*B*, p. 13) by his encounter with Bartleby's first refusal, referring to himself a moment later as 'a man [who] is browbeaten in some unprecedented and violently unreasonable way' (*B*, p. 13). Likewise, he will be 'mortified' (*B*, p. 23) by Bartleby's resistance to his requests. At one point, he offers an amusing literalisation of such metaphors when, having described himself as 'thunderstruck' (*B*, p. 28) by Bartleby's behaviour, he recalls the story of a gentleman from Virginia who was killed by lightning while standing at an open window. In order to neutralise the far greater threat posed by Bartleby, the lawyer must invent a series of ever more implausible expedients that do eventually lead to his achieving an acceptable, albeit bizarre, *modus vivendi* with his antagonist.

No sooner has the lawyer resolved this second crisis, however, than he is faced with a third which is far more redoubtable than the first two. Turkey and Nippers were troublesome but not profoundly menacing, while Bartleby had turned him metaphorically 'to a pillar of salt.' Now, however, the lawyer must face the literal, and profoundly damaging, prospect of losing the respect of his professional colleagues. Although Deleuze alludes to this phase of the story in support of his contention that the liberating encounter between Bartleby and the lawyer is prevented by the intervention of the paternal figure, Melville stresses the fact that this failure – provoked, as it is, by the lawyer's professional associates – is actually of a fraternal provenance:

At last I was made aware that all through the circle of my professional acquaintance, a whisper of wonder was running round, having reference to the strange creature I kept at my office. This worried me very much. And as the idea came upon me of his possibly turning out a long-lived man, and keep occupying my chambers, and denying my authority; and perplexing my visitors; and scandalizing my professional reputation; and casting a general gloom over the premises; [...] as all these dark antici-pations crowded upon me more and more, and my friends continually intruded their relentless remarks upon the apparition in my room; a great change was wrought in me. I resolved to gather all my faculties together, and for ever rid me of this intolerable incubus.

(*B*, p. 32)

This last crisis – portended for the lawyer by 'the unsolicited and uncharita-ble remarks obtruded upon me by my professional friends' (*B*, p. 31) will be resolved by the availability of Bartleby – 'a demented man who already has in some degree turned the tongues, if not the heads of myself and clerks' (*B*, pp. 24–5) – as a surrogate. Thus the 'professional friends' who threaten the lawyer will be miraculously transformed into the 'silent procession' (*B*, p. 37) that accompanies Bartleby to the Tombs. This concluding episode will itself complete the motif of fraternal hostility towards Bartleby that was introduced at the beginning of the story when Turkey advised the lawyer to 'kick him out of the office' and Ginger Nuts dismissed him as 'a little luny' (*B*, p. 14).

As this analysis of the three successive crises faced by the lawyer should make clear, Bartleby, far from being the potential agent of the lawyer's redemption, is simply one among several characters with whom he experiences a potentially threatening conflict. For Deleuze, the culminating event of the story is the lawyer's rejection of the promise of originality that Bartleby had offered him, and his retreat into conformity to paternal law. In fact, however, Melville clearly intends the actual plot of his story to culminate in the decision that permits the lawyer to avoid becoming the object of persecution at the hands of his professional colleagues, by allowing Bartleby to suffer exclusion in his place. Melville stresses the pivotal importance of this act when, in response to a stranger's effort to identify him with Bartleby, the lawyer retorts, 'but really, the man you allude to is nothing to me' (*B*, p. 34), a tactic that echoes the words by which St Peter (similarly motivated by the fear of group hostility) betrayed Christ: 'I know not this man of whom ye speak'.[13] In this way, Melville drives home the contradiction between the requirements of fidelity and the desire for self-preservation that constitute the emotional centre of his story. As the biblical subtext of the story reminds us, the rituals upon which human communities depend for their survival are fundamentally at odds with the ethical teachings that justify their existence. Thus, as Nathalia Wright has pertinently observed, throughout his life Melville was preoccupied with the 'discrepancy between the precepts of the New Testament and the practices of the world, a discrepancy he never, for all his disillusion, ceased protesting' (Wright, p. 114).

Deleuze's insistence upon Bartleby's originality, and his analysis of the failed redemption in which his meeting with the lawyer culminates, lead him to conclude that Melville is sympathetic to his own vision of a society of brothers who have been freed from paternal authority. In this respect, he sees him as representative of a profoundly American spirit: 'L'Américain, c'est celui qui s'est libéré de la fonction paternelle anglaise, c'est le fils d'un père émietté' (Bartleby, p. 109). Melville's vocation, like that of his fellow Americans, is to 'constituer un univers, une société de frères, une fédération d'hommes et de biens, une communauté d'individus anarchistes' (Bartleby, p. 109). The problem with this assumption is that paternal authority is not, in 'Bartleby', the conveniently identifiable stumbling block that Deleuze wishes it to be; that role is continuously played in a more diffuse and uncontrollable way throughout the story by male rivalry.

Melville gives this theme a fundamentally biblical dimension by having the lawyer refer to himself and Bartleby as two 'sons of Adam' (*B*, p. 20) and later allude to 'this old Adam of resentment' (*B*, p. 30)[14] aroused in him by

Bartleby's behaviour. Paternal authority, as represented by the several biblical allusions that Deleuze does not comment on, is, contrary to his thesis, intended as an antidote to the problem of mutual antagonism rather than its cause. Thus the story of Cain and Abel implicitly recalls a God who demystifies rivalry by revealing its fundamental insanity. Likewise, the lawyer's explicit allusion to Christ's words, '[a] new commandment give I unto you, that ye love one another' (*B*, p. 30),[15] serves in the story as a truly revolutionary doctrine which, if acted upon, would spell the ruin, not so much of paternal authority, as of fraternal rivalry.

Deleuze wants to make violence a paternal attribute in order to give legitimacy to a sacrificial ritual that will dispose of the father once and for all. Thus he informs us that 'il n'y a que des pères monstrueux et dévorants, et des fils sans pères, pétrifiés. Si l'humanité peut être sauvée, et les originaux réconciliés, c'est seulement dans la dissolution, la décomposition de la fonction paternelle' (Bartleby, p. 107). In fact, however, the community that Melville presents in 'Bartleby' is, precisely, one in which paternal authority – fundamentally represented not, as Deleuze thinks, by the lawyer, but by biblical allusions that denounce fraternal antagonisms – has been, in effect, 'ruined' by the community of brothers who are guided, in its place, by their own rivalistic impulses. The lawyer, for example, provokes Bartleby into an act of non-cooperation because, as he tells us, 'the evil impulse in me mastered me' (*B*, p. 16). Later, he admits that his behaviour towards Bartleby is governed by what he calls his 'blind inveteracy' (*B*, p. 17). He likewise recognises that he cannot avoid 'falling into sudden spasmodic passions' (*B*, p. 18) with Bartleby. His allusion to the notorious 1841 murder of Samuel Adams by his debtor John C. Colt similarly invokes the determining influence of a malign agency. Thus Colt was 'dreadfully incensed by Adams', which led him to become 'wildly excited' (*B*, p. 30). These are the dystopian symptoms of a fraternal community in which hostile impulses are no longer restrained by effective safeguards, a prospect whose inevitability Freud intuitively recognised but which Deleuze fails entirely to countenance.

As I mentioned at the beginning of this essay, Deleuze interprets 'Bartleby' as expressing Melville's utopian vision of a sacrificial ritual, left unfulfilled by the lawyer's betrayal, that would have disposed of the paternal figure and led to 'une fonction d'universelle fraternité'. Melville, however, has staged Bartleby's demise as a fully achieved ritual expulsion that he presents in such a way as to arouse misgivings in his readers. It is not merely the lawyer, who abandons him, or the landlord, who calls the police, or even the police themselves, who arrest him, that are involved in this act. Rather, guided by a profound intuition in this respect, Melville creates a group of complicitous bystanders:

Some of the compassionate and curious bystanders joined the party; and headed by one of the constables arm in arm with Bartleby, the silent procession filed its way through all the noise, and heat, and joy of the roaring thoroughfares at noon.

(*B*, p. 37)

Thus Melville stages the climactic moment of his story as a fraternal ritual with strongly religious overtones. He does not, however, confer upon this ritual the sacred, redemptive potential that we find in Deleuze's interpretation.

So the larger significance of Melville's story does not reside in the advent of an absolutely original being, or in the emergence of a human community freed from subservience to paternal law that the arrival of this figure makes possible. Rather, it is in the staging of a ceremony – a violent, sacrificial ritual – through which the community will reveal the nature of the deepest bond by which it has always been constituted and maintained in existence. For Melville, the obstacle to the formation of a new kind of human community lies in the profound incompatibility between the aspiration to an ideal community and the necessary reliance of real communities on the practice of ritual exclusion. As he indirectly reminds us in his story's concluding coda, there can be no post office without a 'dead letter office' to which undeliverable mail can be dispatched. By inference, there can be no stable human community without a sacrificial ritual that disposes of its Bartlebys.

Deleuze seems to echo this idea when he argues that Bartleby's profound originality qualifies him as 'le nouveau Christ'. For Melville, however, the crucial attribute of Bartleby is not his originality, but the vulnerability that facilitates his becoming the object of an exclusionary ritual which, while expedient, contradicts the putative moral ideals of this community. Deleuze's divergence from Melville on this point leads, finally, to his advocating precisely the discredited ritual practice – with the father as the chosen object of fraternal wrath – which Melville had led us to experience as untenable. In the role that Deleuze would attribute in his mythology to the 'pères monstrueux', Melville had already, in his deconstruction of this mythology, placed a 'poor scrivener' (*B*, p. 37).

Notes

1 An earlier version of this essay was presented at a meeting of the Centre de Recherche sur la Littérature et la Cognition de l'Université de Paris 8 (St Denis). I wish to thank the director of this research group, Prof. Noëlle Batt, for inviting me to read this paper, and its members for their encouraging responses.
2 Gilles Deleuze, *Nietzsche et la Philosophie* (Paris: Presses Universitaires de France, 1998).
3 Alberto Gualandi, *Deleuze* (Paris: Belles Lettres, 1998) pp. 138–9.
4 Alain Badiou, *Deleuze: La Clameur de l'être* (Paris: Hachette, 1997) p. 30.
5 René Girard, 'Système du délire', in *Critique dans un souterrain* (Paris: L'Age d'Homme, 1976) p. 163.
6 Gilles Deleuze, 'Bartleby, ou la formule', in *Critique et Clinique* (Paris: Editions de Minuit, 1993) pp. 89–114.

7 Sigmund Freud, *Totem and taboo*, in *The Standard Edition of the Complete Psychological Works of Sigmund Freud*, vol. 13, trans. James Strachey (London: Hogarth Press, 1955) p. 144.

8 Bernard Sichère, *Le Moment Lacanien* (Paris: Bernard Grasset, 1983) p. 148.

9 Sigmund Freud, *The future of an illusion*, in *The Standard Edition of the Complete Works of Sigmund Freud*, vol. 21, trans. James Strachey (London: Hogarth Press, 1961) p. 15.

10 See, for example, my later discussion of Cain and Abel, Christ's announcement of the 'new commandment', and Peter's denial of Christ.

11 Nathalia Wright's *Melville's Use of the Bible* (New York: Octagon Books, 1974) offers a useful corrective to this tendency in Deleuze's approach to Melville.

12 Herman Melville, 'Bartleby, the scrivener', in *Billy Budd, Sailor and Selected Tales* (Oxford and New York: Oxford University Press, 1998) p. 19. Hereafter referred to as *B*.

13 See *Mark*, 14:71. Quoted here in the King James version.

14 Compare *Ephesians*, 4:22, and *Colossians*, 3:9.

15 See *John*, 13:34.

10 Knowing one's enemy

Deleuze, Artaud, and the problem of judgement

Catherine Dale

Man plays with god, and god, he plays with himself.[1]

While Deleuze's 'To have done with judgement' modifies the title of Antonin Artaud's essay and radio play 'To have done with the judgement of God', in no way does he alter its sentiment.[2] Likewise, other than introducing God as an object for his scorn, Artaud's critique of judgement differs little from that of Deleuze. Artaud campaigns against God, for he considers him to encompass *all* conditions of judgement, including man's[3] habitual practice of judging and being judged. As he is transcendent, rational and eternal, God epitomises the very form of judgement. Moreover, God presupposes an *ideal* against which everything is measured, making of judgement the confirmation of an obligation, or the settling of a debt. In relation to Artaud's essay, Deleuze's title underscores rather than ignores the omnipotence of God's judgement. Such is its ubiquity, that evocation of his name becomes superfluous. In other words, judgement functions effectively whether or not it relates to God. Thus it matters less that the judgement to be confronted is abstract or divine than that, whether it is in the hands of man or God, judgement is a transcendent, inveterate and formidable opponent.

Deleuze argues that the 'doctrine of judgement', wherein mankind forms judgements every day of his life, is only made possible through the act of suspending to infinity that final day of judgement: 'It is not as if judgement itself were postponed, put off until tomorrow, pushed back to infinity; on the contrary, it is the act of postponing, of carrying to infinity, that makes judgement possible' (*CC*, p. 127). This infinity is the form of judgement itself, an infinity which, other than as the name of God, appears in such guises as Plato's ideal body, the perfection of form or 'spirit' or the universal subject. Within judgement, infinity becomes a body without limits, a body which can only be achieved through death. Accordingly, the subject remains permanently stranded in corporeality while the ideal world lies just out of reach but always in sight. In Christian doctrine, until granted infinite life, man is in this world simply to 'wait it out', knowing 'time' only as the distance between human life and eternal life as lived by God. Thus the infinite can be defined as the impossible measure of man's deficit in relation to God's plenitude.

While Deleuze shows three more authors, namely Nietzsche, D. H. Law-rence and Kafka, to be in confrontation with the postponement of infinity which makes judgement possible, it is Artaud whom he names explicitly as the one who *ceaselessly* sets up 'the operation of having done with the judgement of God against the infinite' (*CC*, p. 127). Artaud not only finds infinity to function ubiquitously as leverage for judgement, he also considers infinity and judgement to be epistemologically intertwined. The answer to both supposedly lies hidden behind the reflection of an endlessly deferrable series of quasi-existential, useless questions and their answers. Artaud asks, 'What is the order of the next world?'

> We do not know. The number and order of possible suppositions in this domain is precisely infinity! And what is infinity? We do not exactly know! It is a word we employ to indicate *the opening* of our conscious-ness towards an inordinate, indefatigable and inordinate possibility. And what exactly is consciousness? We do not exactly know. It is nothingness. A nothingness we employ to indicate when we do not know something from what side we do not know it and so we say consciousness, from the side of consciousness, but there are a hundred thousand other sides.
>
> (*FT*, pp. 71–2)

Presenting infinity as outside consciousness, Artaud then introduces consciousness as a limited position established and maintained through apostolic ignorance. In this way, the transcendence of knowledge delimits a hundred thousand sides of consciousness and acknowledges only one. While the answers formulated here are severely limited, so too are the questions themselves, since it is the desire of monocratic consciousness to think the infinite which makes it a problem in the first place. Attempting to think the entirety of infinity or eternity is a specious problem but also something of a recurrent ruse detracting from the attention paid to life. This terrestrial world is full of what Artaud refers to as 'backward' feelings, passions and institutions where questions concerning existence have become overloaded with significance.

> Existence itself is one idea too many and little by little, softly and bru-tally, philosophers, savants, doctors and priests are making this life false for us. Really, things are without profundity, there is no beyond or here-after and no other abyss than this one into which one is put.[4]

Thus it is not the true answer, declares Artaud, which is the last to be known, but the true problem.[5] Single consciousness, however, awaits only the answer. Judgement plays its part here too, since the life of this world is predicated on a promise of the world to come, on a kind of future blackmail, the representation of a better life and a redeemed spirit. Since life itself does not matter, daily existence is dominated by judgement, which, in appraising every act, however banal, prepares the living for salvation.

Deleuze argues similarly when he points out that judgement is only possible through the doctrine of the immortality of humankind and the infinity of its debt to God. It is Nietzsche, he explains, who reveals that the condition of judgement is 'the consciousness of being in debt to the deity, the adventure of debt as it becomes *infinite* and thus unpayable' (*CC*, p. 126). This infinite debt of mankind is that which he is always repaying but which will never be paid. Henri Bergson alludes to this construction of infinite debt when he recalls Plato's suggestion in *Timaeus* that God gave the world 'time' as 'a moving image of eternity' because he could not make the world eternal.[6] He compares the relation between time and eternity to that 'between a piece of gold and the small change – change so small that payment goes on for ever without the debt being paid off' (*CE*, p. 318). Bergson's example emphasises the gap between man and infinity, wherein man assumes he can think the infinite when he is always only ever approaching it. Likewise, God as the perfect form of man is forever escaping his grasp. In effect, man is unable to make up the change not because he cannot count but because *he himself* is the missing change.

In the third section of 'To have done with the judgement of God', Artaud again addresses man's 'faint idea of the world,' an idea he wants to protect for ever by freezing it. This turns out to be the process whereby man subjugates himself to God's infinity. On the day man stopped the world, writes Artaud, he had 'two roads [...] open to him: that of the infinite outside, and that of the infinitesimal inside. And he chose the infinitesimal inside. ... And god, god himself hastened the movement' (*FT*, p. 69). God hastens the outcome inasmuch as his infinity automatically reduces man to the infinitesimal, the smallest possible quantity. Man's finite consciousness raises God to the idea of a single unity, to an infinity of which man is but an infinitesimal part. Man thinks that he can make up (think) a whole from parts, but this is another specious problem, since man tries to think the whole, which is the single unity of God the infinite, from his own position, which can never be anything but a part. Furthermore, man's redemption is made doubly difficult insofar as the whole and its parts differ as radically as matter does from form.

Artaud's description of the decision to become an infinitesimal portion of God's perfection shows man endeavouring to divide himself into smaller and smaller pieces, well beyond the split between his conscious and unconscious parts, in order to become small enough to evade God's judgement. What happens, however, is that his introspective smallness achieves nothing but the completion of the circle back towards infinity. This is because the infinitesimal *is* the infinite in the same way that the relation between the instant and eternity means that the instant is given only in eternity. If man as infinitesimal can be given only within God's infinite, then the two roads laid out for man offer him a false choice. The infinite outside cannot be contained in consciousness without man's limitation becoming his limitless debt. Ultimately, in order to repay his debt to God and simultaneously become a perfect form, man must die, since only by being rid of his body, of matter, can he join with infinite consciousness. In sum, to use Bergson's terminology, Artaud considers 'man' himself to be a false problem.

In his book on Foucault, Deleuze argues after Nietzsche that as long as 'God exists – that is, so long as the God-form functions – then man does not yet exist'.[7] The man-form is never given a chance to exist, for, as soon as it appears, explains Deleuze, it is already incorporating the death of man in itself. The futility of the man-form appears at the end of the appendix 'On the death of man and superman', within which Deleuze follows Foucault's archaeology of the compositions of a 'God-form', a 'man-form' and a future 'superman'. The first of these, the 'God-form', emerges from the seventeenth-century's creation of several infinities in order to make sense of the diverse limitations of man's own forces. Since man is limited, any encounter between the forces of the infinitesimal inside and the forces of the infinite outside only produces variations of the same God-form. With the nineteenth century, however, new finite forces such as labour, language and science emerge. Deleuze suggests that, as these appear from the outside, man is able to enter into relation with them. The man-form is forged when man's internal forces enter into relation with the outside forces of finitude, thus inaugurating 'a new dimension of in-depth finitude, which then becomes the finitude of man himself' (*Foucault*, p. 128). Although man, in this sense, appeared to be finite, the relation between inside and outside remained one of infinite deferral. Even as a finite form, man cannot catch up with his own image.

In Deleuze's account of Foucault, the idea that the man-form is not even worth saving poses an insistent question: what new forces from the outside do we now risk encountering? Whatever the new form, writes Deleuze, it will be neither God nor man. This is where Deleuze introduces the third form of the trilogy, Nietzsche's 'superman'. The superman, observes Deleuze, 'is what frees life *within man himself*, to the benefit of another form, and so on' (*Foucault*, p. 130). Speculating on the kinds of forces man could enter into relations with, Deleuze declares that it 'would no longer involve raising [man] to infinity or finitude but to an unlimited finity, thereby evoking every situation of force in which a finite number of components yields a practically unlimited diversity of combinations' (*Foucault*, p. 131). The 'superman' results from relations with new forces and, as such, exists in an experimental realm. This is because it is still only a shadow, a vision and a forecast for the freeing of life *within man himself*.

The above threefold genealogy involves first, God basking openly as the unfold; second, man suffering inwardly as the fold, and third, future man appearing as what he terms the *superfold*. Artaud's preoccupation with the materiality of existence formulates a similar triumvirate, but one with a slightly different vision or forecast. The man-form, appearing as a figure of progress, is a symbol Artaud is keen to refute. He suggests that finitude's pioneering opposition to infinity is merely a nominal change. In this way, Artaud appears to fold together the forms of both man and God. He explains, for example, that the new atomic technology of 1946–7 is simply the imposition of a new idea of God presented in the guise of science. 'For, laugh as much as you want to, what men have called microbes is in fact god, and do you know what the Americans and the Russians make their atoms with? They make them with the microbes of god' (*FT*, p. 78). Science, nationhood and capitalism function as God insofar as they use finite forces to represent man and dominate his will.

Artaud's genealogical model of the three phases of man is structured around the one thing God lacks, a human body. First, Artaud presents the God of the infinite as the coward who flees human suffering and change; second, he shows the man of the finite as the body organised in imitation of this, in such a way as to avoid the pain of transformation or change by stopping at every step and thus remaining separated from its will; third, he proposes the 'PURE BODY' of the infinitive as that which, always immanent to its own change, is also the creator of its own will. The latter, the third or 'PURE BODY' contains something of the body of Deleuze's 'unlimited finity'. In this 'PURE BODY', the finite materiality actualised at any given moment already contains and thus provides the makings of its new or future body. Only two kinds of time or existence, the infinite and the infinitesimal, are offered to man. It is the infinitive third body, held from man by the gap between his finite and infinite selves, which Artaud conceives as the only path to take in order to release the body from judgement.

In a letter to the gallery curator Pierre Loeb, written a few months before the composition of 'To have done with the judgement of God', Artaud optimistically declares the coming or returning of the man 'without functions or organs but possessed of will'.[8] The single most important characteristic of Artaud's new and 'PURE' body is its will, which, like Deleuze's superman of 'unlimited finity', is self-creating.[9] It has no parents, is not born from the mother's body – (Artaud claims that he did not come from his mother and that he has no parents) – and it does not represent, signify or classify a man-form nor imitate a God-form. In this way, the 'PURE BODY' moves with a peculiar will to live all its own, a will that is neither man's nor God's. 'Bodies don't come from the evolution of time, but from the will in the middle of time' (*OCXIV*[*], p. 73). This immanent will continuously eludes God's construction of the organs which compose the human body, which is why, in the conclusion to 'To have done with the judgement of God', Artaud refers to it as 'a body without organs'. In the same letter to Loeb, he writes:

> The great lie has been to make man an organism, ingestion, assimilation, incubation, excretion, thus creating a whole order of hidden functions

which are outside the realm of the *deliberative* will; the will that determines itself at each instant…without functions that were hidden, underlying, governed *by the unconscious.*

(SW, p. 515)

Artaud's new or 'PURE' body is made up of diverse forces entering into equally diverse relations with other forces, and it is this *deliberative* will immanent to itself that creates its directions and directs its creations.

The 'PURE BODY', or the 'body without organs', is not, then, an organised body but the body of movement and its affects. Artaud's emphasis on the affective realm in all his work has to do less with changes in feeling than with that aspect of the emotive realm which is less definable. It is only in the infinitive that the movements of difference produced by the relations between the forces of vitality or life can be apprehended. It is the infinitive that Artaud opposes to the infinitesimal, so revealing that which, rather than being deferred till the end of existence, can only be given in the duration of affectivity, the living time of man. In his essay, 'To have done with masterpieces', Artaud suggests that the missing apprehension of affectivity be revised through the theatre. The theatre, he explains, is the place where considerations of the form of an action are willingly overridden by focusing on the impulsion of its forces. Old masterpieces must be forgotten because they petrify contemporary art and drama and keep it from 'making contact with that underlying power, call it thought-energy, the life force, the determination of change, lunar menses, or anything you like'.[10] The theatre, writes Artaud, is *no thing* but a force that makes use of everything.

Because the efficacy of the poetry of the theatre is not easily exhausted (unlike the poetry of a text) and because it is in continual action, it displays the force of life outliving its forms. Artaud declares that the theatre is the only place with no repetition. 'The actor does not make the same gestures twice, but he makes gestures, he moves; and although he brutalises forms, nevertheless behind them and through their destruction he rejoins that which outlives forms and produces their continuation' (*TD*, p. 12). Rather than searching for a way to transcend human existence, Artaud, like Deleuze, finds life in the fleeting glimpses of its activity. But the infinite itself cannot be 'lived' and so, as Artaud will violently demonstrate, in order to create a new affective body, the old one must be remade.

Concluding his diatribe against the judgement of God, Artaud declares that, owing to his bad construction, man must be strapped to the operating table to undergo one last operation 'in order to remake his anatomy. Man is sick because he is badly constructed. We must decide to strip him in order to scratch out this animalcule which makes him itch to death, god, and with god his organs. For tie me down if you want to, but there is nothing more useless than an organ' (*FT*, p. 79). This is where Artaud suggests man make himself a body without organs. The problem is not so much with the organs themselves, for they are useless anyway, so much as the way the organs are organised into the organism known as man or the man-form. Deleuze also distinguishes between this organism, which embodies a relationship between judgement and the sense organs, and the body as a physical system traversed by intensities and affects. As Deleuze points out, the doctrine of judgement supplants the affective body. God steals the dynamic, vivified and wilful forces passing across and through the body and leaves man the rest. Deleuze also points out that the body as organism is produced from the most 'somber organisation' carried out by a priest. Artaud's body without organs, on the other hand, undergoes reconstruction so that it can dance. Once man is given a body without organs, he will be freed 'from all his automatisms', writes Artaud. 'Then you will teach him again to dance inside out as in the delirium of our accordion dances and that inside out will be his true side out' (*FT*, p. 79). Through the intoxication of its frenzied affects, Artaud's 'body without organs' counters the submission of the body to the doctrine of judgement. Despite dancing in anarchic ecstasy, it must be remembered that the 'body without organs' is also a body produced through violence and cruelty. It is an act of cruelty which forces the body onto the operating table, strips it of its organs and then turns it inside out.

In Artaud, cruelty is a precise term around which he constructs a whole theory. His explanation of this concept appears in the 'Letters on cruelty', and a number of essays on 'The theatre of cruelty', in his most famous book, *Le Théâtre et son double*. So significant is cruelty that in his 'To have done with judgement', Deleuze regards all practices acting against judgement to also come under this 'system of cruelty'. Perhaps the clearest description of what Artaud means by cruelty comes from his letters to Jean Paulhan, his friend and then editor of the *Nouvelle Revue Française*. Artaud tells Paulhan, rather ambiguously, that 'cruelty is a matter neither of sadism nor bloodshed, at least not in any exclusive way' (*TD*, p. 101). He warns Paulhan against taking the word in 'the rapacious physical sense that it is customarily given', suggesting instead that it be thought about in a broad or general sense (*TD*, p. 101). Cruelty must be redefined and grasped philosophically: 'From the point of view of the mind, cruelty signifies rigor, implacable intention and decision, irreversible and absolute determination. The most current philosophical determinism is, from the point of view of our existence, an image of cruelty' (*TD*, p. 101). Far from being gratuitous, the practice of cruelty becomes rigorous, definite and irreversible, in contrast to the infinite torture of judgement.

Artaud's 'theatre of cruelty' is designed to wake the audience and actors alike from the sleepy voyeurism of contemporary theatre and its reliance on representation and psychology. In attacking the spectator's sensibility, the theatre of cruelty seeks to scare the audience, so that, on leaving, they feel as though they have just left the dentist's chair. Artaud's life-long plan for the theatre is to treat the theatre as the double of life, which, in terms of the intensity of its affects, means regarding the theatre as life itself. When Deleuze announces that 'Artaud will give sublime developments to the system of cruelty, a writing of blood and life that is opposed to the book' (*CC*, p. 128), the sublime of which he speaks relates directly to Artaud's ambitions for the theatre. Artaud regards the text or script as only one resource amongst myriad theatrical props, voices, gestures, actors and sets. Like the eighteenth-century writer Edmund Burke, Artaud also claims that theatre and poetry contain living forces stronger than those expressed in real life: 'The image of a crime presented in the requisite theatrical conditions is something infinitely more terrible for the mind than that same crime when actually committed' (*TD*, p. 85). In its opposition to judgement, Artaud's cruelty acts in a similar way to Nietzsche's justice, which, as Deleuze explains, involves the *finite* relations between bodies. Nietzsche's creditor/debtor relation is the basis of all exchange, explains Deleuze. In the finite relations between bodies, no one is indebted to God or judgement, they are only indebted to each other. The collision of the forces of bodies changes the finite state of each body and creates an affect. The finite is thus transformed into the infinitive of being affected.

In his last letter, written just a month after the banning of the broadcast, Artaud tells his friend Paule Thévenin that he is done with radio and from now on will devote himself to 'a theatre of blood', where the actors are not performing but doing. 'The theatre is in reality the *genesis* of creation' (*SW*, pp. 584–5). The revolutionary aspect of the theatre of cruelty is its regression to a time when theatre produced a numinous or religious experience for all participants. Artaud's theatrical remedy, which consists in the return to a previous age, recalls Nietzsche's valorisation of a time when mankind was not ashamed of its cruelty and 'life on earth was more cheerful than it is today, with its pessimists'.[11] Guilt and shame are contemporary prerequisites for becoming Christian.

According to Deleuze, Christianity marks the final transformation of judgement. The Christian era is a modernist tragedy where self-punishment comes to characterise judgement, and where judgement is the sole survivor of the forces of man caught up in a relay whereby every judgement creates another. At one point during his incarceration in insane asylums, Artaud embraces God's judgement and his system of morality with such fierce devotion that in a single sitting he swallows over 150 hosts. Accompanying Artaud's religious fervour is the severest form of self-judgement and an equally severe asceticism. Retrospectively, Artaud regarded this time as the product of a nasty trick played on him by God and his beings. What is most interesting about this is that, after he 'recovers', Artaud seems to write more than he has ever written before. According to Thévenin, it was as if Artaud's lifelong problems with thought and language had disappeared.[12] For Artaud to think, he must have done with the judgement of God, for it is God's judgement that traps the body in the mental circularity of infinity and its representation. 'Time only exists from being made by judgement. Without time there is no judgement. Judgement comes from CEREBRAL ACTIVITY, a piece of carbon installed at the summit of the peak'. Man's object of thought is a false eternity, it is that which conditions his existence in carbon in the history of time but which also indicates his ontological inauthenticity as a carbon copy of himself as a representation of God.

In *Difference and Repetition*, Deleuze attributes Artaud with the invention of a transcendental empiricism. The transcendental aspect of the body's empiricism refers to that which can only be enacted within action and that which can only be thought within thought. Artaud bases his theatre of cruelty upon a model of movement, which, like the movement in Balinese dancing, in which Artaud was keenly interested, is not narrative but affective. As Deleuze writes, in the theatre of repetition,

> we experience pure forces, dynamic lines in space which act without intermediary upon the spirit, and link it directly with nature and history, with a language which speaks before words, with gestures which develop before organised bodies, with masks before faces, with specters and phantoms before characters – the whole apparatus of repetition as a terrible power.[13]

Artaud describes his 'theatre of cruelty' as creating 'a metaphysics of speech, gesture and expression, in order to rescue it from its servitude to psychology and "human interest" ' (*TD*, p. 90). The human body, its voice, gestures, attitudes and movements, must all be acted on directly. Moreover, every word, sound, musical note, gesture, light, darkness, shadow, mask, prop, set and costume must be raised to the dignity of a sign. Every element in the theatre becomes a character the moment it makes its entrance. Each character is necessary and cannot be other than it is within the continuous instants of creation.

Cruelty is a process which pits the pain of self-creation and the determination of thought against God's infinity. In a sense, cruelty aims for the rehabilitation of the first force of man, his *élan vital*. Artaud writes: 'I want to be semipiternal, that is, a self that moves and creates itself at every instant and not eternal, that is, having an absolute self which governs me always from the height of its eternity' (*SW*, p. 465). In Artaud's account, to be semipiternal means to be continuously evolving in contingency with one's *deliberative* and determining will. Each decision made by Artaud's *deliberative* will creates a new moment of the body. This means that it is impossible to distinguish between matter and form, since the forming of the body (matter) occurs in the continuity within which the body (form) is created.

A decision is not judgement, declares Deleuze, 'nor is it the organic consequence of a judgement: it springs vitally from a whirlwind of forces that leads us into combat' (*CC*, p. 134). Deleuze introduces the notion of combat as a direct antidote to judgement, but he is careful to distinguish combat against the Other from combat between oneself. 'The combat-against tries to destroy or repel a force (to struggle against "the diabolical powers of the future"), but the combat-between, by contrast, tries to take hold of a force in order to make it one's own' (*CC*, p. 132). The secret is not to destroy or dominate the forces against which one fights but to take them on, to add them to one's own will to power.

Through his perpetual struggles, Artaud shows that the combat between oneself is the most difficult of all, since 'God continues to impregnate human consciousness creating a screen between man and himself' (*OCXIV**, p. 199). Because combat between oneself occurs, according to Deleuze, as 'a powerful, non-organic vitality that supplements force with force', it is always changing and difficult to locate. In a 1946 letter to Peter Watson, an Englishman inquiring about locating Artaud's work in English, Artaud writes, 'Will combat be assessed, judged, justified? No, ... to name the battle is to kill nothing ... and to stop life ... and life will never be stopped'.[14] As Artaud says, a terrible will, the deliberative will, which comes from neither man nor God, must be at work in order to summon up a body to combat the spirit of judgement. This is because in order to fight against the transcendentalism of God's judgement, combat must become a 'perpetual state of battle and assault' (*OCXIV**, p. 172). The will is the determining factor in Artaud's combats between and within. The combat of which Deleuze speaks is this 'indomitable will to live' (*CC*, p. 133). It is the will of the body beyond its organic life, the body God stole, and it assembles itself as an exclusive core of forces. In this sense, the inorganic body without organs, the body unadulterated with organs organised by a dominating will, can be said to be pure

> of all who are incapable of living,/ of all the ignoramuses there are more who have never ever agreed nor wanted to understand reality./ Which is a fight over a possible body and not over a principle or an arbitrary and supposed quality./ There are no states isolated and living by themselves, into which those who toss relentlessly can go./ The body is not definable by a state or interior density/ but by its aggressive and reactive forces.[15]

Artaud posits the 'PURE BODY' of the will to live against the 'PURE SPIRIT' of judgement. In a letter rejecting the help of a priest who offers to support the broadcast of his radio play, he explains that the body is only celebrated in the mass once it has been *consecrated* and *elevated* to the flesh of God (*FT*, pp. 93–5). Artaud points out that the 'PURE BODY' is a working body and has no time for making up the ideas of the 'PURE SPIRIT', which he says are only its voids, the interference 'of absence and want between two movements of a brilliant reality that the body, by its singular presence, has never stopped thrusting forward' (*TM*, p. 111). The continual movement of the 'PURE BODY' is opposed to the theological 'SPIRIT' of judgement. Once again, God becomes the focus of Artaud's combat. In his essay 'Shit to the spirit', Artaud explains that man refuses to live as a 'PURE BODY' of will and simply accepts 'being'. Man is not prepared to suffer the pain of self-creation and so he buries his *deliberative* will, the will which seeks to become itself through its own power, under God's protective and dominating organisation.

Artaud's objectification and reliance on God as his main opponent is not his weakness. On the contrary, it presents his peculiar strength, which is to find in God a worthy enemy with which to do combat. In order to think, Artaud takes the power of theology and discards the form it takes as judgement, in much the same way that God takes the inorganic power of man's body and leaves the rest to slowly die. In this way, Artaud exercises Deleuze's combat perfectly, since he takes God's power and makes it his own.

Notes

1 Antonin Artaud, *Oeuvres complètes*, II, ed. Paule Thévenin, (Paris: Gallimard, 1961) p. 189. All translations from the *Oeuvres complètes* are my own. Hereafter referred to as *OC*, followed by the volume number.

2 Ironically, 'En finir avec le jugement de dieu', which is Artaud's last completed work, received the severest of judgements itself when it was banned the day before it was scheduled for broadcast. The translation used here is from *Antonin Artaud: Four Texts*, ed. and trans. Clayton Eshleman and Norman Glass (Los Angeles: Panjandrum Books, 1982) pp. 61–79 (hereafter referred to as *FT*). The original French can be found in Antonin Artaud, *Oeuvres complètes*, XIII, ed. Paule Thévenin (Paris: Gallimard, 1974) pp. 65–104. Deleuze calls the four authors 'Spinoza's four great disciples' since they all break with the Judaeo-Christian tradition in order to critique it. Deleuze's French text is 'En finir avec le jugement', in *Critique et Clinique* (Paris: Editions de Minuit, 1993), pp. 158–69. The English translation, 'To have done with judgement', appears in *Essays Critical and Clinical* (hereafter referred to as *CC*) trans. Daniel W. Smith and Michael A. Greco (Minneapolis: University of Minnesota Press, 1997) pp. 126–35.

3 In this essay, I have opted for the usage 'man', as a synonym of judgement, rather than 'mankind', which suggests to me an image or model of a person.

4 Antonin Artaud, *Oeuvres complètes*, vol. XIV**, ed. Paule Thévenin (Paris: Gallimard, 1978) p. 80.

5 Antonin Artaud, 'The mistake is in the fact ....', in Jack Hirschman (ed.) *Artaud Anthology* (San Francisco: City Lights Books, 1965) pp. 220–1 (p. 220). Hereafter referred to as *TM*.

6 Henri Bergson, *Creative Evolution*, trans. A. Mitchell (Lanham: University Press of America, 1983) p. 318. Hereafter referred to as *CE*.

7 Gilles Deleuze, *Foucault*, trans. Sean Hand (Minneapolis: Minnesota University Press, 1988) p. 130.

8 Antonin Artaud, 'Letter to Pierre Loeb (April 23, 1947)', in Susan Sontag (ed.) *Antonin Artaud: Selected Writings* (Los Angeles: University of California Press, 1976) pp. 515–19 (p. 515). This volume is hereafter referred to as *SW*.

9 In collaboration with Félix Guattari in *A Thousand Plateaus*, Deleuze produces a separate but intricately related reading of 'En finir avec le jugement de dieu'. Deleuze and Guattari use the single phrase 'the body without organs', to describe a unique and difficult practice of creation. The body without organs is a static plane of immanent creation which Deleuze and Guattari pit against God's transcendentalism.

10 Antonin Artaud, *The Theater and its Double*, trans. Mary C. Richards (New York: Grove Press, 1958) p. 78. Hereafter referred to as *TD*.

11 Friedrich Nietzsche, *On the Genealogy of Morals*, ed. Keith Ansell Pearson, trans. Carol Diethe (Cambridge: Cambridge University Press, 1994) second essay, §6, p. 46.

12 Paule Thévenin, interview with Jean-Jacques Brochier, 'Une Oeuvre en expansion', *Magazine Littéraire*, no. 206 (1984) pp. 34–5 (p. 34).

13 Gilles Deleuze, *Difference and Repetition*, trans. Paul Patton (New York: Columbia University Press, 1994) p. 10.

14 Antonin Artaud, *Oeuvres complètes*, vol. XII, ed. Paule Thévenin (Paris: Gallimard, 1974) p. 236.

15 Antonin Artaud, *Oeuvres complètes*, vol. XXIV, ed. Paule Thévenin (Paris: Gallimard, 1988) p. 192.

Part IV
Beyond theology

11 Pure reserve

Deleuze, philosophy, and immanence

Keith Ansell Pearson

> The most closed system still has a thread that rises toward the virtual, and down which the spider descends.[1]

What would it mean to still believe in the world and in the possibilities of philosophy today, now, as a mark of our contemporaneity? This question will guide the comprehension of Deleuze undertaken in this essay.

Deleuze posits a quite radical and dramatic opposition between philosophy and religion, which concerns philosophy's love of immanence and religion's devotion to transcendence or 'vertical Being'. The death of God is, in Deleuze's terms, the moment of the philosopher's serenity, just as this death provided the 'meaning' to Nietzsche's cheerfulness (the opening of 'our new infinite') precisely because it signals the rebirth of immanence. Here 'God' stands for a centred universe, a fixed hierarchical order, and a substance that is outside of an immanent becoming or evolution; in short, it stands for transcendence. Deleuze, then, is a thinker of the infinite: of infinite movement and of infinite speed precisely because he is a thinker of immanence.

A central task in the contemporary reception of Deleuze must consist, then, in understanding the nature of this thinking of immanence, especially as his thinking can be interpreted as producing the exact opposite, and has been in fact accused of doing just this. To stage an encounter with Deleuze on this burning issue it is necessary to work through a number of related key concepts: immanence, the event, multiplicity, and the virtual. It will be helpful to do this by thinking along with Bergson and the task he gave philosophy as its peculiar vocation, namely, thinking beyond human condition, which means thinking 'beyond' our spatial habits of representation and our attempt to master matter for solely utilitarian ends, and which demands that the primacy of perception be contested. We might ask, however: to what extent is this thinking beyond the human condition itself an affair of transcendence? As this essay unfolds, we shall see how such a questioning can only be answered in terms of a complex response.

Philosophy and perception: thinking immanence

Bergson presents his novel understanding of perception in *Matter and Memory*, and he contests the idea that philosophy must be governed by the primacy of perception in the essays which make up *The Creative Mind*. Deleuze instructs his readers that *Matter and Memory* is one of those highly rare texts of philosophy in which we encounter the 'vertigo of immanence'. It is a work of 'Spinozist inspiration' since it presents a plane containing both the infinite movement of a self-propagating substance and an image of thought that spreads a 'pure consciousness by right' (*WP*, p. 49). The book is an attempt to demonstrate the nature of two differences: that between matter and the perception of matter as a difference of degree, and that between matter and mind or memory as a difference of kind.

Bergson prefaced later editions of *Matter and Memory* with an introduction in which he sought to clarify the nature and ambit of the book, with its unorthodox conception of matter as an aggregate of images. It forms a key component in his non-phenomenological approach: matter is light/energy and it does not need a consciousness to illuminate it and bring it from out of darkness. The entire universe for Bergson is an aggregate of images, with the body constituting a particular image, a local system, or what he calls a 'zone of indetermination'. If one thinks of images as luminosity (propagations of energy), and appreciates that only a few years after Bergson's *Matter and Memory*, Einstein will come up with the equation *matter = energy*, then much of the initial strangeness one encounters with the deployment of the word 'image' disappears and its novel import can be put to work.

Bergson has a number of aims in his opening chapter. One is to show that perception is nothing miraculous, while another is to argue that consciousness cannot be made reducible to the molecular movements of the cerebral mass, which would be to treat it as a mere phosphoresence. Any such privileging of the brain leads to the illusion that, if we could penetrate into its inside, it would be possible by observing the dance of the atoms of the cortex to understand the life of consciousness. This is to commit the error of positing a simple, linear and automatic account of the relation between the mental and the cerebral: (Bergson does not deny there is a relation, simply that it is not one of epiphenomenalism or parallelism). Psychic life varies in accordance with the 'attention to life'; it is made up of diverse tones and rhythms. The key point is this: if we remove the images that compose the material world, we would at the same time 'destroy' the brain:

> To make of the brain the condition on which the whole image depends, is, in truth, a contradiction in terms, since the brain is by hypothesis a part of this image. Neither nerves nor nerve centers can, then, condition the image of the universe.[2]

He likens it to a central telephone exchange that allows and delays communication, 'an instrument of analysis in regard to the movement received and an instrument of selection in regard to movement executed' (*MM*, p. 30). As Deleuze puts it in *Cinema 1*, following Bergson, the brain is an 'interval' between an action and a reaction. It is not a centre of images from which one can begin, but rather one special image among others, constituting a centre of indetermination in an acentred universe of images.[3] Deleuze wishes, in fact, to takes this conception of the interval right down to the micro-level, arguing that at the level of the most elementary life forms one can posit micro-intervals. He writes:

> Smaller and smaller intervals between more and more rapid movements. Moreover, biologists speak of a 'primeval soup', which made living beings possible [...]: it is here the outlines of axes appear in an acentred universe, a left and a right, a high and a low. One should therefore conceive of micro-intervals even in the primeval soup. Biologists say that these phenomena could not be produced when the earth was very hot. Therefore one could conceive of a cooling down of the plane of immanence, correlative to the first opacities, to the first screens obstructing the diffusion of light. It is here that the first outlines of solids or rigid and geometric bodies would be formed.
>
> (*C1*, p. 63)

If matter can be described in terms of an aggregate of images, then the *perception* of matter has to do with these very same images in relation to the eventual action of a particular image, namely, the body, which exists in a state of virtual tension and potentiality. We must avoid the hylomorphic trap which would posit an incomprehensible encounter between a 'formless matter' and a 'matterless thought' (*MM*, p. 23). The modifications of the 'grey matter' cannot be treated as things in themselves, abstractly cut off from the rest of the material universe. This would be to posit a nervous system in isolation from the organism which nourishes it, from the atmosphere in which this organism breathes, from the envelopment of the earth and from the heat, light and energy of the sun. The creation of an isolated material object results in an absurdity, namely that of perception reduced to a purely interior subjective vision. If perception can be said to vary in relation to the movements of the cerebral mass, then, in turn, we must also say that these movements are bound up with the movements of the rest of the material world. To the extent, therefore, that we understand the relation between the two systems, construing local systems in terms of 'centres of real action' and 'zones of indetermination', centres that subordinate images, somewhat in the manner of Nietzsche's will to power, to their position and which are variable with them, then it is possible to see what is, in effect, almost the inevitable occurrence of perception in matter and to adequately understand how it arises.

One of the key claims Bergson advances in the book is that perception does not amount to an addition to the real, but, on the contrary, as a subtraction from it. In the passage or conversion from the virtual to the actual, for example, it is not necessary to throw more light on an object, but quite the opposite, namely, to obscure some of its aspects (*MM*, p. 36). This means that perception subtracts whatever it selects as not being relevant to the interests and functions of the body. A thing is perceived minus that which does not interest the body as a function of its needs. Perception, then, concerns the vital adaptive interests of the body, and these interests are what guide action and instruct its relation with the virtual: 'The body [...] indicates the parts and aspects of matter on which we can lay hold: our perception, which exactly measures our virtual action on things, thus limits itself to the objects which actually influence our organs and prepare our movements' (*MM*, p. 179).

It is in the treatment of the subtractive character of perception that the question of spirit begins to be posed in Bergson's text. It is bound up for him with 'discernment' and with duration. Spirit arises for Bergson out of the very poverty of our conscious perception, that is, out of the fact that it is highly selective and subtractive. Spirit enlarges the domain of possible human action, opening up a field of choice and selection that is not open to the animal which is bound to the sphere of material need. This also refers us to the 'progress of living matter', which consists in a differentiation of function involving the increasing complication of a nervous system that canalises excitations and organises actions. Its also gives rise to the autonomous life of pure memory, that is, memory which does not proceed in accordance with the order of need and habit: 'Memory is, then, in no degree an emanation of matter; on the contrary, matter, as grasped in concrete perception which always occupies a certain duration, is in great part the work of memory' (*MM*, p. 182). For Bergson, life – thought in terms of duration and memory (the prolongation of the past into the present) – belongs, strictly speaking, to mind or spirit (*esprit*) and serves to insert into matter what is required for a creative evolution to take place: *indetermination* in the sense of a reservoir of virtuality.[4] Life can be configured as a rising wave that is opposed to the descending and purely entropic movement of matter, the current of which is converted by matter into a *vortex* (*CE*, p. 269). As we shall see, there is an immanence here between the life of consciousness and the life of the material universe as a whole. The task of philosophy is to reconcile the inert and the living and introduce us into the *vie spirituelle*.

It may now be apparent: philosophy goes beyond the human condition in the specific sense that it is born out of the insufficiency of the faculties of perception. The enlargement of reality it provides is not a moment of transcendence but the opening up of a field of immanence (of duration for Bergson). In this respect, philosophy can be compared to art, in that both show us, in nature and in the mind, things which do not explicitly strike our senses or consciousness. This means that affects and percepts are not reducible to a centred subject of natural perception, to the eye of the actual body and mind.[5] Deleuze draws heavily upon these discoveries of philosophy in his treatment of the movement-image and the time-image that characterise the unanchored perception of cinema. Philosophy breaks with both the fundamental bent of the human intellect and with the habits of science, both of which are geared towards action and neither of which are able to penetrate the reality of duration (the same goes for modern metaphysics, such as the system of Kant, Bergson argues). As Bergson points out, the weakness of a scientific realism is that, in positing the evolution of matter in terms of a mathematical deduction of passing moments, it is unable either to access the dimension of the virtual – (matter is reduced to a series of actuals) – or to develop a point of contact between matter and perception: (matter is once again reduced to homogeneous changes in space). The habit of our intellect is to treat time in terms of space, to strip it of all positive attributes, and to treat matter in terms of a closed system (a system in which duration is absent). This results in the idea – one that Bergson found prevailing in modern physics and biology as well as thought in general – that the future is given in the present and that time is simply an illusion. For science, everything in the universe that cannot be calculated or measured is to be discarded. Now, Bergson does not seek to reduce the evolution of the material universe *to* that of consciousness, but he does want to show that there is an immanence between them in the specific sense that, if we do not discard that which cannot be calculated or measured, then we are 'obliged to ascertain that the states of our material world are contemporaneous with the history of our consciousness' (*CM*, p. 20). For Bergson, there is simply not a question of a split between subject and object, or between consciousness and the material universe. He is opposed to all the philosophical nihilisms of the modern age that would far too easily have us rest content with a 'speck of dust' presence in the universe and within whose immensity we find ourselves lost.[6] No wonder Bergson remains deeply unfashionable within contemporary philosophy, with its relinquishment of metaphysics, its linguistic idealism, and its reduction of the world to human perspectivism! Bergson, in fact, breaks with the two major trajectories of modern thought, namely a materialism that would reduce consciousness (perception and memory) to a cerebral state, and an idealism that reduces the movement of matter to our representations. For Bergson, matter goes beyond our representation of it and the understanding cannot be said to design 'the plan of nature' (*MM*, p. 181).

Immanence in Bergson concerns the nature of duration. This is a duration of continuity and heterogeneity which refers to a creative evolution, a 'perpetual creation of possibility and not only of reality' (*CM*, p. 21). A distinction needs to be made between evolution and unfurling, which amounts to the difference between the radically new and a rearrangement of the pre-existing. It is with this crucial distinction that we can locate the specific character of Bergson's thinking of the event. To think the event in Bergson's terms means to contest the idea that, in order for something to gain reality, it must have enjoyed a preceding possible reality. But to think the radically new – to open up the thought of duration – means recognising that even possibility has to be created. Bergson is contesting the idea that things – whether the work of an artist or the works of nature – are pre-existent to their actualisation. To think the future in terms of a creative evolution is to think in terms of the unforeseeable and the incalculable. Possibility does not precede reality, but it 'will have preceded it once it has appeared' (*CM*, p. 101). The event does not arrive out of nowhere for Bergson. If it does not emerge out of a supreme intelligence, whether real or virtual, he says, that it can only emerge out of duration, and duration is invention or it is nothing at all (*CM*, p. 22). Evolution is something different from the realisation of a programme, and the indetermination of freedom amounts to something more than a competition or choice between possibles, since it is the real which makes itself possible and not the possible which becomes real (*CM*, p. 104). Neither philosophy nor theology are able to make the continuous creation of unforeseeable novelty comprehensible, since both traditions of thought partake of a Platonism in which being is conceived as given once and for all, complete and perfect.

Deleuze on Bergsonism and the event

A key issue in any attempt to think duration, including the duration of the event, is that of the nature of multiplicities. Deleuze is a brilliant and incisive reader of Bergson on this question. He insists that the much-lampooned notion of the *élan vital* is, like duration, neither one nor multiple. Rather, it is a type of multiplicity which needs to be thought substantively and no longer adjectivally. Bergson himself elaborates on this crucial point in helpful terms in *Creative Evolution*. He begins by admitting that the comparison of life to an 'impetus' is drawn from the world of psychology rather than physics simply because images we might borrow from the physical world are inadequate for capturing what is, in effect, a virtual unfolding and enfolding of a 'confused plurality of interpenetrating terms'. Only in space is a distinct multiplicity possible in which any point is absolutely external to another. Space and the categories of the understanding can only, therefore, provide us with an abstract unity and an abstract multiplicity. The key insight is the following one:

> While, in its contact with matter, life is comparable to an impulsion or an impetus, regarded in itself it is an immensity of potentiality, a mutual encroachment of thousands and thousands of tendencies which nevertheless are 'thousands and thousands' only when regarded as outside of each other, that is, when spatialized.

Matter divides what is, and what does not cease to be, a 'virtual multiplicity' (in the English version, 'virtuellement multiple' is translated as 'potentially manifold').[7]

In his engagement with set theory in both the *Cinema* books and in *What is Philosophy?*, Deleuze argues that Bergson's attempt to think the virtual whole makes an important contribution to the construction of a plane of immanence, a plane which might be construed as the open system *par excellence*. The crucial point is articulated by Bergson himself in his essay on 'The possible and the real':

> Once more let me say I am perfectly willing to admit that the future states of a closed system of material points are calculable and hence visible in its present state. But, and I repeat, this system is extracted, or abstracted, from a whole which, in addition, to inert and organized matter, comprises organization.
>
> (*CM*, p. 103)

Deleuze draws on this argument when he insists that the whole is not to be confused with a system or series of 'sets' ('ensembles') since these are always sets of parts that impose an artificial closure on things:

> The whole is not a closed set, but on the contrary that by virtue of which the set is never absolutely closed, never completely sheltered, that which keeps it open somewhere as if by the finest thread which attaches to the rest of the universe.
>
> (*C1*, p. 10)

From the conclusion that the 'whole' is neither given nor giveable, the conclusion is not to be drawn that it is a meaningless and entirely abstract notion. On the contrary, if it is not giveable it is because it is the 'open' whose nature is to constantly change and to give rise to the new. This is precisely what Bergson's thinking of duration, with its related insistence on opening up a virtual multiplicity, demonstrates. Of course, the artificial division of a set or a closed system rests on a well founded illusion. It is owing to the organisation of matter itself that there are systems which are relatively closed, while our deployment of spatial habits makes them necessary for us. But it is in terms of extracting moving parts from their relation to the moving whole – a whole which refers to a 'pure, ceaseless becoming' – that the intellect of both common sense and science is able to perform its spatial operations and carry out its diagrammatic designs upon reality. These are diagrams which enact the movement from the virtual to the actual; Deleuze's diagrams work in the opposite direction. Referring to the new aesthetics and technics of the cinema, Deleuze writes: 'Instead of going from the acentred state of things to centred perception, it could go back upwards the acentred state of things, and get closer to it' (*C1*, p. 58). Thinking beyond the human condition means for Deleuze, then, making this move back upwards from the actual to the virtual.

Set theory can only think in terms of actual or spatial multiplicities; the innovation of Bergsonian philosophy is to think *virtual* multiplicities (*WP*, p. 127). Moreover, Bergson's philosophy is able to provide an account of the possibility of set thinking by showing that it represents a specific extraction and abstraction from the plane of immanence. Closed or finite sets are made possible through the exterior nature of the parts of this plane. But it itself is not a set and can escape the contradiction that revolves around the problem and paradox of the 'set of all sets'. What the science of set theory cannot access is the open whole which cuts across the parts of systems and links up different systems, so preventing absolute closure (*C1*, p. 59). In contrast to science – and Bergson was insistent that science was unable to think duration – philosophy has the task of demonstrating the reality of the virtual. Deleuze states the difference in *What is Philosophy?* in terms of set theory's constitution of a 'plane of reference' and philosophy's construction of a plane of immanence or consistency (*WP*, pp. 119–21). Whereas the first plane approaches chaos in terms of a letting go of infinite speed so as to produce an actualisation of the virtual (so inscribing the limit within the infinite itself), the second gives a consistency to the virtual *qua* virtual and moves at the speed of the infinite (the infinite being another way of describing the 'open whole').

For Deleuze, the contribution of Bergson is misrecognised if it is reduced to the proposition that duration is subjective or merely psychological. Rather, subjectivity belongs only to time itself, so that it is sloppy to say that time belongs to us, but there is something profound in the ordinary phrase 'we live in time': time is not the interior in us, but just the opposite, the interiority in which we are, in which we move, live, and change. 'Subjectivity is never ours, it is time, that is, the soul or the spirit, the virtual'.[8] A strange reversal has taken place: it is the actual which is objective, while the virtual is subjective, precisely because it liberates time from necessity, from the brute fact, from mechanical matter. Virtuality is the time of the event even though the event has a complex relation to time. Deleuze calls it a 'dead time', the meanwhile, an infinite awaiting that coexists with the instant and the time of the accident, a possible world; a superimposition of meanwhiles in contrast to a successive time, which is 'real without being actual, ideal without being abstract' (*WP*, p. 156).

These are two thoughts of the event that rely heavily on a notion of the virtual and which attempt to think beyond the human condition. It should be clear, however, that Deleuze departs from Bergson's thinking of the event in terms of duration in some key respects. A key difference concerns how, for both of them, philosophy is to construct the relation between the virtual and the actual. For Bergson, action and perception are geared towards the actual and informed by the life of the body; thinking beyond the human condition (a Darwinian condition in large part) means going beyond this reduction of creative energy to the order of utility (habit and need) and opening up new possibilities of existence and discovering new potentials of energy. But it also requires bringing about the unity of matter and mind, of matter and duration, and of the actual and virtual. Freedom, for Bergson, has its roots in necessity: 'Spirit borrows from matter the perceptions on which it feeds and restores them to matter in the form of movements which it has stamped with its own freedom' (*MM*, p. 249). Thus, when Deleuze refers to *Matter and Memory* as a work of Spinozist inspiration, he is deflecting attention from Bergson's own aim, which was to constitute the conditions of 'properly *human* experience', which involves seeking experience beyond the decisive turn where the bias in the direction of utility is taken (*MM*, p. 184).

In Deleuze's thinking of the event, by contrast, one persists with the virtual. This is the virtual of a pure plane of immanence relieved of any relation to phenomenological or psychological consciousness: 'The event does not relate the lived to a transcendent subject = Self, but, on the contrary, is related to the immanent survey of a field without subject' (*WP*, p. 48). Deleuze construes a 'nonpsychological life of spirit': this is the nonorganic life that grips the world and renders it acentred and rhizomatic, existing not only beyond the sphere of Darwinian adaptation but also beyond the realm of Bergsonian *durée* and creative evolution. Strictly speaking, the event does not belong to the order of either eternity or of time: 'It is there where nothing takes place, an infinite awaiting that is already infinitely past, awaiting and reserve' (*WP*, p. 158). Within virtuality, nothing happens, says Deleuze, although 'everything becomes'. The event is a dead time and an empty time involving not a succession but the superimposition of 'meanwhiles' which communicate through zones of indiscernibility and undecidability. These are the 'variations, modulations, intermezzi, singularities of a new infinite order' (*WP*, p. 158). Only where there is the event is there … a life. And the task of philosophy is defined as nothing less than one of becoming worthy of this event. What concerns are informing this extraordinary thinking of the event?

Thinking the event: immanence or transcendence?

As in the *Cinema* books, the movement of thought in *What is Philosophy?* takes place in terms of a move from the actual to the virtual, that is, in the opposite direction to natural perception. I wish to note some salient features of this text.

1   The task of philosophy when it creates concepts and entities is always to extract an event, to set up a new event from them and to give them a new event: space, time, matter, thought, evolution, the possible, and possible worlds as events. For example, Nietzsche's concept of 'bad conscience', unfolded and complicated in the second essay of the *Genealogy of Morality*, produces, when thought as an event, a new concept of the human: on the one hand, there is an actual evolution of man as the 'sick animal' (constituted through the internalisation of instincts), but

on the other hand there is a virtual becoming, the forces of which, to be made visible, may require new images of thought (the overhuman, or the will to power posited as a non-Darwinian conception of life and conceived from the perspective of the problem of nihilism).

2   The philosophical concept does not refer to the lived, which is a form of the actual, but rather consists in setting up an event that surveys the whole of the lived no less than every state of affairs. The event is actualised in a state of affairs, in a body, and in the lived, but it is not identical with them, since it enjoys a 'shadowy or secret path' that is either subtracted from or added to any actualisation. An event neither begins nor ends but has only infinite movement to which it gives consistency: (without the virtuality of the event, this movement would be amorphous and lifeless). Moreover, even when it is embodied in a state of affairs, the event remains the pure immanence of what is not actualised or what remains indifferent to an actualisation: (the potentials – that is, the intensities and singularities which make up the event – appear to be inexhaustible on this model). So we have a radical contrast drawn between the event and the state of affairs, and it comes to matter greatly how we construe the relation between the two multiplicities. Philosophy chiefly is, in fact, for Deleuze, a theory of multiplicities.

3   The creation of the concept as an event is only possible in terms of the plane of immanence, for only this plane allows for the becoming of the event as a becoming of the infinite. This plane is acentred and is the image that thought gives itself to find its bearing and to create. If concepts are events, this plane is the absolute horizon and reservoir of events – absolute because it is not ruled by an observer or governed by a state of affairs to which it must conform. A relative horizon would function only as a limit, changing with an observer and enclosing some observable state of affairs. The task is to render the event visible and perceptible, which is why it must be created, and can only be created, on this plane. It is not surprising on this model that Deleuze should insist that the event is 'unlivable'.

Alain Badiou has characterised Deleuze's thinking of the event as Bergsonian in the sense that it is an '*élan vital*', what he describes as 'an immanent activity over a background of totality, a creation, a novelty certainly, but thinkable within the interiority of the continuous', both omnipresent and creative, structural and extraordinary.[9] For Badiou, we need a different thinking of the event, in which the 'excess' of the event does not emerge from the 'inexhaustible fullness of the world' but from its not being part of the world or attached to it; it is separated from it and it interrupts it. This separation for him is consistent with a nonorganic mathematicity of the multiple ('nonorganic' because new axioms are always possible). It is the interruption of chance, part of an infinity to come, naming a postexistence that will bring back to the world the pure separated point of the supplement that the event produces. To the flux, he opposes the 'stellar separation of the event', to creative continuity there is opposed the founding break, to evolution and involution (the fold), there is opposed the 'motionless intricacy of the empty set'. In short, for Badiou, the thinking of the event cannot simply remain within the immanence of a description of the life of the world.

Two critical points need to be noted about this characterisation of Deleuze's thinking of the event. The first is to ask whether Deleuze's thinking on this matter is indeed Bergsonian. We could concur with Badiou that it is, in the sense that it is part of a metaphysics of the world in its becoming; but insist that this is not a metaphysics of the event that is bound up with an unpredictable and inventive duration, and which requires 'the continuous progress of the past which gnaws into the future and which swells as it advances' (*CE*, p. 4). We have seen to what extent the event for Deleuze belongs to a quite different order of reality. It is 'immaterial, incorporeal, unlivable, pure *reserve*' (*WP*, p. 156). The reservoir of virtuality which makes the event possible speaks not of a Bergsonian *durée*, but rather of a becoming of the infinite at any moment. Second, Deleuze is not restricting a thinking of the event to a description of the world; there is no world to describe for Deleuze, only possible worlds to be constructed. The emphasis throughout *What is Philosophy?* is on philosophy as a constructivism.

Nevertheless, in spite of these shortcomings, Badiou's reading remains one of the most serious and incisive. Badiou finds himself compelled, perhaps in line with many readers of Deleuze, to withdraw from the attempt to think beyond the human in accordance with the virtual event since, he understandably argues, the sacrifices it demands of us are too great (its burden is too heavy, we might say): the actual is sacrificed for the sake of the virtual, the virtual cannot be lived and is, his contention goes, rendered transcendent in relation to the irreducibly multiple character of actuality and the spontaneous chance of the actual eruptive event.[10] (Badiou's conception of the event is, ironically, closer to Bergson's than Deleuze's, although it is singularly lacking the richness of Bergson's metaphysics). How does Deleuze respond to Badiou on this matter? By returning the accusation of reintroducing transcendence into the world. Badiou's event is the excess of the void, says Deleuze, and, as such, is entirely inexplicable and mysterious. The theory of multiplicities, he argues, does not support the hypothesis of any multiplicity whatever, such as we find, say, in set theory, which even mathematicians are getting tired of, he says. There are, at least, two types of multiplicity that exist face to face, back to back, side by side: namely the actual states of affairs and virtual events; these are not distributed on an errant line but related to two vectors that intersect (history and becoming, for example, or actualised events and absorbed states of affairs) (*WP*, p. 152). The encounter between Badiou and Deleuze is not, then, exactly as Badiou wishes to stage. It is not an encounter between monism and pluralism, or between unity and multiplicity conceived in terms of the problem of the one and the many (see *D*, pp. 114–16).

Of course, Deleuze allows for the fact that it is the event which might *appear* transcendent in relation to an actual state of affairs. This, however, only reveals the need to expose such an illusion. In contrast to science, then, which is informed and restricted by the function (performing an actualisation of various limits and their observation), the philosophy of the concept traverses the opposite direction, although it is not the same line. This is because philosophy for Deleuze creates out of chaos; it does not rest content with a chaotic virtuality but rather with a virtual that has become consistent, 'an entity formed on the plane of immanence that sections the chaos' (*WP*, p. 156). This is the 'site', conceived as an immanent production and creation, of the event, according to Deleuze.

Philosophy, then, is given the critical and constructivist task of providing the actual with more life than the actual makes actualisable or visible. The relation between the virtual and the actual is clearly the crucial issue, and it is clear for Deleuze that the virtual is *not* transcendent in relation to an actual state of affairs, though it can be said to constitute its transcendent*al* condition: '*A state of affairs cannot be separated from the potential through which it takes effect* and without which it would have no activity or development' (*WP*, p. 153). The demonstration of the life of the virtual, of the germinal event, is, I believe, what informs the *contemporaneity* of Deleuze's practice of philosophy. The becoming of the relation between the virtual and the actual cannot, however, be resolved at the abstract level, and Deleuze's project is not attempting to do this. This is why there can be no conclusive or definitive answer to Badiou's questioning. Philosophy is not an imperialist discipline or practice of thought: for Deleuze, we might say, it either succeeds in opening up the world as a becoming-world or it does not. Invent or perish!, it instructs us. The following telling remark from *What is Philosophy?* strikes me as crucial for staging an encounter with the pretensions and predicaments of Deleuzianism in its thinking of the event, its creation of concepts, and its construction of possible worlds:

> It may be that believing in this world, in this life, becomes our most difficult task, or the task of a mode of existence still to be discovered on our plane of immanence today. […] (We have so many reasons not to believe in the human world; we have lost the world, worse than a fiancée or a god …). The problem has indeed changed.
>
> (*WP*, p. 75)

What draws Badiou and Deleuze together is a shared Bergsonian commitment to a philosophical praxis that shows that the gates of the future are wide open; for Deleuze, however, this is not a historical or an evolutionary future, but an infinite now, a becoming, and the complication of possible worlds. The key issue dividing them is whether the new comes from the world or outside it. For Deleuze, the event is, strictly speaking, neither inside the world nor outside, rather it *becomes* with the world and the world exists and evolves only as a *becoming-world*. It is only because there are events and the pure reserve of the virtual that there is a world and that worlds are created and become. What Deleuze calls *extra*-Being is not a transcendence of, or supplement to, Being, but denotes becoming of Being in its very virtuality.

Conclusion: beyond the human condition?

For Bergson, the life of the mind or spirit, which is not to be confused with intelligence, transcends the order of need, habit and action, but it is not for that reason transcendent to either the evolution of nature or the universe. Rather, it is the expression of certain fundamental immanent tendencies of life conceived as a creative evolution. Deleuze ends up, of course, producing his own peculiar and unique conception of evolution in its transhuman dimension. In fact, he prefers to speak of 'creative becomings' rather than of a creative evolution. He writes constantly, for example, of nonhuman becomings of the human (becoming-animal, becoming-plant, becoming-molecular, etc.) and of zones of indiscernibility where things, beasts and people reach a point that precedes their natural differentiation, and a dissolution of form takes place in which what is animal and what is human is no longer known (*WP*, p. 173). This stress on becomings replaces the emphasis on duration and memory that characterises the work of Bergson. For Deleuze, memory is a 'bad word': we 'hate' memory, he writes (*WP*, p. 168). Deleuze, however, does not completely evacuate the territory of memory but continually reworks it: creative fabulation instead of memory (*souvenir*), becomings instead of memories. But both fabulation and becomings are memory thought as the event: 'Combray like it never was, is or will be lived; Combray as cathedral or monument' (*WP*, p. 168). Combray ... *a life*, as Deleuze wrote, at the end of his life, of 'immanence ... a life'.[11]

In Deleuze, the tasks of philosophy are not bound up with going beyond the human condition in the same way that Bergson conceived, which also involved providing an evolutionary account of that condition and opening up the potentialities for a future creative evolution of human existence. For Deleuze, Bergson still too much restricts the movement and event of immanence to lived experience (see *WP*, p. 132, pp. 149–50, p. 157, pp. 209–10). Reducing the life of immanence to the lived is not to leave behind the world of *doxa*, but simply to produce proto-opinions and perceptual and affective clichés about the world, about the brain and the mind, and about the concept. In opposition to both phenomenology and Bergson, then, Deleuze bestows upon philosophy the task of thinking 'absolute deterritorialization', of thinking immanence in absolute terms, which involves the passing of the Earth into a pure plane of immanence of a 'Being-thought' and a 'Nature-thought' composed of infinite diagrammatic movements. Whatever we make of this remarkable conception of philosophy, in terms of the praxis of a life, we should note its essential unfairness as a critical comment on Bergson. Bergson does not reduce the creative evolution or becoming of the universe to our lived experience but simply shows that there is an immanence between them. It is because there is such an immanence that we are not to consider ourselves lost in the immensity of the universe. (Deleuze himself recognises the identity between the duration of a living being and the duration of the universe in admirably clear and succinct terms in the opening pages of *Cinema 1*, making, for me at least, his comments in *What is Philosophy?* somewhat mysterious.)

Deleuze's thinking of the event is motivated by some real concerns bound up with modernity and with the question of the contemporary. To what extent is the event still possible today in a culture devoted to quantity and homogeneity, to manufacturing the real rather than inventing it, and which thinks that creating concepts is equivalent to a marketing exercise? Postmodern readers of Deleuze are right to detect a conservative tone of lament in the text *What is Philosophy?*. But it is also important that we appreciate the reasons informing the lamentation, as well as the constructivist response laid out in the book. The challenge of this response is to ask: what is our plane of immanence today?; and to suggest that it is not simply that of those who no longer believe in God, since this is to still belong to the old plane as a negative moment. A new plane of immanence, then, is to be created and populated by those philosophers and seers who believe in the world and in its possibilities of movement and intensities, 'so as once again to give birth to new modes of existence, closer to animals and rocks' (*WP*, pp. 74–5).

The key question that needs to be asked of Deleuzianism strikes me as the following: to what extent does it rest *in its desire* (the animal, the rock), not on a denial of the human and its finitude (if this was simply the case then philosophy's own event would never happen) but on a denial of duration and of the virtual actuality and multiplicity of creative evolution? It would seem that Deleuze's strenuous and powerful attempt to think beyond the human condition returns us, once again, but no doubt with a new vision, to the peculiar vocation and habitat of this strange and sick animal. It would appear that a 'becoming-nonhuman' marks out the de-territorialised territory that is the peculiar province of the human.

Notes

1 Gilles Deleuze and Félix Guattari, *What is Philosophy?*, trans. H. Tomlinson and G. Burchell (London: Verso, 1994) p. 156. Hereafter referred to as *WP*.
2 Henri Bergson, *Matter and Memory*, trans. N. M. Paul and W. S. Palmer (New York: Zone Books, 1998) p. 19. Hereafter referred to as *MM*.
3 Gilles Deleuze, *Cinema 1: The Movement-Image*, trans. H. Tomlinson and B. Habberjam (London: Athlone Press, 1986). See pp. 62–3. Hereafter referred to as *CI*.
4 Henri Bergson, *Creative Evolution*, trans. A. Mitchell (Lanham: University Press of America, 1983) p. 126. Hereafter referred to as *CE*.

5 Henri Bergson, *The Creative Mind*, trans. M. L. Andison (Totowa: Littlefield, Adams & Co, 1965) p. 135. Hereafter referred to as *CM*.
6 See Henri Bergson, *The Two Sources of Morality and Religion*, trans. R. Ashley Audra and C. Brereton (Indianapolis: University of Notre Dame Press, 1977) pp. 258–9.
7 See Henri Bergson, *Oeuvres* (Paris: PUF, 1963) p. 714; and *CE*, p. 258.
8 Gilles Deleuze, *Cinema 2: The Time-Image*, trans. H. Tomlinson and R. Galeta (London: Athlone Press, 1989) pp. 82–3.
9 Alain Badiou, 'Gilles Deleuze: *The Fold: Leibniz and the Baroque*', trans. Thelma Sowley, in Constantin V. Boundas and Dorothea Olkowski (eds) *Gilles Deleuze and the Theater of Philosophy* (New York and London: Routledge, 1994) pp. 51–69 (p. 60).
10 Alain Badiou, *Deleuze: La Clameur de l'être* (Paris: Hachette, 1997) pp. 69, 136. Hereafter referred to as *D*.
11 See Gilles Deleuze, 'L'Immanence: une vie … ', *Philosophie*, no. 47 (September 1995) pp. 3–7.

12 Why is philosophy so compromised with God?

Philip Goodchild

It's quite curious to what extent philosophy, up to the end of the 17th century, ultimately speaks to us, all the time, of God. [...] Why is philosophy so
compromised with God [*Pourquoi est-ce que la philosophie s'est-elle tellement
compromise avec Dieu*]? And right up to the revolutionary coup of the 18th
century philosophers. Is it a dishonest compromise or something a little
purer?[1]

Thus spoke Deleuze in a seminar on Spinoza. What is not in question for
Deleuze here is that this speaking of God is a compromise; nor does he
explain why it is a compromise.[2] Rather than posing the question historically,
Deleuze seeks a philosophical motivation: why does philosophy choose to
compromise itself with God?

'With God, everything is permitted'. Deleuze draws an analogy with
religious art: painters such as El Greco make use of the divine in order to
liberate lines and colours from the constraints of representation. This
'enfranchisement' of forms is achieved by the subordination of painting to
Christianity:

> So much so that, in a sense, atheism has never been external to religion:
> atheism is the artistic power at work on religion. With God, everything
> is permitted. I have the distinct feeling that for philosophy it's been
> exactly the same thing, and if philosophers have spoken to us so much
> of God – and they could well be Christians or believers – this hasn't
> been lacking an intense sense of jest. It wasn't an incredulous jesting,
> but a joy arising from the labour they were involved in. [...] God and
> the theme of God offered the irreplaceable opportunity for philosophy
> to free the object of creation in philosophy – that is to say concepts –
> from the constraints that had been imposed on them, ... the simple
> representation of things.

> (Seminar, 25 November 1980)

God, in philosophy, functions as a transcendental ideal which incites us to
take thought beyond the limits of possible experience. For in the empirical
employment of concepts in the simple representations of things, concepts

are added to experience in order to make it intelligible, and then found in experience as if belonging there. Representation thus repeats and confirms concepts, as if they were the only proper way to understand experience; it prevents any opportunity of thinking and acting otherwise. To take concepts beyond experience, to encounter them as things 'in a free and wild state',[3] is to allow the possibility of thinking and living otherwise, to allow the very possibility of philosophy as a critical way of thinking.

The danger which the transcendental ideal of God holds for philosophy is that existing values, virtues and ideals may be instantiated by the representation of their most eminent principle: values are added to experience in order to make judgements, and then extracted from experience in the judgements which are made, thus confirming themselves tautologically. For philosophy, just as concepts must be freed from the simple representation of things, they must be freed from a simple representation of values.

'Atheism is the artistic power at work on religion'. One might draw a strange corollary: Deleuze's atheist philosophy of immanence is an artistic (or creative) power at work on theology. Would such philosophy, then, be a dialectical development of theology? Can it be encompassed or recuperated by theology? If so, is philosophy thus compromised by implicit theological judgements? Or does philosophy acquire a full enfranchisement, escaping any prior theological conditioning?

The issue hinges on the nature of causality which is at work in this history of ideas; indeed, it even hinges on the concept of causality at work. The significance of Spinoza, for Deleuze, is that he abandons theological conceptions of causality, pushing the immanent cause to its own limit.[4] Immanent causality abandons the Aristotelian kinesiological principle, *omne quod movetur ab alio movetur* [all that is moved is moved by another],[5] which forms the centre of Thomist understandings of causality and ontology, so that a cause becomes capable of effecting itself.[6] With an immanent cause, 'we no longer know very well how to distinguish cause and effect', that is to say, we are 'treating God and creature as the same' (Seminar, 25 November 1980). Once one arrives at a philosophy of immanence in Spinoza, philosophy becomes its own virtual cause, with its joy arising from its own labour at work on religion.[7]

It is thus reasonable that Deleuze, an atheist, works with theological concepts, 'immanence' and 'transcendence',[8] in order to construct his concept of philosophy.[9] Indeed, the use of the Latin *immanere* enters philosophy from St Augustine, being developed into the concept of an immanent cause within scholasticism. As we will see, there are specific theological reasons for the way in which the groundwork of the concept is elaborated by Duns Scotus. Moreover, the consonance of the Latin stem with that of the Hebrew messianic name, Immanuel (*Isaiah*, 7:14), meaning God-with-us, can never have been far from the mind of the medieval theologians. What is at stake, in a philosophy of immanence, is whether the concept of an immanent cause passes through a threshold of absolute deterritorialisation, taking leave of the historical territory of theology in which it was formed, or whether the philosophy of immanence still explicates God, as in Spinoza. In short, is 'immanence' an immanent or a theological concept?

Immanuel Kant had distinguished between an *immanent* use of principles, confined entirely within the limits of possible experience, a *transcendental* use of principles, employed beyond the limits of experience, and a *transcendent* use of principles, which takes away these limits, 'or even incites us to tear down all those boundary-fences and to seize possession of an entirely new domain which recognizes no limits of demarcation'.[10] Immanence is normally thought correlatively with a transcendental field: an immanent cause goes beyond the limits of possible experience, because we can no longer very well distinguish between cause and effect. Indeed, Deleuze's plane of immanence is also transcendent in the Kantian sense, being not only a presupposition about the nature of thought, but also a matter of being:

> We will say that *THE* plane of immanence is, at the same time, that which must be thought and that which cannot be thought. It is the nonthought within thought. It is the base of all planes, immanent to every thinkable plane that does not succeed in thinking it. It is the most intimate within thought and yet the absolute outside – an outside more distant than any external world because it is an inside deeper than any internal world.
>
> (*What is Philosophy?*, p. 59)

Moreover, the criteria for absolute immanence and absolute transcendence are the same: they consist in removing all pretenders from the role of the absolute. They are ways of thinking the unconditioned as unconditioned without restriction.

Kant had explicated the principle by which reason moves beyond experience: '*if the conditioned is given, the entire sum of conditions, and consequently the absolutely unconditioned* (through which alone the conditioned has been possible) *is also given*' (*Critique of Pure Reason*, p. 386). He envisaged two ways in which the unconditioned could be attained: either every condition in a series is itself conditioned, but the series itself is unconditioned as an infinite series; or else there is a first condition in the series (*Critique of Pure Reason*, p. 391). The unconditioned is synthesised as the Whole or the One. In either case, if an object is sought corresponding to such a transcendental idea of the unconditioned, then a contradiction results when one attempts to think the unconditioned (*Critique of Pure Reason*, pp. 24, 393–421).

Deleuze's plane of immanence is an attempt to think the unconditioned apart from the Whole or the One. For once being is thought in relation to the Whole or the One, the series of conditions are organised into a hierarchy on a transcendent plane – the organisation of essences transcends the existence of individuals. The consequences of such a metaphysics are immediately political: each individual, in order to exist most fully, must attempt to realise its essence which has been established from without by a hierarchy. So, for example, once Plotinus had subordinated being to the One, such a hierarchy is brought into Thomist metaphysics, via St Augustine, Pseudo-Dionysius, and Avicenna's interpretation of Aristotle, so that effects and causes are subordinated to the pure act which is God, and the Christian God becomes the supreme principle of philosophical intelligibility.[11] The political ramifications of such a move are evident when military analogies are drawn on to explicate divine philosophical causality, as in the case of the Averroist, Boetius of Sweden.[12]

On a philosophical plane of immanence, Deleuze attempts to replace series of conditions with sequences of concepts. This is the project of a *pure ontology*, where being is thought without reference to organisation, the Whole, or the One. This pure ontology is anti-hierarchical, a 'world of immanence'.[13] Deleuze finds a first source for this in Duns Scotus, who re-established the firm separation of philosophy from theology by making metaphysics the science of being as such, separable from the One and all other 'transcendentals' such as 'wisdom'.[14] His aim seems to have been the removal of a transcendent plane of organisation from metaphysics. In the decades after the Condemnation of 1277, aimed at the Averroist tendency implicitly to assert the primacy of philosophy over theology, while the Thomist synthesis was temporarily unavailable as a legitimate option for theologians, Scotus needed to safeguard the principle of the absolute power of God, *de potentia Dei absoluta*. His solution was a theological precursor of Kant's 'Copernican revolution' – for if the unconditioned, the transcendent plane of organisation can be understood by the human intellect, then the unconditioned principle of organisation, God, is conditioned by the human intellect, a clear contradiction. There is a danger that the divine will may be restricted by the nature of creatures. To liberate God from metaphysics, Scotus posited a purely univocal thought and being common to God and creatures. This univocity of being, said only in a single sense, involves a refusal to distinguish between 'the knowledge of *whether a thing is* and *what it is*', a metaphysics beyond the dichotomy of essence and existence (*Opus Oxoniense*, Book 1, d. 3, q. 1, p. 605).[15] The emancipation achieved for God by this move, that God's existence is no longer subordinate to God's essence, is then also achieved for creatures as a fortunate by-product. If God is no longer the condition of, yet conditioned by, a transcendent plane of organisation, then neither are creatures conditioned by it.

Scotus did not fully develop the concept of an immanent cause, but he laid the groundwork for it. In his proof for the existence of God, he appears to fall into the Kantian antimony, claiming the existence of the primacy of a first efficient cause, a final end, and a supreme eminence, on the grounds that an ascending infinite regression is impossible (*Opus Oxoniense*, Book 1, d. 3,

q. 1, p. 607). Subsequently, however, he argues that this primary cause, end, and eminence, is infinite, appearing to embrace both sides of the Kantian antimony (*Opus Oxoniense*, Book 1, d. 3, q. 1, p. 611). What is important here is the way in which Scotus creates the concept of the infinite:

> The more perfect and simple concept possible for us is the concept of unqualifiedly infinite being. This is simpler than the concept of good being or true being or others similar to these, since infinity is not, as it were, an attribute of being or of that of which it is said, but predicates an intrinsic mode of that being; so that when I say 'infinite being', I do not have, as it were, an accidental concept from a subject and an attribute, but rather, a concept of the subject itself in a certain grade of perfection, namely infinity – just as 'intense white' does not predicate an accidental concept such as 'visible white'. Rather, intensity predicates an intrinsic degree of whiteness in itself.
>
> (*Opus Oxoniense*, Book 1, d. 3, q. 1, pp. 605–6)

Although Scotus uses an analogy here, in fact infinite being is immanent within being itself; its concept is constructed by a kind of immanent critique, removing all transcendent or comparative determinations or limitations. If the primacy of the infinite is to be absolute, then Scotus does not think God as the first in a series of discrete conditions, but in intensity, metaphysically, as unconditioned causality, end, and eminence. Transcendence is no longer thought in relation to eminence of the One, but is thought in relation to an intrinsic degree of eminence. 'Infinite' is not an attribute added to an existent 'being'. For Scotus, being is the ultimate determinable concept, the pure form of the determinable (*Opus Oxoniense*, Book 1, d. 3, q. 1, p. 618). Infinite being, by contrast, is not simply determinable (as infinite wisdom, love, etc.) but, as infinite, is undetermined by anything else. This indetermination of the infinite is expressed by Scotus as divine liberty.[16] If God is infinite, all other beings are contingent, and the only conceivable link between them is a will. This introduction of the infinite into the divine breaks the bonds of necessity between God and creatures, allowing the essence of creatures to be conceived in terms of contingency, individuality and singularity. Indeed, Deleuze's anarchic political ontology of pre-individual singularities and individuation by haecceity derives directly from Scotus.

The potential for developing the concept of God as an immanent cause was not developed by Scotus. Deleuze regards Spinoza's ontology as a considerable advance over that of Scotus: being becomes an object of pure affirmation. For Scotus, truth is not predicated definitionally of being; it is merely an attribute – so Scotus' metaphysical concepts are substantives, such as 'causality', the 'producible', and 'haecceity'. With Spinoza, 'univocal being becomes identical with unique, universal and infinite substance: it is proposed as *Deus sive Natura*'. Being is identified with infinite being, a substance, not a substantive. Being is also a being. Spinoza modifies Scotus' formal distinction: 'The attributes behave like real qualitatively different senses which relate to substance as if to a single and same designated'; yet, at the same time, Deleuze reads Spinoza through Scotus:

> And substance in turn behaves like an ontologically unique sense in relation to the modes which express it, and inhabit it like individuating factors or intrinsic and intense degrees. From this follows a determination of modes as degrees of power, and a single 'obligation' for such modes: to deploy all their power or their being *within* the limit itself.
>
> (*DR*, p. 40)

The advantage which Deleuze finds in this is political: modes become expressive and affirmative of their being, which is their power. Being becomes a virtual cause, a power of expression. There is, however, a danger in Spinoza that the freedom attained for creatures by Scotus will be replaced by a new dependency: the modes are dependent on substance (*DR*, p. 40), a single cause. Deleuze specifically tries to remove the idea of the single substance in Spinoza, replacing it with a plane of immanence which is the transcendental field of metaphysics as created by Scotus, now become affirmative, expressing a power. In fact, Deleuze's interpretation of the Spinozist modes – that they are defined by an intensive degree of power – is a direct imposition of Scotist ontology onto a concept where Spinoza himself is far from clear.[17] The danger of Deleuze's use of Spinoza and Scotus is that the concept of God may be smuggled back in.

Pure ontology only finds its truly atheist moment in Nietzsche. Deleuze interprets Nietzsche's doctrine of eternal return not as a cosmological hypothesis, but in a transcendental sense, as a solution to the Kantian problem of moving beyond experience by synthesising a series of conditions so as to attain the unconditioned condition of possible experience. If the series of conditions is subject to recurrence, then there is no place for a first term or any need for an infinite series, for the One or the Whole. Since the series returns on itself, conditions itself, and not as any originary term or as a whole, then it is the repetition of difference, the self-differentiating of the series itself, which liberates a pure ontology from dependence on the Whole or One. Eternal return is the being of an immanent cause; becoming is its mode of being (*DR*, p. 41). All dependence is eliminated, and contingency fully affirmed. A new 'obligation' for modes is determined by selection: modes do not merely deploy their power to the limit; they will only be selected if they are excessive, going beyond the limit, transforming themselves into something else (*DR*, p. 41). Instead of constructing the infinite by removing limitation,[18] repetition is affirmed of that which transgresses limitation, which 'tears down all those boundary-fences' and seizes 'possession of an entirely new domain which recognizes no limits of demarcation'.

The cost of this atheist ontology is a loss of individual modes. Repetition is only said of difference: it is not the modes which return in their individuation of each other, but the 'modal essence' of each corresponding mode, which is distinct from it (*EP*, p. 195). This 'modal essence' is not a possibility, but a physical, virtual reality, an intensive quantity:

> Only a quantitative distinction of beings is consistent with the qualitative identity of the absolute. And this quantitative distinction is no mere appearance, but an internal difference, a difference in intensity. So that each finite being must be said to *express the absolute*, according to the intensive quantity that constitutes its essence, according, that is, to the degree of its power.
>
> (*EP*, p. 197)

Deleuze draws on Scotus' analogy with intense white (*EP*, p. 196; *DR*, p. 39). Intensity can only be known through its representation: 'Intensity is only known as already developed within an extensity' (*DR*, p. 223). Intensity is not normally known in itself, in its original depth, as the absolute. Since intensity always cancels itself in its expression, while at the same time remaining implicated within itself, the highest degree of intensity will be its zero degree of development in extension. Deleuze invokes the concept of the 'body without organs' as a univocal, neuter being in relation to which intensity will be measured. Thus the body without organs 'is nonstratified, unformed, intense matter, the matrix of intensity, intensity = 0' (*A Thousand Plateaus*, p. 153).[19] Since each mode is merely a modification of that neuter being, its mode of determination is purely quantitative. *The concept of intensity is created as quantitative only in relation to representation*; this is merely its *ratio cognoscendi* in relation to a neuter being.

Philosophy thus attains intensity, produces intensity, but such intensity is the unthought within thought. Once produced, each intensity can only be expressed in philosophy as an abstract concept. When reading a philosopher, one finds nothing of the intensity, vitality and creativity which has surged through thought in the concepts themselves, unless one is able to bring thought back to life by working through the concepts oneself. For pure ontology, being simply remains the pure form of the determinable; it does not attain the intensive determinations which arise when it is thought. In defining intensity in relation to zero, Deleuze repeats the Kantian move of determining transcendental ideas, the form of intensity, as indeterminable, as problematic. The transcendental field, the pure plane of immanence, necessarily escapes consciousness because, in immanence, there is nothing which can reveal it ('Immanence: a life ... ', p. 3). It contains only virtuals. Deleuze calls it *a life*, that is, a determinable life, a life which determines itself as an immanent cause.

Yet, when Deleuze writes that 'the virtuals communicate immediately above the actual which separates them',[20] epitomising the extent to which the action always happens out-of-frame in his philosophy (from the philosophical commentaries, through the co-authorship with Guattari, to the cinema books), then his work sounds like a theology of the indeterminable. Being, liberated from the Whole or the One, is thought in relation to the Indeterminate. As such, there is a resonance here with Scotus' theology of the infinite being. Unrestricted affirmation is achieved by removing determinations at the most impersonal level of thought.

By contrast to these scholastic considerations, one of the most personal moments in Deleuze's oeuvre is to be found in his television interviews, *L'Abécédaire*,[21] when Claire Parnet, out of long personal experience, asks under the topic of 'joy' why Deleuze, as a philosopher of affirmation, complains all day long. Deleuze says that if he had not been a philosopher, he would have been a professional wailer (*une pleureuse*). A complaint, he says, can conceal joy; it can be 'an adoration, like a prayer'. It says, 'What's happening is too great for me' [*Ce qui m'arrive est trop grand pour moi*]. One passes the limits of experience, for Deleuze, not by formulating a transcendental idea, as in Kant, but by encountering within experience something which is 'too great'. The indeterminable, for Deleuze, is the 'too great': 'an immanent life that is pure power and even beatitude through the sufferings and weaknesses' ('Immanence: a life ... ', p. 5).

Let us return, then, to the problem of taking thought beyond the limits of possible experience, the very problem of creation in philosophy, the very question of philosophy itself.[22] If this is done by constituting metaphysics as the science of being *qua* being, following Avicenna and Scotus, then the transcendental field is constituted within thought alone, and being itself remains forever problematic or indeterminable. Modal distinction is quantitative when what is distinguished lacks intensity, is neuter. Just as Scotus thinks metaphysics in relation to an abstract and neuter being, and just as Kant schematises thought in terms of time defined as an abstract linear succession, Deleuze seems to construct his ontology around determinations of such a neuter being, or such a pure and empty form of time, or in relation to a zero degree of intensity.

There is, however, an alternative way of reading Scotus the theologian. While neuter being has a certain primacy over all other concepts, the primacy of commonness and virtuality (*Opus Oxoniense*, Book 1, d. 3, q. 3, p. 618), infinite being, as an intrinsic mode of being, has the primacy of eminence and perfection over being. There thus remains an objective uncertainty in the way in which Scotist metaphysics is to be understood – whether neuter being is privileged over God, leading to the independence of philosophy from theology, or whether God is privileged over neuter being, in the sense that the final cause of metaphysics is knowledge of God, subordinating philosophy to piety, even if not to theology. Following Scotus' emphasis on infinite being, one can thus comprehend intensity, no longer in relation to degree zero, but in the mode by which infinite being is implicated within that mode. Each finite being may then be said to express the infinite according to the intensity that constitutes its essence. Such a determination of intensities is neither qualitative, as in St Thomas' hierarchy of essences based on analogy, nor quantitative, as in Deleuze.

Infinite, intensive being is simply the mode by which the infinite is implicated within that mode. Here, the infinite is indeterminable in relation to a determinate mode of determination, possibly determinable in relation to an undetermined mode of determination, and actually determined in relation to itself, where 'itself' designates the infinite. As such, the infinite is the immanent cause of being. On the one hand, the infinite is only said of its modes; on the other hand, the modes themselves are infinite determinations. Thus modes, instead of being defined in relation to a zero degree, are defined in relation to the intensive modes which they implicate.

To transcend the limits of possible experience is not simply to abstract thought; it is to rediscover the real determinations of experience as themselves transcendental conditions of possible experience. On a plane of immanence, the transcendental becomes objective while the object becomes a transcendental. So, for example, one does not abstract being from wisdom as the matter for thinking, without rediscovering a determinate mode of wisdom as an intensity, a condition of possibility for abstract thinking. The need for wisdom returns when the virtual is no longer regarded as that which completely and necessarily determines our modes of existence, but as admitting a certain degree of contingency within the virtual. Instead of the contingency of intensive quantities, which is a world of chaos, we now have the contingency of responsibility – where one's mode of transcending the limits of experience is an ethical gesture. Then the question of being is inseparable from the question of wisdom: the univocity of being develops into a strange monism where ontology, ethics and theology are identified. For to raise the question of transcendence *qua* transcendence, even if encountered implicitly as an intensive mode on a plane of immanence, is to raise a theological question. In its most rigorous purity, philosophy finds itself once more compromised with God.

Notes

1 Gilles Deleuze, Seminar, 25 November 1980, trans. Timothy S. Murphy, at website: http://www.imaginet.fr/deleuze/TXT/ENG/251180.html.
2 The four great illusions of philosophy described by Deleuze each recall the elaboration of the concept of God in philosophy deriving from Christian thought: the illusions of transcendence, of universals, of the eternal, and of discursiveness. See Gilles Deleuze and Félix Guattari, *What is Philosophy?*, trans. H. Tomlinson and G. Burchell (London: Verso, 1994) p. 49.
3 Gilles Deleuze, *Difference and Repetition*, trans. Paul Patton (London: Athlone, 1994) p. xx. Hereafter referred to as *DR*.
4 Thus Spinoza begins the *Ethics* with a definition of *causa sui*, the cause of itself, which is a meaningless concept for the Thomists.
5 See Thomas Aquinas, *Summa Theologiae*, Ia, q. 2, a. 3.

6 Stephen Crocker has explored the significance of this move for Deleuze in a paper, 'Ab alio movetur: on Deleuze's reversal of time and movement', delivered at the 'Rhizomatics, Genealogy, Deconstruction' Conference, Trent University, May 1999.

7 Deleuze himself would appear to be among those least concerned with religion of his own generation. Nevertheless, the philosophical tradition to which he is the heir has formed itself in its work performed on religion – this is evident above all in the work of Spinoza, Leibniz, Hume, Kant, Marx, Nietzsche, Freud and Bergson. This heritage is re-dramatised in Deleuze's work in the confrontation of immanence with transcendence.

8 There are no entries for 'immanence' and 'transcendence' in the recently published *Routledge Encyclopedia of Philosophy*, ed. Edward Craig (London: Routledge, 1998) whereas entries do feature in Mircea Eliade (ed.) *Encyclopedia of Religion* (London: Macmillan, 1993).

9 See especially Gilles Deleuze and Félix Guattari, *A Thousand Plateaus*, trans. Brian Massumi (London: Athlone, 1988) pp. 265–72; Gilles Deleuze and Félix Guattari, *What is Philosophy?* (London: Verso, 1994) chapter 2; Gilles Deleuze, 'Immanence: a life ... ', *Theory, Culture & Society*, 14, 2 (May 1997) pp. 3–7.

10 Immanuel Kant, *Critique of Pure Reason* (Basingstoke: Macmillan, 1929) p. 299.

11 *Deus est esse omnium, non essentiale, sed causale* [God is the essence of all, not essentially, but causally]. Thomas Aquinas, I *Sentences*, d. 8, q. 1, a. 2. Etienne Gilson brings out the full consequences of this move, as cited by Eric Alliez, *Capital Times* (Minneapolis: University of Minnesota Press, 1996) pp. 192–3.

12

This Prime Principle is to this world as the father of a family is to his house, the commander is to his army and the common weal to the City. And just as the army is one in the unity of its chief, and as the good of the army is in its chief intrinsically, and in the others only according to rank, so also the unity of this world is intrinsically in this Prime Principle, but it is in the other beings of this world only according to their participation in this Prime Principle and to their rank in relation to it, so that there is not, in any being in this world, any good which is not a sharing in the Prime Principle. [...] As to the said Prime Principle, it is God, the glorious, the sublime, who is blessed throughout the centuries. *Amen*.

(Boetius of Sweden, as cited in Etienne Gilson, *History of Christian Philosophy in the Middle Ages* [London: Sheed and Ward, 1955] pp. 400–1)

13 See Gilles Deleuze, Seminar, 12 December 1980.

14 See Duns Scotus, *Philosophical Writings* (Edinburgh: Thomas Nelson, 1962) pp. 1–12. In Deleuze scholarship, Scotus' doctrine of the univocity of being is occasionally confused with that which it opposes, a neoplatonised metaphysics in which there is One Being. Scotus specifically argues that the determinable concept of being and the ultimate differentia such as 'one' are primarily diverse, so that one includes nothing of the other. Duns Scotus, *Opus Oxoniense*, Book 1, d. 3, q. 3, in Arthur Hyman and James J. Walsh (eds) *Philosophy in the Middle Ages* (Indiana: Hackett, 1973) p. 618.

15 Indeed, we may note in passing that such a metaphysics cuts through the heart of Kant's critique of proofs for the existence of God, since we no longer have to admit, 'as every reasonable person must, that all existential propositions are synthetic' (*Critique of Pure Reason*, p. 504).

16 Scotus explores contingency through the will of both God and creatures: 'There is no reason why this agent has this mode of action (i.e. free, though necessary) except that it is that sort of active principle' (Duns Scotus, *God and Creatures: The Quodlibetal Questions*, trans. Felix Alluntis and Allan B. Wolter [Princeton: Princeton University Press, 1975] 16.46, p. 385). Scotus thus has an 'immanent' conception of the will.

17 See Gilles Deleuze, *Expressionism in Philosophy: Spinoza* (New York: Zone, 1990) p. 196, hereafter referred to as *EP*; see also Gilles Deleuze, *Difference and Repetition* (London: Athlone, 1994) p. 39.

18 Deleuze immediately goes on to discuss the work of Hegel and Leibniz as having proceeded the furthest in this regard. See Gilles Deleuze, *Difference and Repetition* (London: Athlone, 1994) pp. 42–50.

19 See also Gilles Deleuze and Félix Guattari, *Anti-Oedipus*, trans. Robert Hurley, Mark Seem and Helen R. Lane (London: Athlone, 1984) p. 21.

20 Gilles Deleuze, 'L'actuel et le virtuel', *Dialogues* (Paris: Flammarion, 1996) p. 185.

21 Gilles Deleuze, *L'Abécédaire* (edited videotape of filmed discussions between Deleuze and Claire Parnet, directed by Pierre-André Boutang, broadcast on Arte channel between 1994 and 1995) Vidéo Editions Montparnasse, 1996.

22 'So, the question of philosophy is the singular point where the concepts and its creation are related to each other' (Gilles Deleuze and Félix Guattari, *What is Philosophy?* [London: Verso, 1994] p. 11).

13　The doctrine of univocity

Deleuze's ontology of immanence

Daniel W. Smith

'If God does not exist, everything is permissible.' Deleuze likes to invert this Dostoyevskian formula from *The Brothers Karamazov*, because, he says, the opposite is in fact the case: it is *with* God that everything is permissible. This is obviously true morally, since the worst atrocities have always managed to find a divine justification, and belief in God has never been a guarantor of morality. But it is also true aesthetically and philosophically. Medieval art, for example, is filled with images of God, and it would be tempting to see this merely as an inevitable constraint of the era, imposed from without by the Church. Deleuze suggests a different hypothesis. In the hands of great painters like El Greco, Tintoretto and Giotto, this constraint became the condition of a radical emancipation: in painting the divine, one could take literally the idea that God must not be represented, an idea that resulted in an extraordinary liberation of line, colour, form, and movement. With God, painting found a freedom it would not have had otherwise – a properly pictorial atheism.[1]

The same was true in philosophy. Until the revolution of the eighteenth century, philosophers were constantly speaking of God, to the point where philosophy seemed completely compromised by theology and the demands of the Church. But, in the hands of great philosophers such as Spinoza and Leibniz, this constraint became the condition of an equally extraordinary liberation. With God, philosophical concepts were freed from the traditional task that had been imposed on them – the representation of things – and allowed to assume fantastic dimensions. With the concept of God, everything was permissible. Or almost everything, for thinkers (like Spinoza) who went too far with the concept, or went too fast, often did so at their own peril. Deleuze thus harbours neither the antagonism of the 'secular' who find the concept of God outmoded, nor the angst or mourning of those for whom the loss of God was crisis-provoking, nor the faith of those who would like to retrieve the concept in a new form. He remained fascinated with theological concepts, and regarded medieval theologians in particular as a magnificent breed of thinkers who were able to invent, in the name of God, remarkable systems of logic and physics. Indeed, at several points in his writings, he picked up on certain 'heretical' paths of theological thought closed off by orthodoxy and seemingly abandoned, and set them to work philosophically in a different context.

Deleuze's appropriation of the medieval concept of univocity is the most obvious and important example of this unorthodox use of the Christian theological tradition. The doctrine of the 'univocity of Being' was an ontological theory developed in the thirteenth century by Duns Scotus, following Henry of Ghent, in his magnum opus entitled *Opus Oxoniense*, which Deleuze calls 'the greatest book of pure ontology'.[2] In the Middle Ages, univocity was a heterodox position, constantly at the borders of heresy, and had limited currency outside the Scotistic school (the English word 'dunce' is derived from the term of approbation used to describe the followers of Duns Scotus).[3] The concept has a rather curious history in Deleuze's own work. The term was not even mentioned before 1968, when univocity suddenly became an important theme in almost all of Deleuze's writings. It first appears in *Expressionism in Philosophy: Spinoza*, where it forms the 'keystone' of Deleuze's interpretation of Spinoza (even more than the title concept of 'expression').[4] It then assumes an even more prominent role in *Difference and Repetition* and in *The Logic of Sense*, where Deleuze not only identifies an entire tradition of univocity in the history of philosophy, running from Duns Scotus (against Thomism) through Spinoza (against Cartesianism) to Nietzsche (against Hegelianism), but also presents his own ontology as a univocal ontology, thereby, as it were, identifying himself as the most recent inheritor of that tradition. And then, equally abruptly, and without explanation, the concept disappears, almost without a trace; it is scarcely mentioned in any of Deleuze's subsequent works.

What role does the doctrine of univocity play in Deleuze's thought? And why does the concept have such a short-lived but intense trajectory in Deleuze's writings, like a flashing meteor? Despite Deleuze's provocative claim, there is no 'tradition' of univocity in the history of philosophy, apart from the one he himself creates; there is hardly a secondary literature on the concept outside of Scotistic studies. Deleuze was more accurate when he remarked, in a seminar, that univocity is 'the strangest thought, the most difficult to think, *if it has ever been thought*'.[5] In what follows, I attempt to follow the life of this 'strange' concept as it appears, matures, and then passes away within the flow of Deleuze's thought, creating unexpected 'traversals' between otherwise disconnected thinkers and problems. Were one to 'dramatise' the movement of the concept, it could perhaps be staged in four separate acts.

Act One would take us back to the medieval articulations of the concept. For Duns Scotus, as for many Scholastic philosophers, the object of theology was God, while the object of philosophy, or rather of the metaphysics crowning it, was *Being* as Being. In developing his theory of univocity, Duns Scotus was injecting himself into a lively thirteenth-century debate concerning the nature of Being: Being is said of beings, but in what sense? The Scholastics used three precise terms to designate the various ways of resolving the problem: equivocity, univocity and analogy. To say that Being is equivocal means that the term 'Being' is said of beings in several senses, and that these senses have no common measure: 'God is' does not have the same sense as 'man is', for instance, because God does not have the same type of being as man. By contrast, to say that Being is univocal, as Duns Scotus affirmed, means that Being has only one sense, and is said *in one and the same sense* of everything of which it is said, whether it be God or man, animal or plant. Since these positions seemed to lead to scandalous conclusions – (equivocity denied order in the cosmos, univocity implied pantheism) – a third alternative was developed between these two extremes: Being is neither equivocal nor univocal but analogical. This became the position of Christian orthodoxy, as formulated by Thomas Aquinas: there is indeed a common measure to the forms of Being, but this measure is analogical, and not univocal.

Why did Deleuze revisit this seemingly obscure Scholastic debate? The answer seems clear: the three books Deleuze published in 1968–9 (*Expressionism in Philosophy: Spinoza, Difference and Repetition* and *The Logic of Sense*) mark, among other things, the culmination of Deleuze's confrontation with Heidegger. This confrontation had been present in Deleuze's work from the start, even if Heidegger's name receives only passing mention in the texts.[6] As always, Deleuze brings a *contemporary* problematic to bear on his work in the *history* of philosophy. Heidegger (who wrote his own thesis on Duns Scotus) famously inaugurated the modern renaissance of ontology by posing the question of the 'ontological difference': what is the difference between Being and beings? Or, more precisely: how is Being distributed among beings? During the Middle Ages, this ontological problem had been intertwined with a similar, though not identical, set of theological questions: what is the difference between God and his creatures? Or put logically, in terms of the 'divine names' tradition: in what sense can we predicate of God the same terms (e.g. goodness) that we use of his creatures? The concept of univocity was situated at the nexus of this complex set of philosophical and theological questions.

According to Deleuze, however, although Heidegger revived the question of ontology and gave 'renewed splendor to the univocity of Being', he did not effect the necessary conversion according to which 'univocal Being belongs only to *difference*' (*DR*, p. 66).[7] Heidegger, in other words, was unable, or perhaps unwilling, to push the problematic of ontological difference to its necessary conclusion. This is the project that Deleuze takes up as his own in *Difference and Repetition*. In this sense, univocity must be seen as one of the concepts Deleuze uses in order to state and resolve Heidegger's ontological problematic in his own manner. For Deleuze, the only pure and fully realised ontology *must* be a univocal ontology, and only a univocal ontology is capable of thinking difference-in-itself, or of providing difference with its own concept. As Foucault put it, in his well known essay on Deleuze, the univocity of Being is 'the principal condition which permits difference to escape the domination of identity'.[8] But this link between univocity and difference might seem obscure: if Being is univocal, what constitutes the *difference* between beings? Why does a philosophy of difference require a univocal ontology?

In the second act, Deleuze begins to respond to these questions by turning, not to Duns Scotus, who plays the role of a precursor, but rather to Spinoza, who, according to Deleuze, gave the concept of univocity its fullest expression. 'Univocity', Deleuze claims, 'is the keystone of Spinoza's entire philosophy' – even though the word does not appear even once in Spinoza's texts.[9] Deleuze, however, often employs this 'topological' method in his historical monographs: when he interprets Bergson in terms of the concept of 'difference' (as formulated by Heidegger), or Leibniz in terms of a theory of 'singularities' (borrowed from Albert Lautmann), or Spinoza in terms of 'univocity' (imported from Duns Scotus), he is using a 'foreign' concept, not explicitly formulated by the thinkers at hand, to bring out aspects of their thought that might otherwise remain obscure.

Deleuze's affinity with Spinoza here is not incidental. Heidegger himself wrote notoriously little on Spinoza – a surprising omission, it would seem, since the *Ethics* is a work of pure ontology that poses the problem of ontological difference in terms of the difference between infinite substance (Being) and finite modes (beings). Deleuze's work on Spinoza, from this viewpoint, can be read as his means of working through the problematic of ontological difference in a new manner, just as *Difference and Repetition* could be read as a response to *Being and Time* (for Deleuze, Being is difference, and time is repetition). Where Heidegger returns to the Greeks (the origin), Deleuze turns to Spinoza (the middle). According to Deleuze, univocity assumes three figures in Spinoza's philosophy: univocity of the attributes, univocity of cause, and univocity of modality; they are the three important scenes of the second act. The first two, however, are particularly important in showing how Spinoza overturned the medieval theological tradition, at the price of his condemnation.

In the Middle Ages, as Heidegger says, ontology became an onto-theo-logy: the question of the Being of beings tended to be forgotten in favour of the thought of God as the supreme (ontic) being. The Christian concept of God was the inheritor of the Platonic 'Good' and the neoplatonic 'One', which were 'above' or 'beyond' Being (*hyperousios, epikeina tes ousias*), that is, transcendent to Being. Christian theology thus oscillated between a double requirement: *immanence* (the ontological requirement that the first principle be a *being*) and *transcendence* (the more powerful requirement that the transcendence of God be maintained, as the One *beyond* Being). The 'divine names' tradition, in turn, was concerned with the manner in which the traditional divine attributes (e.g. goodness, love, wisdom, power, etc.) could be predicated of God – negatively or positively? As conditional affirmations, or negations marking the ablation of some privation? The Christian tradition identified two extreme (and heterodox) responses to this question: pure transcendence would imply the equivocity of terms; pure immanence, their univocity. Between these two poles, orthodoxy developed a *via media* approach to the problem, centred in large part on the strategies of negation, eminence and analogy. These five ways – equivocity, negation, eminence, analogy, univocity – entered into historically varying combinations in Christian thought, though two general approaches assumed the status of orthodoxy: a way of negation and a way of affirmation.

The way of negation, which came to be called 'negative theology' (following Pseudo-Dionysius), admits that affirmations are able to designate God as cause, subject to rules of immanence, but insists that God as substance or essence can only be defined negatively, according to rules of transcendence. Meister Eckhart, for instance, prefers to say 'God is not' rather than 'God is', because 'x is' is a statement that is said of beings, whereas God is eminently superior to Being, beyond Being.[10] This allows God to appear in his 'supra-substantial' or 'supra-essential' eminence, as far from all negation as from all affirmation. Negative theology can therefore be defined by its dynamics: one goes beyond affirmations (God is good) via negations (God is not good in the human sense of the term), and beyond both affirmations and negations to attain God's *eminence* (God is good with an 'incomparable' or 'ineffable' goodness). By contrast, a theology with more positive ambitions, like that of Thomas Aquinas, relies on *analogy* to found new affirmative rules. Positive qualities can indeed belong to God substantially, but only insofar as they are treated 'analogically', either in terms of an ordered relationship between two proportions, e.g. the divine goodness is to God as human goodness is to man (analogy of proportionality); or by reference to a focal meaning or 'prime analogate' e.g. 'goodness,' which God possesses eminently and creatures only derivatively (analogy of proportion). The way of affirmation must likewise be defined by a specific dynamic: it maintains the strength of the negative and the eminent, but comprehends them within analogy.[11]

The audacity of Spinoza's 'heresy' was to have rejected both these orthodox approaches – the negative and the positive, the apophatic and kataphatic – and to have set against them the heterodox doctrine of the univocity of the divine attributes. For Spinoza, we know only two of God's infinite attributes (thought and extension), and these attributes are common forms predicable univocally of *both* God and his creatures. Though formally distinct, the attributes are ontologically univocal. To say that the attributes are univocal means, for example, that it is in the *same* form that bodies imply extension, and that extension is an attribute of the divine substance (the position of immanence). If Spinoza radically rejects the notions of eminence, equivocity, and even analogy, it is because they imply that God possesses these perfections in a form *different* from that implied in his creatures, a 'higher' form (the position of transcendence). Spinoza's genius lies in his having provided a profound explanation for his rejection of these orthodox positions: the problem they were attempting to solve, he says, was an altogether false one, and this for two reasons.

On the one hand, as Spinoza argues in the *Short Treatise*, theologians had tended to confuse God's attributes with his *propria*. Following Aristotle, Spinoza defines a *proprium* as that which belongs to a thing, *but can never explain what it is*. The attributes that have traditionally been ascribed to God are not attributes, Spinoza explains, but mere *propria*. They reveal *nothing* of the divine essence. The *Short Treatise* distinguishes three types of *propria* of God: the first type are modalities of the divine essence that must be affirmed of all God's attributes (cause of itself, infinite, perfect, immutable, eternal, necessary, etc.), or of a specific attribute (omniscience is affirmed of thought; omnipresence is affirmed of extension); the second type are those that qualify God in reference to his products or creations (cause of all things, predestination, providence); the third type, finally, do not even belong to God, but designate extrinsic determinations that merely indicate the way we imagine God, failing to comprehend his true nature (justice, charity, compassion). The basic error of theology is that it confuses God's essence with these *propria*, and this confusion pervades the entire language of eminences, negations and analogies. When *propria* are given a substantial value that they do not have, the divine substance is given an inexpressible nature that it does not have either. And this error, in turn, has compromised the whole of philosophy. Even Descartes was content to define God as infinite perfection, though perfection and infinity are merely modalities of the divine essence (*propria* of the first type).[12]

On the other hand, Spinoza offers a genetic account of this theological error in the *Tractatus Theologico-Politicus*. Why was the nature of God denatured in this way? Because, Spinoza explains, his predecessors lacked a proper *historico-critical method* for interpreting Scripture. They simply presumed that God had revealed his nature in Scripture. But in fact, the aim of Scripture is to give us models of life, to make us obey, and to ground our obedience through its warnings, commandments and rules. 'Revealed theology' concerns itself exclusively with *propria* of the third type, which appeal to our imaginations to make us serve a God of whose nature we remain ignorant. As for God's true attributes (thought and extension), they are made known through the light of Nature, not revelation. The nature of God is made manifest in the order of Nature, not in the teachings of the Bible. Spinoza likes to remind us that the prophets were men with vivid imaginations but weak understandings: Adam, Abraham, and Moses were not only ignorant of the true divine attributes, but also of most of the *propria* of the first and second type.[13] According to Harry Wolfson, the *Tractatus* overturned a long hermeneutical tradition that had been inaugurated centuries earlier by Philo: after Spinoza, Scripture could and would no longer be treated as a properly *philosophical* authority.[14]

The univocity of the attributes entails the absolute immanence of God and Nature, *Deus sive natura*, stripping God of any transcendence (it matters little whether this is understood as pantheism or atheism). What Deleuze finds in Spinoza, prior to Hume and Kant's critiques of theology, or even Nietzsche's 'death of God', is a quiet and confident philosophy of immanence, the consequences of which he will pursue throughout his writings. But already, one can sense Deleuze manoeuvring between Scylla and Charybdis: univocity is as opposed to the negative eminence of the neoplatonists as to the positive analogies of the Thomists, both of which have their modern counterparts.

The second figure of univocity Deleuze finds in Spinoza is the univocity of cause: God is cause of all things *in the same sense* that he is cause of himself. Broadly speaking, medieval philosophy distinguished between three types of causes: a transitive cause, an emanative cause, and an immanent cause. A *transitive* cause is a cause that leaves itself in order to produce, and what it produces (its effect) is outside of itself. Christianity held to the idea of a real distinction between God and the world: if God created the world, and the world is exterior to God, then God must come out of himself in order to create the world; it therefore needed to see God as a purely transitive cause (creationism). An *emanative* cause, by contrast, is a cause whose effect is exterior to it, but which nonetheless remains within itself in order to produce its effect. The sun, for example, remains within itself in order to produce, but what it produces (light) comes out of it. Such metaphors of luminosity are frequent in Plotinus and the neoplatonists, who pushed an emanative conception of cause to its furthest point. An *immanent* cause, finally, is a cause that not only remains within itself in order to produce, but one whose produced effect also remains within it. This is the conception of causality developed by Spinoza.

Here again, Christian theology adopted a syncretic solution: is God a transitive cause, an emanative cause, or an immanent cause?[15] Orthodoxy insisted that God is a transitive cause, transcendent to the world (creation *ex nihilo*). How then does God create the world? He would have to have a model or idea of the world in his understanding, and he would create the world, in conformity with this model, through a free act of the divine will. But this is a fully immanent causality: the model or idea must remain in God's understanding, and God must remain in himself in order to contemplate it. To reconcile these two movements, one requires the idea of an emanative causality between the model of the world in God's understanding and the real world produced in conformity with this model. Medieval thinkers consequently had to combine the three types of causality in varying permutations. The idea of an immanent causality, Deleuze suggests, functioned as a kind of internal theoretical limit for philosophers and theologians up to the Renaissance (Nicholas of Cusa, Erigena, Bruno, Eckhart) – a limit, however, that was always repulsed, out of a concern to avoid pantheism, through the doctrines of creation (by a transcendent being above his creatures) and emanation (from a transcendent One beyond Being). Spinoza was the sole thinker to take causality to this immanent limit, at the price of his condemnation.

What are the consequences of an immanent causality? In an emanative causality, the One is the cause of Being, but the cause (the One) remains beyond its effect (Being). This is the sense of Plotinus' notion of the *gift*: Being is a gift or donation of the One, but the One necessarily remains beyond Being. Ontologically, the universe is in this way rendered hierarchical – beings having more or less reality depending on their distance from or proximity to the One as the transcendent first principle (the 'great chain of Being'). Morally, it allows Being to be judged because there is an authority higher than Being itself (the 'system of judgement'). The One is thus inseparable from a negative theology or a method of analogy, which are required to maintain this eminence of the cause. Heidegger seems to have remained tied to a certain conception of eminence in his famous lecture on 'Time and Being,' where he developed the theme of the *es gibt*, that is, the 'gift' (*Gabe*) of time and Being by the It.[16] Jacques Derrida, in his later works, has moved towards a philosophy of transcendence, influenced by Levinas and linked to the theme of a negative theology.[17]

Deleuze has followed a very different path. In Spinoza's immanent causality, not only does the cause remain in itself, but its effect remains 'immanate' within it, rather than emanating from it. The effect (mode) remains in its cause no less than the cause remains in itself (substance). Hence Deleuze's fondness for the 'expressionistic' Renaissance notions of *complicare* and *explicare*, which he adopts for his own purposes in *Difference and Repetition*: all things are present to God, who complicates them, and God is present to all things, which 'explicate' and 'implicate' him. In an immanent ontology, Being necessarily becomes univocal: not only is Being equal in itself, it is equally and immediately present in all beings, without mediation or intermediary. There is no distant cause, no 'chain of Being', no hierarchy, but rather a kind of anarchy of beings within Being. 'The rock, the lily, the beast, the human equally sing the glory of God in a kind of crowned anarchy'.[18] One must not be led astray (as Alain Badiou seems to have been) by the prefix 'uni' in the term 'univocity': a univocal ontology is by definition irreconcilable with a philosophy of the One, which necessarily entails an equivocal concept of Being.[19]

These then, in brief, are the three figures of univocity Deleuze identifies in Spinoza: the univocity of the attributes (the attributes are said in one and the same sense of God and his creatures), the univocity of cause (God is cause of himself in the same sense that he is cause of all things), and the univocity of modality (God is necessary in the same sense that all things are necessary). I will leave it to readers to explore the heretical conse-quences of the denial of free will in the third figure of univocity. Taken together, they effect what Deleuze calls a 'pure' ontology, that is, *an ontology in which there is nothing beyond or outside or superior to Being*. But this is only the first half of the unfolding of the concept of univocity in Deleuze.

'Have I been understood? – Univocity versus Analogy': such is the Nietzschean gauntlet Deleuze throws down in *Difference and Repetition*, the third and most important act in the story of univocity. *Difference and Repetition* links the project of a pure ontology, as developed by Spinoza, with the problematic of difference, as formulated by Heidegger, and in the process goes beyond both Spinoza and Heidegger. The conversion Deleuze effects from identity to difference is as important as Spinoza's move from transcendence to immanence. According to Klossowski's thesis, the concept of God has always functioned as a guarantor of the principle of identity.[20] Even in Spinoza, modes are modifications *of* substance, and the concept of substance (or God) can still be said to maintain the rights of identity over difference. Deleuze's philosophy of difference must thus be seen as a kind of Spinozism *minus* substance, a purely modal or differential universe.[21] *Difference and Repetition* is an experiment in metaphysics whose aim is to provide a (transcendental) description of the world from the viewpoint of a principle of difference rather than the principle of identity. 'In accordance with Heidegger's ontological intuition', Deleuze writes, 'difference must be articulation and connection in itself; *it must relate different to different without any mediation whatsoever* by the identical, the similar, the analogous or the opposed' (*DR*, p. 117). Despite his indebtedness to Heidegger, however, Deleuze never subscribed to the theme of the 'overcoming of metaphysics'. He describes himself as a 'pure metaphysician',[22] a classical philosopher who sees his philosophy as a system, albeit an open and 'heterogenetic' system.[23] Though obviously indebted to such metaphysical thinkers as Spinoza, Leibniz and Bergson, Deleuze appropriates their respective systems of thought only by pushing them to their 'differential' limit, purging them of the three great terminal points (God, world, self) of traditional metaphysics. Deleuze's historical monographs, in this sense, are preliminary sketches for the great canvas of *Difference and Repetition*.

Aristotle appears as an important *dramatis persona* in *Difference and Repetition*, and for good reason. Aristotle held a famous thesis concerning difference: *different things differentiate themselves only through what they have in common*. This subordination of difference to identity can be seen in the schematisation of Aristotle's ontology known as Porphyry's Tree (Figure 1). In the middle regions of the tree, specific difference allows a genus or concept to remain the same in itself (identity) while becoming other in the opposing predicates (differences) that divide it. This process of specification in turn reaches a limit at either end of the table. At the lower end, a plurality of different individuals can be placed under a single concept only on the condition that a sensible resemblance between the individuals can be perceived. At the upper end, the differences between the highest genera or 'categories' can be related to the concept of Being only through an operation

	Being			
	Substance, etc.* (the categories)		generic difference (highest determinable concepts)	ANALOGY of judgement
Corporeal		Incorporeal	specific difference	
	Body		subaltern genus	
Animate		Inanimate	specific difference	IDENTITY in the concept
	Living thing		subaltern genus	
Sensitive		Insensitive	specific difference	
	Animal		subaltern genus	OPPOSITION of predicates
Rational		Nonrational	specific difference	
	Human		infima species (smallest determined concepts)	
Socrates	Plato	etc.	individual difference (individuals)	RESEMBLANCE in perception

*Aristotle's ten categories: substance, quality, quantity, relation, place, time, position, state, activity, passivity.

Figure 1 Porphyry's Tree

Adapted from E. M. Curley (1969) *Spinoza's Metaphysics: An Essay in Interpretation*, Cambridge MA: Harvard University Press, p. 29.

that would come to be known as analogy. Aristotle thus subordinates difference to four interrelated principles: identity in the concept and the opposition of predicates (specific difference), resemblance in perception (individual difference), and the analogy of judgement (generic difference). Readers will recognise this quadripartite structure of 'representation' as one of the recurring motifs of *Difference and Repetition*.

Deleuze contrasts the 'univocity of Being' point by point with Aristotle's theory of the 'analogy of Being,' which dominated medieval philosophy prior to Spinoza. Is Being distributed among beings univocally or analogically? This question concerns a very specific problem: the relation of Being to the 'categories'. Kant defined a category as a concept that can be said of every object of possible experience (causality is a category because every object has a cause and is itself cause of other things). Aristotle's formulation amounts to the same thing: the categories are the different senses in which Being is said of beings, *they are different senses of the word Being*.[24] In Heidegger's formulation, the categories are the fundamental 'determinations of the Being of beings', the fundamental ontological predicates.[25] But what then is the relation of Being, as the most general concept, to the categories, as the highest genera? Aristotle recognised that Being cannot be a univocal genus in relation to the categories, and this for a precise reason: because *differences 'are'*. To predicate Being as an overarching genus would deny the being of difference; or rather, it would mean that the genus 'Being' would have to be predicated twice, once to its species, and once to its own differentiae.[26] Generic difference must therefore be of another nature than specific difference: whereas a genus in relation to its species is univocal, Being in relation to the categories is necessarily equivocal. The categories, Aristotle concluded, must therefore be related to each other *analogically*. Every philosophy of the categories, from Aristotle through Kant and Hegel, implies an analogical ontology.

In Aristotle, the analogy of Being has two fundamental forms, both of which would be taken up theologically by later thinkers such as Aquinas. On the one hand, the concept of Being has no content in itself, but only a *distributive* content that is proportional to the formally different categories of which it is predicated (analogy of proportionality). The 'proportionality' involved here need not be understood in a strict mathematical sense (a:b:c:d), since the categories do not need to have an equal relation to Being, but only an internal relation. On the other hand, Being therefore tends to form a hierarchical series, insofar as the category of substance assumes the role of the primary category or the first sense (*pros hen*) of Being: everything that 'is' is a substance, and in turn everything that is a substance has a quality, a quantity, a place, and so on (analogy of proportion).[27] These two forms of analogy are what Deleuze terms, respectively, the distributive 'common sense' and the hierarchical 'good sense' (or first sense) of Being.[28]

What is wrong with Aristotle's analogical vision of the world? Put simply, it provides an inadequate solution to the Heideggerian problematic of ontological difference. On the one hand, *it cannot posit Being as a common genus* without destroying the very reason one posits it as such, that is, the possibility of *being* for specific differences; it can conceive the universality of Being only as a quasi-identity. On the other hand, it has to relate Being to particular beings, *but it cannot say what constitutes their individuality*: it retains in the particular (the individual) only what conforms to the general (the concept). An equivocal or analogical concept of Being, in other words, can only grasp that which is univocal in beings. A true universal is lacking, no less than a true singular: Being has only a distributive common sense, and the individual has no difference except a general and reflexive one in the concept.[29]

Deleuze's thesis in *Difference and Repetition* is that only univocity can provide us with a truly *collective* sense of Being (and not merely a distributive sense) by giving us a comprehension of the play of *individuating differences* within beings (and not mere generalities in a network of resemblances). But this brings us, precisely, to the fundamental problem of a univocal ontology. If Being is said in *one and the same sense* of everything that is, then what constitutes the difference between beings? There can be no categories in a univocal ontology: if we distinguish beings by their substance, or their form, or their generic and specific differences, then we are back in the analogical vision of the world. Yet if we say that Being is univocal, that there is no categorical difference between the senses of the word 'Being', then we seem to fall into the thought of infamy: the thought of the inessential, the formless, the non-specific, the non-generic, the non-categorical. Between God and man, plant and animal, there can be no difference of category, no difference of substance, no difference of form. This is why Deleuze insists that univocity is such a difficult concept to *think*: how can we say that there are differences between beings, and nonetheless that Being is said in one and the same sense of everything that is?

Not surprisingly, it was Spinoza who foresaw the only possible type of solution to this problem. At this point, the only difference conceivable is difference as a *degree of power* or intensity. The power or intensity of a being is its relation to Being. Why is the idea of difference as a degree of power linked to that of the univocity of Being? Because beings that are distinguished solely by their degree of power realise *one and the same* univocal Being, except for the difference in their degree of power or its withdrawal. Difference as a degree of power is *a non-categorical* difference in that it preserves the univocal sense of Being.[30] Beings are no longer distinguished by a qualitative essence (analogy of Being) but by a quantifiable degree of power (univocity of Being). We no longer ask what the essence of a thing is (for instance, man as a 'rational animal' or 'featherless biped'), but rather what its affective capacities are, since the power of an existing individual is expressed in a certain capacity for being affected.

This move already marks an important practical conversion in philosophy, which Deleuze describes as a shift away from a *morality* to an *ethics*. For Deleuze, morality is fundamentally linked to the notion of essence and the analogical vision of the world. In Aristotle, man's essence is to be a rational animal. If he nonetheless acts in a irrational manner, it is because there are *accidents* that turn him away from his essential nature: man's essence is a *potentiality* that is not necessarily realised. Morality can therefore be defined as the effort to rejoin man's essence, to realise one's essence. In an ethics, by contrast, beings are related to Being, not at the level of essence, but at the level of existence. Ethics defines a person not by what they *are* in principle (their essence), but by what they *can do*, what they are *capable* of (their power). Since power is *always* effectuated – it is never a potentiality, but always in act – the question is no longer: what *must* you do in order to realise your essence?, but rather: what are you *capable* of doing by virtue of your power? As Eric Alliez has put it, if analogy is theological (onto-theology), univocity is ethical (onto-ethology).[31] The political problem, in turn, concerns the effectuation of this power: what conditions allow one's power to be effectuated in the best fashion? Conversely, under what conditions can one actually desire to be separated from one's power? One can see clearly how these ontological questions form the basis for the ethico-political philosophy (and corresponding 'existential' notions) developed in *Capitalism and Schizophrenia*.

We might note here that Deleuze and Emmanuel Levinas, with their respective philosophies of immanence and transcendence, represent two very different approaches to the question of ethics in contemporary thought. If the *other* is the fundamental problem of transcendence, *difference* is the fundamental problem of immanence. For Levinas, ethics *precedes* ontology because it introduces an element of transcendence (the wholly other) that is necessarily 'otherwise' than Being. For Deleuze (and Spinoza) ethics *is* ontology because beings are immediately related to Being at the level of their existence (intensity or degree of power as the element of immanence). This is why Spinoza entitles his pure ontology an *Ethics* rather than an *Ontology*: his speculative propositions concerning univocity can only be judged practically at the level of the ethics they envelop or imply.

But these ethical concerns are derived directly from the univocal ontology developed in *Difference and Repetition*, and the solution it offers to the problem of the ontological difference. Being must not only be able to account for the external difference between beings, but also the fact that beings themselves are multiplicities marked by an 'internal difference'; and the ontological difference must not only refer to the non-categorical difference between Being and beings, but also the internal difference of Being *from itself*. The ontological concepts developed in *Difference and Repetition* are all non-categorical notions that preserve the univocity of Being by comprehending this co-articulation of Being and difference within themselves: 'difference in intensity, disparity in the phantasm, dissemblance in the form of time, the differential in thought: opposition, resemblance, identity, and even analogy are only effects produced by these presentations of difference' (*DR*, p. 145).[32] This is the meaning of Deleuze's formula 'monism = pluralism' (univocity of Being = equivocity of difference).[33] It is true that if analogy denies Being the status of the common genus because (specific) differences 'are', then conversely, univocal Being is indeed common only in so far as (individuating) differences 'are not' and must not be. This is the second fundamental problem of a univocal ontology that Deleuze confronts and takes to its limit: the (non-)Being of difference is in fact the reality of the *virtual* or the *problematic*. Univocal being, in other words, always presents itself in a 'problematic' form. If one consigns 'difference' to the actual or the empirical, to individuals constituted in experience, one inevitably falls back into an analogical or equivocal ontology, and subordinates difference to the rights of identity and negation. A reading of Deleuze's ontology, yet to be written, would have to focus on these two fundamental problems.

But why, finally, in the fourth and final act, does univocity disappear from Deleuze's writings? The reason, in the end, is not difficult to discern. Other concepts, like that of the 'simulacrum', meet similar fates.[34] Deleuze used Klossowski's concept of the 'simulacrum' to think through the problematic of anti-platonism; outside that context, the concept no longer held any 'interest' (since beings no longer 'simulate' anything), and was replaced, as it were, by the concept of the *agencement* or 'assemblage'. The same is true for univocity. Univocity was an arrow first shot by Duns Scotus, and which Deleuze then picked up and aimed elsewhere, using it to interpret Spinoza's philosophy, critique orthodox theology, and think through Heidegger's problem of ontological difference through a confrontation with Aristotle. Once its (already considerable) work was done, Deleuze's moved on. In *A Thousand Plateaus*, for instance, the logic of *est* ('is') gives way to a conjunctive logic of *et* ('and'), which 'overthrows ontology', and places relations 'outside everything which could be determined as Being, One, or Whole' (*ATP*, p. 25; cf. p. 98).[35] This is not an appeal to transcendence, but rather a deepening of immanence, requiring, in later works, the invention of new concepts such as the 'plane of immanence', the 'outside', the 'interstice', and so on.[36] What the drama of univocity exemplifies is the dynamic nature of Deleuze's thought, which must be defined and comprehended in terms of its *movement*.

Notes

1 See Gilles Deleuze, *Francis Bacon: Logique de la sensation* (Paris: La Différence, 1981) vol. 1, pp. 13–14, as well as Deleuze's seminar of 25 November 1980. Transcripts of Deleuze seminar sessions at Vincennes are being made available on the Web by Richard Pinhas at http://www.imaginet.fr/deleuze, with English translations by Timothy S. Murphy, Melissa McMahon, Charles Stivale and others. They are an invaluable resource for understanding Deleuze's thought.

2 Gilles Deleuze, *Difference and Repetition*, trans. Paul Patton (New York: Columbia University Press, 1994) p. 39. Hereafter referred to as *DR*. (Pages 35–42 contain Deleuze's well known analysis of the 'tradition' of univocity.) See also Gilles Deleuze, *The Logic of Sense*, trans. Mark K. Lester with Charles Stivale, ed. Constantin V. Boundas (New York: Columbia University Press, 1990) pp. 177–180.

3 Deleuze's interpretation of Duns Scotus relies primarily on Etienne Gilson's definitive *Jean Duns Scot: Introduction à ses positions fondamentales* (Paris: J. Vrin, 1952). In English, see Gilson's historical discussions in *History of Christian Philosophy in the Middle Ages* (London: Sheed and Ward, 1955) pp. 454–71; and *Being and Some Philosophers* (Toronto: Pontifical Institute of Mediaeval Studies, 1952) pp. 84–95.

4 Gilles Deleuze, *Expressionism in Philosophy: Spinoza*, trans. Martin Joughin (New York: Zone Books, 1990). Deleuze almost certainly developed the notion of univocity while researching his 'secondary' thesis on Spinoza for the Doctorat d'Etat.

5 Gilles Deleuze, 'Scholasticism and Spinoza', seminar of 14 January 1974, trans. Timothy S. Murphy. The seminar includes Deleuze's discussion of the Scholastic approaches to the concept of Being.

6 Deleuze's 1956 essay, 'Bergson's conception of difference', trans. Melissa McMahon, in John Mullarky (ed.) *The New Bergson* (Manchester: Manchester University Press, 1999) for example, is a reading of Bergson through the prism of Heidegger's problematic of ontological difference. See Constantin V. Boundas' analyses in 'Deleuze-Bergsonian ontology of the virtual', in *Deleuze: A Critical Reader*, ed. Paul Patton (London: Blackwell, 1996) pp. 81–106, which makes the comparison.

7 In the preface to *Difference and Repetition*, Deleuze cites 'Heidegger's ever more pronounced orientation toward a philosophy of ontological Difference' (p. ix) as one of the factors that led him to write the book. The only direct confrontation, however, is the long footnote in chapter 1 (pp. 64–6), which concerns the notion of difference in Heidegger's thought. The note was apparently inserted at the insistence of Deleuze's thesis advisers, who no doubt recognised the subterranean battle lines being drawn in the book.

8 Michel Foucault, 'Theatrum philosophicum', in *Language, Counter-Memory, Practice: Selected Essays and Interviews*, trans. Donald F. Bouchard and Sherry Simon, ed. Donald F. Bouchard (Oxford: Blackwell, 1977) p. 172.

9 Gilles Deleuze, *Spinoza: Practical Philosophy*, trans. Robert Hurley (San Francisco: City Lights Books, 1988) p. 63. To my knowledge, Deleuze is the only commentator to have drawn this link between Duns Scotus and Spinoza on the question of univocity.

10 See Reiner Schürmann, *Meister Eckhart: Mystic and Philosopher* (Bloomington: Indiana University Press, 1978) especially pp. 172–92. While recognising Eckhart's affinities with immanence (see pp. 176, 252, n56) and with an immanent causality (p. 177), Schürmann attempts to provide a qualified analogical interpretation of his teachings (p. 179).

11 For Thomas Aquinas' formulations of analogy, see *Summa Theologica* 1.13.5. The way of affirmation found its greatest literary expression in Dante's *Divine Comedy*, and perhaps its most important modern proponent in Charles Williams.

12 See Baruch Spinoza, *Short Treatise*, in *The Collected Works of Spinoza*, ed. Edwin Curley (Princeton: Princeton University Press, 1985) pp. 65–90, as well as Deleuze's commentary in *Spinoza: Practical Philosophy*, pp. 104–5, and *Expressionism in Philosophy: Spinoza*, pp. 49–51, 55–61, 70–7.

13 See Baruch Spinoza, *Tractatus Theologico-Politicus*, trans. Samuel Shirley (Leiden: E. J. Brill, 1984) particularly chapter 2.

14 See Harry Austryn Wolfson, *From Philo to Spinoza: Two Studies in Religious Philosophy* (New York: Behrman House, 1977).

15 On the distinction between these three types of causality, see Deleuze's seminar of 22 March 1983.

16 Martin Heidegger, *On Time and Being*, trans. Joan Stambaugh (New York: Harper & Row, 1972).

17 See in particular Jacques Derrida, *On the Name*, trans. Thomas Dutoit (Stanford: Stanford University Press, 1995). John D. Caputo has analysed Derrida's theological appropriations in his book *The Prayers and Tears of Jacques Derrida* (Bloomington: Indiana University Press, 1997).

18 Gilles Deleuze, 'Les plages d'immanence', in *L'art des confins: Mélanges offerts à Maurice de Gandillac*, ed. Annie Cazenave and Jean-François Lyotard (Paris: Presses Universitaires de France, 1985) p. 79.

19 In his *Deleuze: The Clamor of Being*, trans. Louise Burchill (Minneapolis: University of Minnesota Press, 2000), Alain Badiou rightly notes the influence of Heidegger on Deleuze, but wrongly presents Deleuze's 'univocal ontology' as if it were a neoplatonic 'philosophy of the One'. For instance, when Badiou writes that, in Deleuze, 'the paradoxical or super-eminent One engenders, in an immanent manner, a procession of beings, whose univocal sense it distributes' (p. 26), he is giving an exact description of an *emanative* ontology, not a univocal one. In general, Badiou combines transitive, emanative and immanent elements in his treatment of univocity, thereby seeming to confirm Deleuze's adage, cited above, that univocity is 'the strangest thought, the most difficult to think'.

20 See Deleuze's essay on Klossowski in the *Logic of Sense*, especially pp. 292, 294, where he contrasts the 'order of God' with the 'order of the Anti-Christ'.

21 See *Difference and Repetition*, pp. 40–1. Similarly, if Deleuze is Leibnizian, it is only by eliminating the idea of a God who chooses the 'best' of all possi-

ble worlds, with its pre-established harmony; in Deleuze, incompossibilities and dissonances belong to one and the same world, the only world, our world.

22 See Deleuze's interview with Arnaud Villani in the latter's *La Guêpe et l'Orchidée: Essai sur Gilles Deleuze* (Paris: Belin, 1999) p. 130: 'Bergson says that modern science hasn't found its metaphysics, the metaphysics it would need. It is this metaphysics that interests me'.

23 See Gilles Deleuze, 'Lettre-préface', in Jean-Clet Martin, *Variations: La Philosophie de Gilles Deleuze* (Paris: Payot & Rivages, 1993) p. 8: 'I believe in philosophy as system. For me, the system must not only be in perpetual heterogeneity, it must be a *heterogenesis* – something which, it seems to me, has never been attempted'.

24 See Aristotle, *Categories*, 4, 1 b 25, and *Physics*, I, C.2, 185 a 21: 'Being is said in several senses'.

25 Martin Heidegger, *Hegel's Phenomenology of Spirit*, trans. Parvis Emad and Kenneth Maly (Bloomington: Indiana University Press, 1988) p. 102; cf. p. 117.

26 See Aristotle, *Metaphysics*, III, 3, 998b, 22–7:

> It is not possible that either unity or being should be a single genus of things; for the differentiae of any genus must each of them both have being and be one, but it is not possible for the genus taken apart from its species (any more than for the species of the genus) to be predicated of its proper differentiae; so that *if unity or being is a genus, no differentia will either have being or be one.*

27 See Aristotle, *Metaphysics*, IV, 2, 1003 a 33–34: 'Being is said in several senses, but always with reference to a single term (*pros hen*)'.

28 On the relation between 'common sense' and 'good sense,' see *Difference and Repetition*, p. 269; and *Logic of Sense*, pp. 75–9.

29 For Deleuze's summary of his criticisms of Aristotle, see *Difference and Repetition*, pp. 269–70.

30 The interpretation of Spinoza's 'degree of power' in terms of the concept of intensity is another Deleuzian innovation. In *Difference and Repetition*, however, the concept of intensity is no longer linked to that of substance, as in Spinoza, but takes on an autonomous status, defined formally (following Kant) as a difference that divides into itself, an *individuating difference*, in relation to a limit where intensity = 0.

31 See Eric Alliez, *La Signature du monde* (Paris: Cerf, 1993) chapter 3, 'Onto-éthologiques', pp. 67–104.

32 One could conserve the notion of a 'category' in a univocal ontology, as does Whitehead (see *Difference and Repetition*, pp. 284–5), on the condition of defining categories in a new manner, as differential concepts. From this viewpoint, Deleuze suggests, the conclusion to *A Thousand Plateaus* could be read as a 'table of categories' (in the Whiteheadian-Deleuzian sense, not the Aristotelian-Kantian sense). The theory of the concept formulated in Gilles Deleuze and Félix Guattari, *What is Philosophy?*, trans. H. Tomlinson and G. Burchell (London: Verso, 1994) is the direct result of Deleuze's rethinking of the problem of the categories. See Deleuze's comments in Villani, pp. 130–3.

33 Gilles Deleuze and Félix Guattari, *A Thousand Plateaus*, trans. Brian Massumi (Minneapolis: University of Minnesota Press, 1989) p. 20. Hereafter referred to as *ATP*.

34 See Gilles Deleuze, 'Lettre-préface', in Jean-Clet Martin, *Variations: La Philosophie de Gilles Deleuze* (Paris: Payot & Rivages, 1993) p. 8: 'It seems to me that I have completely abandoned the notion of the simulacrum'.

35 See Gilles Deleuze and Claire Parnet, *Dialogues*, trans. Hugh Tomlinson and Barbara Habberjam (New York: Columbia University Press, 1987) p. 57.

36 See, for instance, Gilles Deleuze, *The Time-Image*, trans. Hugh Tomlinson and Robert Galeta (Minneapolis: University of Minnesota Press, 1989) p. 180: 'The whole undergoes a mutation, because it has ceased to be the One-Being, in order to become the constitutive "and" of things, the constitutive between-two [*entre-deux*]'.

14 Deleuze's impersonal, hylozoic cosmology

The expulsion of theology

Eliot Albert

Deleuze and Guattari's work is distinct in contemporary philosophy in a multitude of striking ways. Here, however, I shall concentrate on the relationships between three strands in their work. First is their pursuit of an ontological materialism, a materialism that refuses the image of matter foisted upon it by transcendence, and that seeks to exempt itself from Georges Bataille's charge that most erstwhile philosophical materialisms have remained within the conceptual structure of idealism by giving in to 'an obsession with the *ideal* form of matter'.[1]

The second element to be considered is Deleuze and Guattari's positive response to the event of nihilism, or the conflagration of transcendent values, a response which refuses to treat it as a site of mourning – of so many 'deaths of' and 'ends of' – but takes it as a uniquely productive beginning of philosophy, of an infinitely constructive exploration of the resources of immanence. Deleuze rigorously refuses the funereal atmosphere that characterises the response of much contemporary French philosophy to this event of nihilism, by insisting that he has 'never worried about going beyond metaphysics or the death of philosophy',[2] and by adopting a diametrically opposed position, that of a Nietzschean cheerfulness. Speaking of his book on Foucault for example, Deleuze insists that it is 'not a work of mourning'; after all, 'non-mourning takes even more work' (*Negotiations*, p. 84). This work is a call to continue doing philosophy, 'never being bothered with the death of metaphysics or the overcoming of philosophy: it is just pointless, idle incoherencies [*d'inutiles, de pénibles radotages*]'.[3]

The third element of Deleuze and Guattari's work to be considered is their critique of the pernicious infiltration of theological argumentation into philosophical thought. In a sense, then, one of the implicit aims of this essay will be to explore how, and why, the phrase 'materialist philosophy' is a tautology for Deleuze and Guattari, for whom philosophy can only, and must, be a materialism.

According to Deleuze, the two intimately linked prizes of philosophy are the attainment of a Nietzschean 'cheerfulness' (*Heiterkeit*) at the death of God, and the concomitant abolition of transcendent values.[4] In a significant passage, Deleuze and Guattari make a sweeping assault upon the founda-

tions of the different forms of the dominant philosophical tradition, 'that is
to say, the tradition that justifies Power and exalts the State',[5] consisting as
they do in varying proportions of Judaeo-Christian theology, Aristotelian
formalism, Kantian schemas, and liberal politics, and the many varieties of
what Bataille felicitously calls its 'metaphysical scaffolding' (*OCI*, p. 220).
Deleuze and Guattari write: 'For philosophers neither atheism nor the death
of God are problems. [...] That philosophers still take the death of god to
be a tragedy is astonishing. Atheism is not a drama, but the philosopher's
serenity and philosophy's achievement' (*WP*, p. 92; my translation).

From this perspective, Deleuze's attitude towards theological thought can
be characterised as being relatively straightforward; he identifies theology
with transcendence, and philosophy with immanence. As such, philosophy
and theology have quite distinct objects, for 'whenever there is transcendence, vertical Being, imperial State in the sky or on earth, there is religion;
and there is philosophy whenever there is immanence' (*WP*, p. 43). A whole
string of philosophemes to which Deleuze has consistently set his thought in
opposition appear here, amongst them Platonism, judgement, and representation. These three, all of which are taken to be manifestations of transcendence, are attacked from Deleuze's first writings onwards under the rubric of
reversing Platonism. It is important to note that he sees this reversal as
already being prefigured, and indeed begun, in some of Plato's own work,
most notably at the end of *The Sophist*, where it becomes impossible to
distinguish Socrates from his imitators, and where, for a brief and vertigi-
nous moment, the Eleatic Stranger raises the thought that lies at the heart of
anti-Platonism: 'And to increase our perplexity we were plunged into a whirl
of confusion by the apparition of an argument that called into question all
these terms and disputed the very existence of any copy or image or
semblance'.[6]

Deleuze writes that, in this moment,

> the different, the dissimilar, the unequal – in short, becoming – may well
> be not merely defects which affect copies like a ransom paid for their
> secondary character [...] but rather models themselves, terrifying mod-
> els of the *pseudos* in which unfolds the power of the false.[7]

Needless to say, this possibility, this moment, in which Plato himself 'pointed
out the direction for the reversal of Platonism'[8] is quickly laid aside.
Prevailing against this rejected possibility, Deleuze diagnoses a problem
inherited by post-Platonic philosophy, since the setting of the 'popular and
technical images of the philosopher' (*Logic*, p. 127). This inheritance, the
'poisoned gift of Platonism',[9] consists of the introduction of 'transcendence
into philosophy', what Deleuze describes as the Platonic provision of a
'plausible philosophical meaning' to transcendence (*Critical*, p. 137).
According to Deleuze, the dominant forms of modern philosophy labour
under this 'plausibility' and, as such, facilitate the 'triumph of the judgement

of God', becoming in the process so many versions of Kant's 'renovated theology'.[10]

This theological infiltration has not, however, gone entirely unchallenged, for, as Deleuze never tires of demonstrating, there is a philosophical current that stands in permanent opposition to it, in the form of the 'philosophies of pure immanence' that 'escape Platonism – from the Stoics to Spinoza or Nietzsche' (*Critical*, p. 137), and, we might add, Bruno and Bergson. Philosophy's linked concerns, then, must be to seek a 'restoration of immanence' and, in so doing, forbid 'the return of any transcendence' (*Critical*, p. 137). Things, however, are never so simple, for amongst the various features that unite these, otherwise disparate, escapes from Platonism to which Deleuze continually looks for a 'dose of immanence' (*WP*, p. 45), is the accusation cast against them, in varying forms, of pantheism, or, more recently, of vitalism.

The continual repetition, and difference, of a set of arguments and counter-arguments throughout this essay from seemingly widely differing cultural and political contexts, is not to be taken as either the construal of a teleological progression of argumentation, or as the comparison of a series of philosophers abstracted from their historical contexts. Rather, this continual movement is an exemplification of what Deleuze and Guattari mean when they argue that one must replace the *history* of philosophy with a study of its *time*, a time that is characterised, they argue, as being *stratigraphic* – a product of the replacement of genealogy with a geology (*WP*, p. 44). This claim must be made emphatic, for what is at stake here is, in many ways, *the* problem of philosophy, that of immanence, 'the burning issue of all philosophy because it takes on all the dangers that philosophy must confront, all the condemnations, persecutions and repudiations that it undergoes' (*WP*, p. 45). To practise philosophy with Deleuze and Guattari is to accept the claim that concepts are only formulated in conjunction with problems, are flat with, or immanent to, problems, such that the concept is meaningless if 'it is not connected to other concepts [...] linked to a problem that it resolves' (*WP*, p. 79).

Deleuze and Guattari's concepts are produced in concrete analyses, and bear an immanent relationship to a body of knowledge, of historical, technical and political procedures. The immanent character of Deleuze and Guattari's concepts is posed in direct contradistinction to Kant's declaration that 'reason is never in immediate relation to an object, but only to the understanding; [...] it does not, therefore, *create* concepts (of objects) but only *orders* them'.[11] To expand briefly upon the relationship between judgement and transcendence: Deleuze and Guattari follow Antonio Negri in showing that the ontological is absolutely identical with, and not just analogous to, the political. Hence Kant is seen as the philosopher of the state *par excellence*, credited with 'turning the philosopher into the judge' (*WP*, p. 72), and identifying the spuriously sovereign subject with the legislator, such that the ' "proper usage of the faculties" mysteriously coincides with these established values: true knowledge, true morality, true religion' (*Nietzsche*, p. 92). In the same way, Kant's investment of philosophy with a juridical form and his 'tracing its doctrine of faculties onto the organs of state power'[12] is the classical example of the raising of *doxa* to the level of transcendent judgement.[13]

The features of Deleuze's philosophy that we have identified as being part of his project of reversing Platonism are taken up in another, more superficially constructive element of his work: the attempt to construct a transcendental field constituted by 'impersonal and preindividual nomadic singularities' (*Logic*, p. 109). Deleuze's location of singularities as a conceptual core of his philosophy of energetic materiality is an attempt to guarantee its being founded on two principles: immanence and intensity. This whole account is predicated upon an energetic basis, for the critical problem with transcendental philosophy in its Kantian form, as identified by Deleuze, lies in its metaphysical dependence upon a choice between '*either* an undifferentiated ground, a groundlessness, formless nonbeing, or an abyss without differences and without properties, *or* a supremely individuated Being and an intensely impersonalised Form' (*Logic*, p. 106).

As such, the claim that Kantian transcendental philosophy is still to be characterised as theological rests upon the argument that it is incapable of offering a coherent account of genesis or individuation, and so is incapable of thinking matter without imposing upon it any one of that series of diktats (e.g. spirit, the subject, Platonic form, species, Kantian categories) that Deleuze and Guattari condemn as the strata or 'the judgements of god', the generalities to which a thought of singularity is opposed. This imposition of form reveals the great stakes, both political and philosophical, involved in the maintenance of the hylomorphic schema in transcendental thought, and correspondingly in the critique of that hylomorphism. This latter critique, the advocacy of hylozoism, a philosophy ascribing immanent power to matter, is a vital constant in the counter-tradition to which Deleuze allies himself.

Kant is conventionally seen as transcending and unifying competing strands in philosophy (represented in Kant's own account by Rousseau and Hume). However, this was achieved on the basis of a hegemonised hostility to Spinozism, and the silencing of Spinozist questions. This silencing, though, was not entirely homogeneous and contained substantial cracks, most notably Schelling, Marx and Nietzsche. Regardless of the massive differences between these figures, it is their common attempt to think the Spinozist prioritisation of the body, of materiality, that is of concern here.

Vitalism split

In what became known as the 'Pantheism Controversy',[14] Schelling had argued that there are two distinct ways of interpreting pantheism, and that the second 'concept of Pantheism has not yet been assessed. To assess this task is the task of philosophy itself'.[15] I have also suggested that Deleuze makes a similar move with vitalism. As Deleuze and Guattari continually insist, vitalism has never been one, but multiple, having

> always had two possible alternatives: that of an Idea that acts, but is not
> – that acts therefore only from the point of view of an external cerebral
> knowledge (from Kant to Claude Bernard); or that of a force that is but
> does not act – that is therefore a pure internal Awareness (from Leibniz
> to Ruyer). [...] The second interpretation seems to us to be imperative.
> (*WP*, p. 213)

The variant of vitalism, described on occasion as a 'technological vitalism' (*Thousand*, p. 407) that is being suggested is not the vitalism that is usually baldly counterposed to mechanism. Indeed, as some contemporary biologists have recognised, the alternative to mechanism is not vitalism, but complexity, and this latter is an imperative component of the contemporary *superior materialism* that Deleuze sought to provide. This is a vitalism that has ceased to posit entities mobilised by an extra, or metaphysical, force (a 'supplementary dimension' in Deleuze's terminology), but rather one that opens entities to the outside, and stands in counterposition to the theological and metaphysical legislation of the one. It is a thought of infinite variation and modal being, *pace* Spinoza, a thought set in opposition to any ontology predicated upon static entities; it is, rather, one that conceives of bodies as a locus of force, a condensation of affects, a thought that makes *potentia* constitutive.

The tradition in which Deleuze's philosophy of matter is best placed is one that he describes as being 'always subject to the charge of pantheism'.[16] Seen in more contemporary terms, this is the accusation of vitalism that has been levelled at, *inter alia*, Spinoza, Leibniz and Bergson, all of whom figure as Deleuze's philosophical heroes. As such, he is happy for his own philosophy to run the risk of this accusation, apparently lethal insofar as it is equivalent to that of irrationalism or mysticism, and to be subject to it is to run the risk of expulsion beyond the bounds of sound philosophy and science. For Deleuze, however, there is a vitalism subject to the power of nonorganic life, 'a profound link between signs, events, life and vitalism. [...] Everything I've written is vitalistic, [...] and amounts to a theory of signs and events' (*Negotiations*, p. 143).

Lexicon of hylomorphism

For constructing a plane of immanence that is 'the purest, the one that does not hand itself over to the transcendent, or restore any transcendence, the one that inspires the fewest illusions, bad feelings, and erroneous perceptions' (*WP*, p. 60), Spinoza is the 'Christ of philosophers' (*WP*, p. 60); and, because he 'never compromised with transcendence and [...] hunted it down everywhere' (*WP*, p. 48), he is the 'prince of philosophers'. Furthermore, having made the crucial discovery that 'immanence was only immanent to itself' Spinoza was able to teach the critical lesson that 'whenever immanence is interpreted as immanent *to* Something, we can be sure that this Something reintroduces the transcendent' (*WP*, p. 45).

Ever since *The Logic of Sense*, Deleuze had identified philosophy with a naturalism in which there is no space whatsoever for the gods, who 'shout at us promising eternal punishment' (*Logic*, p. 277), a naturalism understood as an 'enterprise of "demystification" ' (*Logic*, p. 279), a 'philosophy of affirmation [...] and the practical critique of all mystifications' (*Logic*, p. 279). Philosophy's task is 'always a matter of denouncing the illusion, the false infinite, the infinity of religion and of the theologico-erotic-oneiric myths in which it is expressed' (*Logic*, p. 278). Spinoza's system, Deleuze always insists, is one that is utterly resistant to the claims of transcendence to which most philosophies succumb, including those which shout loudest about their being wedded to immanence or materialism.

Both Bataille and Negri have presented strong arguments to show that most materialisms have ultimately been idealisms or systems of transcendence, precisely because their image of matter is one reclaimed from idealism. As already noted, Georges Bataille argues that most materialisms have remained idealist insofar as they 'situated dead matter at the summit of a conventional hierarchy' and so 'gave into an obsession with the *ideal* form of matter' (*OCI*, p. 179). This argument is, however, anticipated by Schelling in his *Ideas for a Philosophy of Nature*, in which it is suggested that all hitherto existing philosophies – with the possible exception of Spinozism – have been beholden to a concept of matter derived from the lexicon of hylomorphism, the groundplan of all dualisms and hence of transcendence. Schelling writes:

> From the inception of philosophy up to the present day, in very different forms, admittedly, but always recognisably enough, matter, in by far the majority of so-called systems, has been assumed as a mere given, or postulated as a manifold, which has to be subordinated to the supreme unity, as an existing stuff, in order to comprehend the formed universe in terms of the action of the one upon the other.[17]

It is precisely in his apprehension of matter, beyond the strictures of hylomorphic dualism and transcendence, that Schelling descends most deeply into the 'abyss of Spinozism' (*HMP*, p. 66). The first element of Schelling's quietly devastating twofold critique of Kant is that, by adhering to the doctrine of the *Ding an sich*, he is rendered incapable of gaining any 'real knowledge of the supersensuous' (*HMP*, p. 103). Second is the claim, repeated by both Nietzsche and Deleuze, that, in spite of his claims to the contrary, Kant's system ends up smuggling God back in. Schelling writes, 'Kant is known, after he has expelled God from the theoretical philosophy, to have nevertheless brought Him back via the practical philosophy' (*HMP*, p. 105). It is in accord with this claim that Deleuze describes Kantianism as a 'renovated theology' (*Nietzsche*, p. 93), and that Nietzsche writes that, since Kant,

> transcendentalists of every kind have once more won the day – they have been emancipated from the theologians: what joy! – Kant showed them a secret path by which they may, on their own initiative and with all scientific respectability, from now on follow their 'heart's desire'.[18]

This Nietzschean construal of the theological stakes in Kantianism is decisive for Deleuze and Guattari, who will see in Kant the founder of a new theology and a new humanism, and the discoverer of 'the modern way of saving transcendence' (*WP*, p. 46), in whom 'both God and the I underwent a practical resurrection' (*Difference*, p. 87). It is his identification of this clandestine theology in Kant that leads Schelling to engage with Spinoza, and, to a lesser degree, with Giordano Bruno. Whilst the general grounds for this engagement are the need to move beyond Kantianism, the specific spur is the need to overcome the irrevocable distance that Kantianism had opened up between man and the cosmos. The Spinozism elaborated by Schelling functions as a sign for a thought of active matter, or hylozoism, and as the principal means of making man into an active part of nature. It is in the name of this Spinozism that Deleuze remarks that he and Guattari wish to 'produce a sort of philosophy of nature, now that any distinction between nature and artifice is becoming blurred' (*Negotiations*, p. 155); given the framework sketched here, it is quite clear that the philosophy alluded to is one in which nature will be conceived as a site of production, metamorphosis, creation. Deleuze and Guattari's nature or plane of immanence will be one which 'does not make any distinction at all between things that might be called natural and things that might be called artificial. Artifice is fully a part of nature'.[19]

Such a Spinozism effects a dissolution of any boundary between man and nature; it is a philosophy on the scale of the cosmos. This productivist immanentist vision is developed by Deleuze and Guattari thus:

> Man and nature are not like two opposite terms confronting each other – not even in the sense of bipolar opposites within a relationship of causation, ideation, or expression […]; rather, they are one and the same essential reality, the producer-product. Production as process overtakes all idealistic categories and constitutes a cycle whose relationship to desire is that of an immanent principle.[20]

The philosophy of nature produced here, with its reintegration of man into cosmos and its flattening of ontological hierarchies, is one that is at the deepest levels explicitly anti-theological. A similar insight leads Michel

Serres to remark that 'nothing distinguishes me ontologically from a crystal, a plant, an animal, or the order of the world; [...] this is complexity itself, which was once called being'.[21] Thus Serres' complexity is that which certain currents in contemporary biology, as I have suggested, are elaborating as a means to escape from the stultifications of mechanism.

Ontogenesis precedes ontology

Taking their lead from his critique of the complex of ideas characterised, since Aristotle, as hylomorphism, Deleuze and Guattari's philosophy of nature is animated by Simondon's prioritisation of what he calls *ontogenesis* (the process of individuation) over and above ontology. For Simondon, 'ontogenesis becomes the point of departure of philosophical thought: it really will be first philosophy [...]. Ontogenesis precedes ontology'.[22] Deleuze's turn from the sovereign Kantian subject to the cosmic and inorganic, via a philosophy based upon the principles of an order immanent to matter[23] and of the impersonal, is precisely indebted to this prioritisation of ontogenesis. It leads him to write of the necessity to 'stop thinking of yourself as an ego in order to live as a flow, a set of flows in relation with other flows, outside of oneself and within oneself' (*Critical*, p. 51).

Simondon's starting point is a critique of all philosophies that remain attached to a transcendent principle, on the basis that, in varying forms, they all rely upon the ontological presupposition that the concept of an individual is a meaningful one, claiming that 'it is the individual as already constituted individual that is the reality of interest, the reality to be explained'.[24] Kant, for example, insists that 'one must make one's beginning something that human reason is utterly incapable of deriving from any previous natural causes, [...] one must begin with man as a *fully formed adult*'.[25] Simondon continues by arguing that scientific work carried out on such assumptions 'accords an ontological privilege to the already constituted individual' (*Individu*, p. 21).

For Simondon, then, the problem to be addressed is that of the assumption of the unified one as the starting point of any philosophy or science; in opposition to this, he proposes that philosophy start from 'the idea of a *principle of individuation* [...] which would provide a sufficient explanation of how the individual had come to be an individual and account for its singularity (haecceity)' (*Individu*, p. 21). It is this critique that was adopted by Deleuze in his positing of difference in itself, a materialist guarantee against the assumption of an original ground of plenitude to which we can return, or a telos to which we are heading, or equally of a truth that we can discover. Deleuze's world, governed by the eternal return, the groundless 'law' of a world which is a 'monster of energy', 'excludes the assignation of an originary and a derived as though there were a first and second occurrence, because the sole origin is difference, [...] the absence of any assignable origin – in other words, the assignation of difference as the origin' (*Difference*, p. 125).

Following Simondon on this point, Deleuze and Guattari are led to take the individual, the entity, or whatever it might be in the case under consideration, out of its ontological founding and replace it with the resolutely materialist set of concepts deployed by Simondon. For Simondon, philosophy must shed its concern with the (post-)metaphysical categories of Being, identity, absence and presence, and focus instead upon diagramming becoming, singularity, and assemblage. Central to Simondon's own agenda is the consignment of the former set of categories to the reservoir of redundant metaphysical baggage, the 'metaphysical bog where', Bataille reminds us, 'it sometimes seems a serious person would only go for a good laugh'.[26] 'Unity and identity', Simondon writes, 'are useless in helping us to discover the process of individuation itself' (*Individu*, p. 24), and in their stead he proposes the concepts of metastability, potential energy and entropy.

As Simondon goes on to argue, the terms and concepts of classical ontology are utterly incapable of comprehending individuation: they are too static, too rigidly dualist and, as a consequence, in Nietzsche's words, 'none of them can completely explain to me the simple process of becoming'[27] – as such new concepts must be invented. Simondon is clear: 'We will have to use both new methods and notions' and refuse to 'construct the essence of a given reality by means of a *conceptual* relation' (*Individu*, p. 30). Relation must be understood as constitutive, as part of the entity under consideration. As such, Simondon argues, ontology only perceives a diminished being 'due to its having been separated out into milieu and individual. They do not refer to the whole [...], to the totality that will be formed later by the individual together with the milieu' (*Individu*, p. 30). It is on the basis of this Simondonian critique of ontology that Deleuze and Guattari suggest that 'what is real is the becoming itself, the block of becoming, not the supposedly fixed terms through which that which becomes passes' (*Thousand*, p. 238).

Lifeless matter

Antonio Negri has argued that 'the general framework' of Deleuze and Guattari's work 'seems at first to be an animist, hylozoist, pre-Socratic one', in which 'vitalism finds itself inverted at the very moment that it is asserted, [...] placed at the service of the production of singularity, of the emergence of singularity'.[28] From this perspective, Kant can be seen to be desperate to hold onto the metaphysical inheritance which, by rendering matter as *lifeless*, refuses outright this possibility of an inverted vitalism, of a hylozoism. Kant insists that 'the possibility of a living matter is quite inconceivable [...] since lifelessness, *inertia*, constitutes the essential characteristic of matter'.[29] Schelling notes that this phobic reaction was inherited by Jacobi, who combined a self-confessed inability to even '*think* matter as living' with 'a panic-stricken terror of nature' (*HMP*, p. 173). Here we see Kant offering not an argument but a bald assertion derived from ideological necessity, that hylozoism is atheism: matter cannot be living because matter is defined by inertness.

The conceptual chasm, revealed by this Kantian definition, between Bruno, Spinoza, Schelling and Nietzsche on the one hand, and Kant (and, for that matter, Jacobi) on the other, is given by Deleuze in his distinction between two different 'conceptions of the word "plan" '. For Deleuze,

> any organisation that comes from above and refers to a transcendence, be it a hidden one, can be called a theological plan: [...] it will always be a plan of transcendence that directs forms as well as subjects, and that stays hidden, [...] always has an additional dimension; it always implies a dimension supplementary to the dimensions of the given.
>
> (*Practical*, p. 128)

On the other hand, 'a plane of immanence has no supplementary dimension; the process of composition must be apprehended for itself, through that which it gives, in that which it gives. It is a plan of composition, not a plan of organisation or development' (*Practical*, p. 128).

Much of twentieth-century philosophy can be characterised as a choice between two essentially nineteenth-century alternatives: Husserl or Frege. It is in his rejection of these two alternatives that the radicality of Deleuze's project lies, for it is conceived as a profound rejection of the two major, essentially still theological, responses to the various crises of conviction that wracked the nineteenth century. This essentially is what Toni Negri is suggesting when he writes that *A Thousand Plateaus* attempts to 'construct the terrain upon which to redefine the materialism of the twenty-first century' (*GFPJ*, p. 86), a philosophy adequate to the challenges of a complex future, the only serious philosophical project that attempts to think that future. To read the history of philosophy with Deleuze, to make it stratigraphic, is to scour it for those singularities where heretical thought seeks to challenge the thought of the state, the 'tradition that justifies Power and exalts the State' (*Notes*, p. 61). It is an attempt to marshal the resources of that thought as part of a war machine mobilised on the terrain of contemporary philosophy. This hidden, or heretical, tradition is the means given to us by Deleuze to enable us to leap over, and out of, the theological mire in which the philosophical alternatives are stuck – the perpetual ruminations over the 'death of' this, the 'end of' that – and into the twenty-first century. Philosophy, when conceived along the lines sketched out above, is an imperative to the invention of new beginnings, the activation of potentialities from the rubble of the contemporary, and a perpetual reinvention of philosophical history which is, and will be, the future – a 'counter-philosophy of the schizophrenic laughter and revolutionary joy of the great books'.[30]

Notes

1 Georges Bataille, *Oeuvres complètes*, I and II, ed. Denis Hollier (Paris: Gallimard, 1970–88) vol. I, p. 179; my translation. Hereafter referred to as *OC*, followed by volume number.

2 Gilles Deleuze, *Negotiations*, trans. Martin Joughin (New York: Columbia University Press, 1995) p. 88. Hereafter referred to as *Negotiations*.

3 Gilles Deleuze and Félix Guattari, *What is Philosophy?*, trans. Graham Burchell and Hugh Tomlinson (London: Verso, 1994) p. 9. Hereafter referred to as *WP*.

4 Friedrich Nietzsche, *The Gay Science*, trans. Walter Kaufmann (New York: Vintage Books, 1974) §343, p. 279. Hereafter referred to as *GS*.

5 Antonio Negri, 'Notes on the evolution of the thought of the later Althusser', trans. Olga Vasile, in Antonio Callari and David F. Ruccio (eds) *Postmodern Materialism and the Future of Marxist Theory: Essays in the Althusserian Tradition* (Hanover NH: Wesleyan University Press, 1996) pp. 51–68, (p. 61). Hereafter referred to as *Notes*.

6 Plato, *The Sophist*, in *The Collected Dialogues*, ed. Edith Hamilton and Huntingdon Cairns (Princeton: Princeton University Press, 1989) pp. 957–1018 (p. 1012, 204d).

7 Gilles Deleuze, *Difference and Repetition*, trans. Paul Patton (London: Athlone Press, 1994) p. 128. Hereafter referred to as *Difference*.

8 Gilles Deleuze, *The Logic of Sense*, trans. Mark Lester with Charles Stivale (London: Athlone, 1990) p. 256. Hereafter referred to as *Logic*.

9 Gilles Deleuze, *Essays Critical and Clinical*, trans. Daniel W. Smith and Michael Greco (London: Verso, 1998) p. 137. Hereafter referred to as *Critical*.

10 Gilles Deleuze, *Nietzsche and Philosophy*, trans. Hugh Tomlinson (London: Athlone Press, 1983) p. 93. Hereafter referred to as *Nietzsche*.

11 Immanuel Kant, *Critique of Pure Reason* (1781) trans. Norman Kemp Smith (London: Macmillan, 1929) A 643/B 671, p. 533.

12 Gilles Deleuze and Félix Guattari, *A Thousand Plateaus: Capitalism and Schizophrenia*, trans. Brian Massumi (Minneapolis: University of Minnesota Press, 1987) p. 376. Hereafter referred to as *Thousand*.

13 The relationship between transcendent thought and the power of the state is given its most extensive treatments in *Thousand*, p. 376, and in *Critical*, pp. 126–35. Deleuze and Guattari's position is, as they acknowledge, derived from Nietzsche's essay 'Schopenhauer as educator', 'the greatest critique ever directed against the image of thought and its relation to the State' (*Thousand*, p. 376).

14 The definitive account of the controversy and its intellectual context is Frederick Beiser, *The Fate of Reason: German Philosophy from Kant to Fichte* (Cambridge MA: Harvard University Press, 1987). Beiser writes:

> Until the middle of the eighteenth century it was de rigueur for every professor and cleric to prove his orthodoxy before taking office; and proving one's orthodoxy demanded denouncing Spinoza as a heretic. Since attacks on Spinoza became a virtual ritual, there was an abundance of defamatory and polemical tracts against him. Indeed, by 1710 in the German states there was a *Catalogus scriptorum Anti-Spinozanorum*. And in 1759 Trinius counted, probably too modestly, 129 enemies of Spinoza in his *Freydenkerlexicon*.
>
> (*Fate*, p. 48)

15 Friedrich von Schelling, *On the History of Modern Philosophy*, trans. Andrew Bowie (Cambridge: Cambridge University Press, 1994) p. 74. Hereafter referred to as *HMP*.

16 Gilles Deleuze, *Expressionism in Philosophy: Spinoza*, trans. Martin Joughin (New York: Zone Books, 1992) p. 16.
17 Friedrich von Schelling, *Ideas for a Philosophy of Nature*, trans. Errol E. Harris and Peter Heath (Cambridge: Cambridge University Press, 1988) p. 179.
18 Friedrich Nietzsche, *On the Genealogy of Morals* and *Ecce Homo*, trans. Walter Kaufmann (New York: Vintage Books, 1969) III, §25, p. 156.
19 Gilles Deleuze, *Spinoza: Practical Philosophy*, trans. Robert Hurley (San Francisco: City Lights Books, 1988) p. 124. Hereafter referred to as *Practical*.
20 Gilles Deleuze and Félix Guattari, *Anti-Oedipus: Capitalism and Schizophrenia*, trans. Robert Hurley, Mark Seem, and Helen R. Lane (Minneapolis: University of Minnesota Press, 1983) p. 5.
21 Michel Serres, 'The origin of language: biology, information theory and thermodynamics', in *Hermes: Literature, Science, Philosophy*, ed. Josué V. Harari and David F. Bell (Baltimore and London: Johns Hopkins University Press, 1982) pp. 71–83, (p. 83).
22 Gilbert Simondon, *L'Individuation psychique et collective* (Paris: Aubier, 1989) p. 163. Translations from Simondon are my own.
23 See the references to the Stoic *logos spermatikos* in *Thousand*, p. 165.
24 Gilbert Simondon, *L'Individu et sa genèse physico-biologique* (Paris: Aubier, 1995) p. 21. Hereafter referred to as *Individu*.
25 Immanuel Kant, 'Speculative beginning of human history' (1786) trans. and ed. Ted Humphrey, in *Perpetual Peace and other Essays on Politics, History and Morals* (Cambridge: Hackett, 1983) p. 49.
26 Georges Bataille, 'Sacred sociology and the relationships between "Society", "Organism", and "Being" ', in *The College of Sociology 1937–39*, ed. Denis Hollier, trans. Betsy Wing (Minneapolis: University of Minnesota Press, 1988) pp. 73–84 (p. 79).
27 Friedrich Nietzsche, *Untimely Meditations*, trans. R. J. Hollingdale (Cambridge: Cambridge University Press, 1983) p. 188.
28 Antonio Negri, 'On Gilles Deleuze and Félix Guattari, *A Thousand Plateaus*', trans. Charles Wolfe, *Graduate Faculty Philosophy Journal*, 18, 1 (1995) pp. 93–109, (p. 99). Hereafter referred to as *GFPJ*.
29 Immanuel Kant, *Critique of Judgment* (1790) trans. James Creed Meredith (Oxford: Clarendon Press, 1952) §73, p. 46.
30 Gilles Deleuze, 'Nomad thought', trans. David B. Allison, in *The New Nietzsche*, ed. David B. Allison (Cambridge MA: MIT Press, 1992) pp. 142–9 (p. 147).

Appendix

Michel Tournier on Deleuze

Introduction to Michel Tournier, 'Gilles Deleuze'

Walter Redfern

Tournier, who became a novelist almost by default, whereas his youthful ambition was to be a philosopher, ('a little metaphysical Tarzan, drumming on his pectorals',[1] or the irresistible 'Popeye of philosophy', as he described himself on his return from several years' immersion in German philosophy in 1950[2]), met Gilles Deleuze at school during the War. These two and their birds of a feather rejected *en bloc*: science, religion, humanism and psycho-analysis.[3] The whole groupuscule were obsessed with rational systems which, in their downplaying of causalism, they preferred to view as superior to their devisers: the author as end-product. I am unsure to what extent Deleuze would have agreed with Tournier's analogy between the clear lines of a philosophical system and the picked-clean bones of a skeleton: the reduction to an essence or framework.[4]

Pascal was the much-derided bogyman, and most forms of philosophy they dismissed as 'strip-cartoons' (*VP*, p. 159). All were bowled over by Sartre's *L'Etre et le Néant* (1943), which seemed to offer the incontrovertible system they longed to find. Sartre's later attempt to present existentialism as a new humanism, however, disgusted these newborn parricides.

When Deleuze provided a postface[5] for Tournier's first novel, *Vendredi* (1967), Tournier was not in complete agreement with his reading of 'perversion' in this text, by which Deleuze meant the structure of the other, which breaks down in this revamped story. Deleuze was mainly taken with the psychosexual development of this variant, un-Puritan Robinson Crusoe, and his switch to a radically new form of existence. For Deleuze, this version of the Crusoe myth is forward-looking rather than a return to sources. In fact, Deleuze wilfully minimises this novel's heavy stress on regression. Deleuze wants Robinson to be more of a Leibnizian monad, and a nomad-on-the-spot, than the text justifies. All the same, Deleuze is highly responsive to his friend's slippery ambivalences. The two certainly saw eye-to-eye on the question of upending the usual hierarchy of model and copy, so that the whole issue of originality is skewed. On the other hand, Deleuze rears up against synthesis, for which Tournier hankers. Furthermore, Deleuze distinguishes nomads from migrants, the purposeless travellers from the purposeful, though Tournier himself at times blurs the distinction, as in his favourite oxymoron of the 'stationary vagabond'.[6]

Notes

1   'Ces coups de poing tambourinant mes pectoraux de petit Tarzan métaphysique'. Michel Tournier, *Le Vent Paraclet* (Paris: Gallimard, 1977) p.180. Hereafter referred to as *VP*.

2   Michel Tournier, cited in M. Braudeau, 'L'Ogre Tournier', *L'Express* (29 May 1978) p. 147.

3   In Tournier's words, they managed to 'jeter ensemble par-dessus bord la science et la religion, l'humanisme et les moiteurs de la "vie intérieure" ' [throw overboard science, religion, humanism and the ooziness of 'inner life'] (*VP*, p. 158).

4   See Tournier's interview with G. Dumier: 'Portrait d'un ogre', *Le Nouvel Observateur* (30 November 1970) p. 46.

5   See 1972 edition of Michel Tournier, *Vendredi* (Paris: Gallimard).

6   See, for example, Michel Tournier, *Le Vagabond immobile* (1984).

Gilles Deleuze

Michel Tournier
Translated by Walter Redfern

In 1977 I had occasion to mention Gilles Deleuze in my book *Le Vent Paraclet*. I was inhibited by feeling sure that those few lines would annoy him, like anything else that might be said or written about him, at least about his private life. My embarrassment has altered in nature since his death, but it has still not gone away. How difficult it is to speak of those we love!

In 1941 I was in the *philosophie* class at the Lycée Pasteur under the gentle, luminous rule of Maurice de Gandillac. Gilles Deleuze – who lived with his parents in the rue Daubigny – was in the lower sixth at the Lycée Carnot. There was only one month (December/January) between our ages, but it fell in such a way that I was in the year ahead of him. A mutual friend who became a doctor, Jean Marinier, brought us together. I can say with some pride that it was through me that Gilles first heard about philosophy. But this small headstart did not last. Scarcely had he made contact with philosophy than he was head and shoulders above the rest of us. Let me quote from my *Vent Paraclet*:

> The ideas we threw about like cottonwool or rubber balls he returned to us transformed into hard and heavy iron or steel cannonballs. We quickly learnt to be in awe of his gift for catching us red-handed in the act of cliché-mongering, talking rubbish, or loose thinking. He had the knack of translating, transposing. As it passed through him, the whole of worn-out academic philosophy re-emerged unrecognisable, totally refreshed, as if it had not been properly digested before. It was all fiercely new, completely disconcerting, and it acted as a goad to our feeble minds and our slothfulness.

We saw a great deal of each other over the next fifteen years. When I settled for a spell in Germany so as to follow philosophy courses at the University of Tübingen – where I was soon joined by Claude Lanzmann and Robert Genton – I managed to entice him there for a brief stay. I think that may have been his only trip abroad. On my return to France in 1950, he took a room at the Hôtel de la Paix, 29 quai d'Anjou, on the île Saint-Louis, where I myself lived. I introduced him to Karl Flinker, who was later to open two splendid art galleries, and it was through him that Gilles got to know the woman who would become his wife.

We often ate at the restaurant La Tourelle, in the rue Hautefeuille. The owner, Mme Gallas, rummaged about frenetically in the kitchen and put the fear of God into Simone the waitress, who was curvaceous but hardly aware of it. We were often joined by Evelyne Rey, the sister of Claude and Jacques Lanzmann. She was an actress. She had spent one summer on the Côte d'Azur, just long enough to appear as the heroine in a photo romance. The following winter, Simone picked her out in the woman's weekly – *Nous Deux* or *Intimité* – that she daydreamed over. Every time she saw Evelyne after that, she told her about the chapter she had just read, as if it were the diary of Evelyne's real-life adventures. 'Ah,' she'd say to her, 'This young man who's courting you, I wouldn't trust him. You must be careful!' Or again: 'Ah, when I saw you getting into his car, I thought: "Let's hope nothing happens to her!" '

We would meet in a bar on the island that we had chosen because its window bore the seductive words MONAD TAKEAWAY. Our chinwags were thus placed under the august patronage of Leibniz whom Claude Lanzmann was studying for his postgraduate diploma.

Our rooms were next to each other, and Gilles used to plague me to translate pages from German books for him, or to type his manuscripts. I did it under protest and making critical comments. When I finished typing out his first book, *Empirisme et Subjectivité*, he expressed surprise at how manuscripts shrink in size when typed. That's how I got this dedication which is on my desk before me:

> For Michel, this book which he typed, and criticised, and scoffed at, and perhaps even shortened, because I'm sure it was longer, but which is also to some extent his book insofar as I owe him a great deal (not for Hume) as regards philosophy.

One summer, I took him off to Villers-sur-Mer. He hardly ever took his scarf or his city shoes off. He did have one dip in the sea. 'I swim with my head straight up out of the water to show that I am not in my natural element,' he said. There was an athletic beach-attendant rejoicing in the name of Ingarao, who lifted enormous weights. I can still see Gilles fascinated by the heaviest one of them. 'Want to have a go?' Ingarao asked him. 'No,' replied Gilles, 'my idea of sport would be something like table-tennis.' 'Table-tennis needs good reflexes,' Ingarao commented helpfully. 'Yes,' said Gilles, 'but I'm afraid my reflexes couldn't lift that thing up.'

His very first publication was in 1947 in the review *Poésie 47*, edited by Pierre Seghers: a long article (heavily influenced by Sartre's *L'Etre et le Néant*) entitled 'Dires et profils'. At that period, he was not above writing short, mocking, enigmatic poems in the style of Raymond Queneau. Here are two of them:

Statement of the Middling Narcissus

Unreachable chaste one,
like a pricking conscience that can't be scratched
like a reminder to me of vile finitude,
of the fact that
          I am not God
this thing in me which is not me
like the refusal in me playing under the skin
the shoulder-blade noumenon
immune to twisting

Statement of the Mime-Artist

He stood before the attentive, fertile mirror,
and then twisted his eye
and made a different eye grow
on the end of his nose
There was an electrical power failure
like a cosmic blinking of the eyelids
and so precise
that I ask God
to make me blink like a light-bulb.

If I had to recall an incident from our teenage years, I would probably pick the performance of Sartre's *Les Mouches*, one Sunday afternoon in 1943 at the Théâtre de la Cité (also known as the Sarah Bernhardt).

The part of Jupiter was played by Charles Dullin. At one point, he suddenly cried out loud to Oreste: 'Young man, do not indict the gods!' Just then, the Paris air-raid sirens began to wail. The curtain came down and the lights went up. Everyone dutifully left the theatre, and cards were given out so that people could come back in after the all-clear. Everyone went down to basement air-raid shelters, except for us of course. When you're eighteen you're above that sort of precaution. It was brilliantly sunny. We strolled along the river-banks of an absolutely deserted Paris: it was like midnight in full daylight. And the bombs began to rain down. It was the Renault factories at Billancourt that the RAF were targeting. It was unlikely the île de la Cité would be hit. On the other hand, the German anti-aircraft guns started firing, and shell fragments fell dangerously close to us. We could see mushroom shapes forming on the waters of the Seine over and over again. We were aristocratically disdainful of the whole thing. We made absolutely no comment on this paltry incident. All we were concerned with was the dispute between Oreste and Jupiter over the invasion of 'flies'. Half an hour later the sirens sounded the all-clear, and we went back to the theatre. The curtain went up again. Jupiter-Dullin was on stage. He cried out for the second time: 'Young man, do not indict the gods!'

These are snapshots from our youth, which is falling away in great chunks each year with the death of this one, that one, or a third. Evelyne, Michel Foucault, François Châtelet, Karl Flinker, Gilles Deleuze, I can see you all gathered on the other side of the river, talking to each other, but without me. I know you are expecting me. Be patient, old friends, I'll soon be there!

Index